BY HIS OWN HAND
UPON PAPYRUS

A NEW LOOK AT
THE JOSEPH SMITH PAPYRI

by

CHARLES M. LARSON

Institute for Religious Research
Grand Rapids, Michigan

CONTENTS

Foreword

ONE OF THE MOST EXCITING events in modern Mormon history was the rediscovery of some of the Egyptian papyri which the Prophet Joseph Smith had in his possession when he produced his Book of Abraham translations. Long thought to have been destroyed in a fire in Chicago, they had in reality found their way to the Metropolitan Museum of Art in New York City where they resurfaced in 1967. Their rediscovery established for certain that Joseph Smith had authentic Egyptian documents on which he based his translation of the Abrahamic work now published in the Pearl of Great Price.

The rediscovery of these "Joseph Smith Papyri," as they have come to be known, sent scholars rushing in all directions to explore the meaning and full implications of these texts. Articles and books have flooded the market examining every facet of these documents.

For a long time the average reader has needed someone to bring into manageable form this mass of material. Charles Larson has had the patience and skill to render us this service. Complications have been reduced to understandable terms, various theories have been set forth and evaluated, and the essential facts have always been kept before the reader's eyes. To do these things with clarity requires more than a brief pamphlet, yet Mr. Larson has kept the task within a commendably brief span. The reader who stays with this book until the final sentence will find himself amply rewarded with a knowledge of all the facets of these most significant documents.

Unlike the gold plates of the Book of Mormon, which scholars were never able to examine, these Egyptian texts give us the actual documents from which Joseph Smith was working in making his translation. Therefore, they give us the first real opportunity to examine the Prophet's claims objectively and scientifically. Mr. Larson has provided us with all the pertinent data we need to reach our own conclusions on this much discussed and important topic.

Wesley P. Walters

Part I

BACKGROUND

CHAPTER ONE

How It All Began:
The Mormon Story

T HE MORMON CHURCH BEGAN with a man who claimed a vision. For nearly eighteen centuries God had been silent; neither his voice nor his messengers had been heard upon the earth since the days of Christ's apostles. For long ages the world had to depend upon only the Bible as a spiritual guide, a record which many believed was poorly preserved, often improperly translated, difficult to understand, sprinkled throughout with additions made by men, and with many plain and precious parts lost. Forced to depend upon such a standard, the inevitable happened. Different opinions arose, factions erupted, and the one, True Church was racked by apostasy and division. Many splinter churches sprang up, each putting forth its own interpretation of the Bible.[1]

But one event was about to change all of this. A new, latter-day prophet — a young man named Joseph Smith — was about to appear who would claim he had been given the mission of restoring the one, True Church and the fullness of the Gospel.

An angel had appeared to Joseph Smith four years earlier and revealed the hidden location of a sacred record, written on plates of gold.[2] These plates, when translated, would settle once and for all the disputes which had arisen because of apostate Christendom's sole reliance upon the Bible. This revelation, given by supernatural power to

Joseph Smith, was to become a new scripture to mankind. It would be a book pure and undefiled, translated from its ancient tongue by the gift and power of God operating through Joseph Smith.[3]

Smith was now on his way to recover the hidden records. The time had arrived. It was the twenty-second day of September in the year 1827.

The golden plates turned out to be a record of the former inhabitants of the Americas, ancestors of the American Indians, who had journeyed to the new world from the land of Israel hundreds of years before the time of Christ. They had left a vivid account of their travels and wars, and of the teachings and visions of their prophets, and even of Christ's visit and ministry among them following his crucifixion and ascension on the other side of the world,[4] knowing that these writings would one day come forth and speak to men "low out of the dust, as the voice of one having a familiar spirit."[5]

The record, however, could not be translated by normal means or by an ordinary man. Written in a strange, long-forgotten language called *Reformed Egyptian,* only a person called and blessed of God could read and understand it.[6] Joseph Smith could do so, but because of all the excitement and misunderstanding that the discovery of the strange plates caused, and the persecutions and moving he was forced to endure, it was more than two years before his translation was completed and ready for publication.

Finally, in the early spring of 1830 the Book of Mormon first appeared in print and shortly thereafter the one, True Church of God was re-established on the earth.[7]

But circumstances were not favorable for the little church as it struggled to grow in those early days. The world seemed generally either hostile or indifferent to the claim of the Restoration of the Fullness of the Gospel, and after many months of heartfelt labor proselytizing throughout the area around Joseph Smith's home in upstate New York, his little group had scarcely enlisted the membership of a handful of families from his own neighborhood.[8] The missionaries ranged farther and farther afield, selling their books and seeking their harvest of souls.

Then, for a while things began to look up. Word came from Ohio that the leader of a communal religious society had read the Book of

Mormon and converted himself, his family, and several hundred of his followers.[9] Joseph soon moved the center of the Church from New York to the town of Kirtland, Ohio, where the missionary effort was redoubled. One group was sent westward to preach to the Indians. These missionaries, after passing through the wilderness of Missouri, sent back a report of the vast, unspoiled beauty of that sparsely settled region.[10] The Prophet received the word of the Lord that Missouri was to be Zion, the site of the City of New Jerusalem,[11] and a fast growing colony of Latter-day Saints was soon established there in Jackson County. People from far away began to hear of this marvelous work, and steadily, more and more came to see whether God had indeed raised up a new prophet among men.

Things seemed to be going well, but this good fortune did not last long. Angry mobs rioted against the Saints in Jackson County and drove them from their homes as winter began to settle in. Joseph again received the word of the Lord, this time that he was to gather together an army from among the Saints in Ohio and march to reclaim their inheritance in Zion, where he said the Lord had promised them a mighty victory over their enemies.[12] The army set out in the spring with Joseph at its head, but by the time it arrived in Missouri an outbreak of cholera had begun to rage through its ranks, dashing all hopes of redeeming Zion.[13] Defeated, the weary soldiers drifted back to Ohio when they were well enough to travel, their homes and crops already neglected far too long. The word of the Lord given again by Joseph, explained that they had been turned back because of their unwillingness to be totally obedient to God's commandments.[14] But many had started to lose faith in Joseph's calling as a prophet.

Once back in Kirtland, the murmuring against Joseph and the Church increased. There had always been some scoffing by the unbelieving in the neighborhood (the "gentiles," as the Saints called them), but now there were "apostates" at work as well. Though few in number, the growing sound of their voices as they joined the gentiles in deriding the prophet and his followers was having it's effect on Joseph's leadership. "How do we really *know* the Book of Mormon is what you say?" they would pointedly ask. "Show us the *plates* — if there ever *were* any!" Of course Joseph could not do this; as he always maintained, he had given the gold plates back to the angel after finishing the translation,[15] since he had no further use for them and they were the property of the angel in the first place.

There was also a certain amount of uneasiness and concern over some of the newer commandments being taught in the church — things not a part of the Prophet's teaching in the beginning, when many had been baptized — but which they now had to accept as Church doctrine.[16] Joseph continued to receive new revelation from God, or at least said he did. But many seriously wondered how they could be *sure* without something tangible backing up Joseph's new teachings. Something . . . *scriptural?* Something *more* than the Book of Mormon, perhaps?

Though newcomers continued to arrive in Kirtland, the back door had now been opened and others were leaving. The growth of the Church became stagnant, and for a while it looked as though a stalemate was about the best that could be hoped for.

That is, until something truly incredible happened.

July 4, 1835, was an unusually eventful day in Kirtland. The talk all over town was about the Irishman who had arrived in the village the day before, and had now set up an exhibit of, of all things, four *Egyptian mummies.*[17] It was spectacular! For a small price you could actually see and touch mysterious carvings, fragments of ancient writings, and even mummified human corpses, all of which had been on the earth since Bible times! The exhibit was extremely popular, and Mr. Chandler, the Irishman, did everything he could to accommodate the Saints during his stay.

The four mummies were probably the most colorful objects displayed, but several of the prominent brethren of the Church were even more intrigued by the scraps of ancient writings. In the Book of Mormon, they recalled, Mosiah had described a *seer* as "a man that can translate all records that are of ancient date" (Mosiah 8:13). Joseph, they knew, had been called of God as "Prophet, *Seer,* and Revelator" back when the Church was first organized. Joseph should be able to read and understand this writing! What a wonderful way of silencing his critics for good! Having been told of the Mormon leader's reputation of deciphering the ancient text of the Book of Mormon, Chandler was invited to show some of his Egyptian writings to Joseph, if he would care to learn their meaning. To this the Irishman happily consented.

Some of the writings were taken to Joseph Smith, who told Chandler that he could indeed translate them, though to do so properly

would take some time. Joseph explained that a few of the figures were more immediately recognizable to him than the rest, possibly because of their similarity to the engravings on the gold plates. These he proceeded to interpret for Chandler, who thanked him profusely and even wrote down on a piece of paper for Joseph the following:[18]

KIRTLAND, July 6, 1835

This is to make known to all who may be desirous, concerning the knowledge of Mr. Joseph Smith, Jun., in deciphering the ancient Egyptian hieroglyphic characters in my possession, which I have, in many eminent cities, showed to the most learned; and, from the information that I could ever learn, or meet with, I find that of Mr. Joseph Smith, Jun., to correspond in the most minute matters.

MICHAEL H. CHANDLER
Traveling with, and proprietor of, Egyptian mummies

This was just the sort of thing the brethren had been hoping for, and they were confident that this certificate would help to strengthen the Prophet's reputation and undo some of the harm that had occurred. On further reflection, however, it occurred to them to go a step farther. Pooling their resources, they raised $2400 to actually *purchase* Chandler's exhibit — the writings, the mummies, everything — which they then presented to Joseph.[19] Now, surely, any who ventured to question the Prophet's God-given ability to translate ancient records would be able to see for themselves.

But even their wildest hopes could not have prepared these faithful brethren for what the newly acquired Egyptian writings turned out to be, as identified by their prophet. The astonishing discovery is best described by Joseph Smith himself, who later wrote of the incident:

> . . . with W. W. Phelps and Oliver Cowdery as scribes, I commenced the translation of some of the characters or hieroglyphics, and much to our joy found that one of the rolls contained the writings of Abraham, another the writings of Joseph of Egypt, etc. — a more full account of which will appear in its place, as I proceed to examine or unfold them. Truly we can say, the Lord is beginning to reveal the abundance of peace and truth.[20]

The news sped like an electric shock through the community. All the Saints were beside themselves with joy over the fact that God should so preserve and direct these things unto them through his holy Prophet. The Church's local periodical printed a letter by Oliver Cowdery, one of Joseph's scribes in the work, in which he reported:

> Upon the subject of the Egyptian records, or rather the writings of Abraham and Joseph, I may say a few words. This record is beautifully written on papyrus with black, and a small part red ink, or paint, in perfect preservation.[21]

Describing some of the artwork on the record identified as the Book of Joseph, he excitedly continued:

> The serpent, represented as walking, or formed in a manner to be able to walk, standing in front of and near a female figure, is to me one of the greatest representations I have ever seen upon paper, or a writing substance; and must go so far towards convincing the rational mind of the correctness and divine authority of the holy scriptures . . . as to carry

away, with one mighty sweep, the whole atheistical fabric . . . Enoch's Pillar, as mentioned by Josephus, is upon the same roll . . .[22]

Translation of the papyri commenced almost at once, though not with the record of Joseph that had so impressed Cowdery. Instead, Joseph Smith turned to what would have been the more ancient record of Abraham. Day after day, as much as time would allow, the Prophet occupied himself with the ancient writings.[23] Besides the translation manuscript, which grew steadily, Joseph also undertook the preparation of an alphabet and grammar of the Egyptian language. This was the first work of its kind in the world, since all knowledge of ancient Egyptian writing had been lost to mankind for centuries.

People were duly impressed with the translation project, and eventually a brother named Warren Parrish was called upon to assist Joseph full-time as his principle scribe, aiding the work of Phelps and Cowdery.

Scores of visitors, both Saints and gentiles alike, would call upon the Prophet to see for themselves these wondrous things. Joseph endeavored to give to all "a brief history of the manner in which the writings of the fathers, Abraham and Joseph, have been preserved, and how I came in possession of the same — a correct translation of which I shall give," he promised, "in its proper place."[24]

In the meantime, however, problems continued to plague the Church. During the next few years the Saints would experience some severe setbacks, including economic chaos brought on by the fall of the Church-sponsored Kirtland Safety Society bank, the resulting abandonment of the town of Kirtland, the apostasy and excommunication of the three witnesses to the Book of Mormon and other prominent brethren (including Joseph's scribe, Warren Parrish), the eventual expulsion of the Saints from the state of Missouri, and even the arrest and imprisonment of Joseph and several other Church leaders for treason.

Yet the Church would endure these things and more. And while there were doubtless a number of reasons why the Church survived adversity, the one common element was its *credibility* with its members, a credibility now bolstered for hard times ahead in large part by the miraculous existence of the Prophet's Egyptian records, and of his obviously God-given ability to understand and translate things hidden from the world.

If Joseph could decipher the Egyptian characters on the papyri, then surely he had been able to translate the writings on the golden plates of the Book of Mormon, just as he said he did. And if he had translated the Book of Mormon, he really was called of God as a true prophet. What more proof could a person ask?

CHAPTER TWO

The Book of Abraham:
A Timely Document

T HE SMALL ASSORTMENT OF brittle, faded papyri that Joseph had acquired strengthened his reputation as a prophet and translator at a time when such support was greatly needed; but the little work now known as the Book of Abraham was to have an even more far reaching effect upon the Church.

As published today, the Book of Abraham is a small work, containing only about fifteen printed pages (including the "facsimiles," or pictures adapted from the papyri, which accompany the text). It was apparently never completed, as it ends abruptly in the middle of the beginning sequences of the Garden of Eden story. Possibly Joseph was killed (June 1844) before the remainder could be produced; we cannot be certain. That he had intended to do more with the papyri at a later time seems likely, for the portion completed was the product of two separate, relatively brief but intense periods with an interruption of several years between them.[1]

From the beginning, Joseph revealed to his scribes that the papyrus record was an expanded version of the Genesis account of the life of Abraham as found in the Bible.[2] It showed that Moses, in compiling the Pentateuch, had apparently relied upon the very same account which Joseph Smith now possessed. Moses evidently abridged and condensed the record as he wrote, omitting considerable detail. Either that, or the original writings of Moses had suffered the same ravages of time through careless and dishonest scribes thought to have affected the rest of the Bible.

But no matter. If Joseph was correct, the Church now had before it the very work from which Genesis had been derived; nothing less than the original, first-hand journal that had been kept by Father Abraham himself.[3]* And this account, now slowly unfolding as the Prophet labored to translate it — first in Kirtland, later in Nauvoo — not only cast new light on the background and experiences of the great biblical patriarch, it also gave scriptural authority to a number of new doctrines and teachings Joseph had recently introduced.

During the first phase of the translation process, which took place from the time he acquired the papyri in July 1835 to the latter part of the same year, Joseph was able to dictate approximately forty percent of what he would eventually produce. His scribes in Kirtland faithfully recorded the words as Joseph read them off, filling nearly ten full manuscript pages. The translated portion appeared neatly alongside a narrow column on the left side of the paper that displayed a hand-drawn copy of the Egyptian symbol from which Joseph derived the text.

The opening section of the Book of Abraham, which reads today through Abr. 2:18, gives Abraham's first person account of the conditions in his homeland, the idolatry and famine which preceded his rescue by the Lord from an altar of sacrifice, and the subsequent command to depart from his homeland and go to a land which the Lord would show him. The account Joseph produced from the papyri greatly expands upon the Bible's version of the same events, to the extent that only a half-dozen or so corresponding Bible verses (Genesis 12:1-6) are detectable.

The sheer volume of this newly discovered Bible-related material

---

*This would mean that the frail papyrus from which Joseph Smith translated the Book of Abraham is the only existing "autograph" (author's original copy) of a Scriptural book. Also, Abraham is dated about 2,000 B.C., while the book of Genesis was authored by Moses between 1440-1400 B.C. This would mean the Book of Abraham predates the first book in the Bible by over 500 years.

was surely impressive enough to establish, once and for all, Joseph's continued favor with God. But to the joy of Joseph and the faithful, they noted that Abraham made repeated references to his lineal priesthood authority, which he referred to simply as *the Priesthood*. This was highly significant, for some within the Church had begun to criticize Joseph for introducing back in mid-1831 the office of "High Priest" within the Church. These dissenters argued that the whole matter of priesthood had always been a *temporal* affair, developed in the days of Moses and strictly confined to the Levites until the time of Christ, when it was abolished.[4] These critics were the same people who had refused to accept as scripture some of the writings of Moses rewritten by Joseph in 1830 under the influence of direct revelation. In these, Joseph had argued that the Priesthood was an *eternal* power. In his attempts to reason with these dissidents, Smith pointed out the revelation contained in Doctrine and Covenants 27, which referred very plainly to the bestowal of the priesthood upon both himself and Oliver Cowdery in the spring of 1829. This, he argued, occurred long before there had been any question of authority. In response, his critics charged that the revelation had simply been altered more recently to include these teachings *after* they had already been put into practice.[5]

But the Book of Abraham changed all this, for it stated clearly that Abraham had held the Priesthood of God long before the Levites existed. And if any still cared to question the matter, the original manuscripts themselves were on display for all to see. The challenge had been met and answered. Both Joseph's status as a prophet and the doctrine of the priesthood authority within the Church had been vindicated by the timely appearance of the Book of Abraham.

Nor was this the only instance when Joseph was so vindicated, for Abraham's record continued in a most gratifying manner to justify the still newer doctrines of the Church when Joseph again took up the task of translating in early 1842. By this time the Saints, having been forcefully expelled from the state of Missouri, had settled in Illinois. There, on a peaceful bend in the Mississippi River, they began to build up a new city which they called Nauvoo; and there, at least for a season, it looked as though the Church would be left alone to take care of its own affairs. Then the Lord could reveal through the Prophet

Joseph Smith the further light and knowledge he desired his people to have.

Most of these additional teachings were made public and were embraced by the membership as soon as they were revealed. However, some (and one very special teaching in particular) were of such a sacred nature that they could not be taught publicly, nor could their existence even be acknowledged, as the time had not yet come, their leaders said, when people could understand these new truths.

The major new issue was polygamy — the practice of a man having more than one wife at a time. Joseph said he had been commanded of the Lord to enter secretly into the practice of this principle at least as early as 1841, and possibly much earlier — the surviving records are unclear. He had also been told to instruct certain select, faithful brethren around him in the same practice. But as might be expected, this presented a dilemma to the Prophet and the others who had been initiated. How were they to practice something secretly in order to be counted righteous of God, and at the same time be able, in honesty, to deny that they were practicing it? Joseph and many of the brethren were being forced into the position of having to deny publicly that polygamy was being taught and practiced in Nauvoo in order to prevent persecution from their gentile neighbors and dissent from uninitiated fellow Mormons.[6]

When translation of the Book of Abraham began again, the answer to this dilemma became obvious. The Bible described how Abraham, when he first entered Egypt, had deceived the Egyptians into thinking that Sarai, who was very beautiful to look upon, was his *sister* — not his wife. He did this because he feared the Egyptians would kill him and take his wife (Genesis 12:11-13). This same incident was described in the papyri when Joseph began translating the second time, but with a significant change: according to the papyri version of the narrative it had actually been the *Lord himself* who had instructed Abraham to tell the Egyptians that Sarai was his sister (Abraham 2:22-25). This demonstrated that God sometimes justifies deceit in those instances when a righteous purpose is served.

But this was only the beginning. Following the episode concerning Abraham's wife and the Egyptians, the translation of the ancient record broke off from any semblance of paralleling the biblical sequence of events, and instead recounted an entirely new episode. In an elaborate vision, the Lord is described as instructing Abraham on the principles of astronomy, whereby the heavens are likened unto *eternal progression,* the *pre-existence of spirits,* and the governing of the *Celestial Realms by Deity* (Abraham 3:1-21).*

It provided insight into God's plan for organizing the earth and peopling it for a *second estate* by the spirits of mankind, gave further details of Lucifer's rebellion, and an account of a resulting war in Heaven over the issue of man's *free agency* (Abraham 3:22-28).

The Prophet was just beginning to teach many of these ideas in 1842, the period when the translation project was taken up again. Significantly, the parts of the Book of Abraham dealing with these concepts formed the basis for virtually all of Joseph's subsequent teachings about an area of doctrine known as the *plan of progression,* and the eventual exaltation of those men who would go on to become gods themselves in the *Celestial Kingdom.*

The final chapter of the Book of Abraham, also completed at this time, was a continuation of Abraham's vision. It appeared to Joseph and his scribes to correspond to — and thus be the original source for — the creation account found in the first two chapters of Genesis. Joseph had once (back in 1830) corrected, by inspiration, this same passage of biblical text, along with other portions of the Bible (producing what is known as the *Joseph Smith Translation* or the *Inspired Version,* of the Bible). But now, as they translated the Book of Abraham creation story, the Prophet and his scribes found that it contained some noteworthy and startling differences from both the Bible's account and Joseph Smith's earlier, inspired restoration. This only served to emphasize how significantly the original writings of Abraham (as they were now being translated by Smith) differed from

---

*It is here that *Kolob,* the great governing sphere near to the place of the residence of God, is first mentioned. In fact, the *only* place that Kolob is ever mentioned in LDS scripture is in the Book of Abraham, where it is discussed in both the text and in the inspired explanation of one of the three facsimiles that are included in this part of the Mormon canon of scripture. In explaining the facsimile that depicts Kolob, the Prophet also made a number of references to the secret phrases and passwords connected with the ordinances of the Temple, subjects he was just beginning to teach privately among the Saints at that time.

the biblical version authored by Moses.

What were some of the significant differences? When the book of Genesis had been corrected by the Prophet the first time in 1830, the text he produced retained the Bible's (and Moses') emphasis that there is *only one God.* Joseph's 1842 translation of portions of the Book of Abraham, however, distinctly taught the *plurality of gods* — a concept of deity Joseph had started teaching a few years earlier, but one which many Saints neither understood nor appreciated.[7]

The Book of Abraham also introduced the first and only scriptural basis for denying the priesthood to Blacks, the Church's official position until 1978. It described Pharaoh and the Egyptians as descendents of Ham and Canaan (understood to be the progenitors of the Negro race), and under the curse of Canaan and disqualified from the priesthood (Abraham 1:21-22, 26-27).

The entire text of the translation, together with woodcuts of the three facsimiles and their explanations, created a sensation when they appeared in print for the first time in *Times and Seasons,* a publication of the Mormon Church. The paper featured bi-weekly installments of the Book of Abraham text, starting in its March 1, 1842 issue. The value and impact of the Book of Abraham was recognized at once by the faithful, and Joseph continued to expound upon its contents in lectures, sermons, and other teachings for two full years, right up to the time of his death.

For several years after Joseph and his brother Hyrum were killed by a mob at the Carthage jail, there was a period of confusion and contention among the Saints. Without Joseph to hold the Church together, these confrontations soon erupted into a series of permanent divisions over doctrines and leadership that would split the Saints forever.

Several dominant groups emerged, with varying numbers of followers.[8] The majority of the Saints aligned themselves with the Apostles under the leadership of Brigham Young. These people tended to endorse the doctrines of the Priesthood, pre-existence, eternal progression, and the plurality of gods. They favored the principle of plural marriage once they were introduced to it, and they upheld the Book of Abraham as a vital revelation from God. Those who followed other leaders tended, with a few exceptions, either to reject, ignore, or modify these newer doctrines, and to cast the Book of Abraham into a state of limbo.

But to the followers of Brigham Young — those who would eventually become the Utah-based Church of Jesus Christ of Latter-day Saints — the value of the Book of Abraham was incalculable. It could never be laid aside without forfeiting some of that Church's most sacred and distinctive doctrines. It was published a second time in 1851 by the overseers of the branches of the LDS Church in England, appearing in pamphlet form as part of a small collection of writings entitled *The Pearl of Great Price*. This collection was later re-issued in a slightly edited form in Utah in 1878 under the same title. Two years later, in October of 1880, it was officially canonized by unanimous vote at a session of the Church's semiannual General Conference in Salt Lake City.

Maintaining the divine authority of the Book of Abraham is every bit as vital to the doctrines and theology of the Church of Jesus Christ of Latter-day Saints today as it was in the days of Joseph Smith, Brigham Young and their successors. As the late Apostle Bruce R. McConkie (one of the Church's most prolific scriptural spokesmen) so succinctly stated, the Book of Abraham:

> . . . contains priceless information about the gospel, pre-existence, the nature of Deity, the creation, and priesthood — information which is not otherwise available in any other revelation now extant.[9]

CHAPTER THREE

Charges and Rebuttals: The Challenge Begins

NEARLY FORTY YEARS WERE TO PASS from the time Joseph translated the Book of Abraham until it was officially recognized as sacred Scripture of the Church. However, during this period something occurred which neither Joseph nor any of his contemporaries could have foreseen. After many years of dedicated work on the Rosetta Stone and other sources, scholars were able to decipher the ancient Egyptian language. It was now possible to translate accurately Egyptian texts with virtually the same degree of comprehension as Greek or Latin texts.[1]

Initially, though, it did not appear likely that this new development would impact the Mormon Church or the Book of Abraham. Living in the shelter of their Great Basin kingdom, the Saints for much of the second half of the nineteenth-century were both physically and culturally isolated from the rest of the country. In spite of such developments as the introduction of the railroad and increased gentile enterprises and settlements in the region, the Saints lived in a rigidly structured state of near-total dependence on Church authority. Many of their teachings and practices (such as polygamy) only served to reinforce the barriers established between the Saints and their neighbors.

For their part, the Saints trusted the word of the prophet and felt no particular need to vindicate his work to the rest of the world. And even if they had desired such vindication, Joseph's papyri collection was unavailable; it had passed into the hands of his widow, Emma, who refused to follow the leadership of Brigham Young, and had remained in Nauvoo.[2] So, as far as the Utah Saints were concerned, the world could simply go its own way with its knowledge, and the Saints would go on their way with theirs. *Surprising*

Except that the rest of the world was not to be quite so obliging.

It was sometime during the year 1856, about five years after the Pearl of Great Price had been printed in England, when one of the small pamphlets found its way to the Louvre in Paris. There the facsimiles from the Book of Abraham, together with Joseph's accompanying explanations, were brought to the attention of M. Theodule Deveria. As one of the pioneers in the field of Egyptology, Deveria was asked to offer any comments on them he cared to make.

To Deveria the project probably did not seem worth the minimal effort it would require. However, he proceeded, and immediately recognized all three drawings as copies of rather common Egyptian funerary documents, of which he had examined hundreds. To be sure, most of the hieroglyphic and hieratic figures had been too poorly transcribed to be of much use for translation, and some elements in several of the drawings appeared to Deveria to be guesswork, probably incorrect restorations of missing sections of the original papyri. Still, most of the major elements fit very well into the established pattern associated with Egyptian mythology and the preparation of common funerary documents. Enough of the writing was legible for Deveria to decipher the names and titles of various Egyptian gods and goddesses, and on one of the drawings (Facsimile No. 3) he was able to determine the name of the deceased Egyptian for whom the scroll had originally been prepared. Concerning Facsimile No. 3 he wrote:

> The deceased led by Ma into the presence of Osiris. His name is Horus, as may be seen in the prayer which is at the bottom of the picture, and which is addressed to the divinities of the four cardinal points.

Deveria dismissed Joseph's explanations as rambling nonsense. His comments first appeared in French in a two-volume work by Jules Remy entitled *Voyage au Pays des Mormons* (Paris, 1860). Understandably, they caused very little concern within the Church, if LDS officials were even aware of the book. However, the following year an English translation of Remy's work appeared, published in London under the title *A Journey to Great Salt Lake City*. Perhaps it was through this account that certain Church leaders first became aware of the results of Deveria's investigation, though no deliberate effort appears to have been made at that time to answer his charges. Possibly they felt criticisms raised by such an obscure work did not warrant a reply. Furthermore, the Saints could reason, if the scholarship of Christendom could not recognize and correct the corruptions in the text of its own Bible, how could anyone expect the "learned" to have even a faint understanding of the subject matter of the Book of Abraham?

But then, in 1873, a man by the name of T. B. H. Stenhouse wrote a book which brought Deveria's study back into the public eye again. *The Rocky Mountain Saints: A Full and Complete History of the Mormons* seemed to hit the market at just the right time to become a popular success. Published in New York and later issued in two editions in London, it finally presented — at least to the gentile mind a serious challenge to the Book of Abraham. Many eyes turned to the Mormon Church to await an official response. Many no doubt hoped to catch the Church making a retraction of some of the more bizarre doctrines it had helped to formulate. Some critics, no doubt even went so far as to predict the eventual collapse of the entire Mormon system.

The response of the Church was to disappoint such critics, however. Back in the original *Times and Seasons* article of 1842, the text of the papyri translation had been preceded by the heading:

A Translation of some ancient Records that have fallen into our hands from the Catacombs of Egypt, purporting to be the writings of Abraham, while he was in Egypt, called the Book of Abraham, written by his own hand upon papyrus. THE BOOK OF ABRAHAM.

This same heading had been used in the (first) 1851 edition of The Pearl of Great Price, the source that had been available to the critics. But in 1878, when the second edition was being prepared for publication in Salt Lake City, Apostle Orson Pratt edited out the words "purporting to be" from the heading. This emphasized even more strongly the Church's position that the book was nothing less than the divinely translated record of Abraham, and not merely some pagan funeral text as the non-Mormon scholarly world was asserting.[3]

The following year (1879) George Reynolds, a president of the LDS Council of Seventy, wrote an article for the Church entitled, "The Book of Abraham: Its Authenticity Established as a Divine and Ancient Record." In it Reynolds suggested that the papyrus,

> . . . had at least two (but more probably three) meanings, the one understood by the masses — the other comprehended only by the initiated, the priesthood and others; which latter conveyed the true though hidden intent of the writer.*

The following year the Book of Abraham was officially recognized as scripture. The position of the Saints was firm: Deveria's 20-year-old conclusions were misleading and lacked the authority of Latter-day Saint enlightenment. This was, after all, the only real authority the Saints could properly recognize.

This was not to be the end of the matter, however. Though each passing decade tended to put Deveria's work further out of reach, it was included in Stenhouse's book when it was republished in 1900. Apparently in response, the Church once again voted on and sustained the latest edition of the Pearl of Great Price at its October 1902 Conference. At this rate the subject might well have continued to seesaw back and forth until one side grew too weary to respond.

At least that was how the Rt. Reverend Franklin S. Spalding, Episcopal Bishop of Utah, saw the situation in 1912. It was in that year that he decided to send copies of the three facsimiles from the Book of Abraham to some of the world's leading scholars of Egyptology, asking each for an independent assessment of Joseph Smith's interpretations.

The eight Egyptologists and Semitists who responded were unani-

---

*Cf. George Reynolds and Janne M. Sjodahl, *Commentary on the Pearl of Great Price.* (Salt Lake City: Deseret Book Co.) 1980, pp. 280, 281.

mous in their scathing verdict: "Joseph Smith's interpretation of these cuts is a farrago of nonsense from beginning to end," came the report from the Metropolitan Museum of Art in New York, which added that "five minutes study in an Egyptian gallery of any museum should be enough to convince any educated man of the clumsiness of the imposture;"[4] ". . . difficult to deal seriously with Smith's impudent fraud," wrote another from Oxford, England. "Smith has turned the Goddess into a king and Osiris into Abraham."[5] From Chicago, ". . . very clearly demonstrates that he (Joseph Smith) was totally unacquainted with the significance of these documents and absolutely ignorant of the simplest facts of Egyptian Writing and civilization."[6] And from London, ". . . the attempts to guess a meaning are too absurd to be noticed. It may be safely said that there is not one single word that is true in these explanations."[7]

On and on the critiques went, giving the most comprehensive portrayal ever assembled of exactly what Joseph's papyri actually were: common Egyptian funerary texts. Spalding published the results of his survey as *Joseph Smith, Jr. As a Translator*, adding enough fuel to the fire to keep the controversy burning hot for many years to come. *The New York Times* featured a major exposé on the Book of Abraham in December of that year; other articles and pamphlets soon began to appear in print as well.

The Church's response was quick and sharp: Charges *simply not valid*. Church spokesmen vehemently charged the scholars with using erroneous criteria. Their methods were faulty, their motives questionable. In 1913, Mormon writer John Henry Evans pointed out in an article in the Church-sanctioned *Improvement Era*, that less than one-seventh of the whole Book of Abraham was represented by the facsimile portion, and even that only as an accompaniment to the text. Evans argued that in order to give a fair test of Joseph's true ability to translate Egyptian, and before the scholars could get away with charging that the entire Book of Abraham was a false translation, "they would have to examine the original papyrus, or a copy of it, from which the Book of Abraham was translated."[8]

B. H. Roberts, the well-known Church historian, took special exception in the same magazine to remarks quoted in the *Times* article by Dr. Albert Lythgoe, head of the Department of Egyptian Art at the

New York Metropolitan Museum. Dr. Lythgoe had suggested that the scene Joseph interpreted as a "wicked priest attempting to sacrifice Abraham upon an altar" was a false reconstruction, because "the god Anubus, bending over the mummy, was shown with a human and strangely un-Egyptian head, instead of a jackal's head usual to the scene. And a knife had been drawn into the god's hand"[9] (see Facsimile No. 1 on p. 33). Dr. Lythgoe's observations were virtually identical to those Deveria made a half-century earlier. Deveria had also noted that the bird in the picture, to correctly represent the soul of Osiris, "should have a human head."

"*. . . should have a human head,'*" wrote Roberts caustically about both critics. "Yes, or the head of an *ass,* then it could be made to mean *something else* than what these other learned men describe it as meaning . . . '*should have a jackal's head.*' Yes, or some *other* change might be suggested, and by such process some *other* meaning may be read into the plate and make it *different* from the translation of *Joseph Smith.*"[10]

Such strongly worded pronouncements from respected Church authorities would, under most circumstances, have been sufficient to erase doubt from the minds of even the most wavering Saint, and adequate to frustrate the arguments of the most adamant critics. But this was far from an ordinary situation. In reality, the Church's best arguments not only looked and sounded ridiculous to the gentiles — hardly a tenable position for a missionary-minded church — but a surprising number of members seemed to recognize the sad fact that even the best minds in the Church were simply unable to respond credibly to the charges of scholarly professionals.

The Church was openly vulnerable, and the frustration that accompanied that vulnerability led its leaders to do something they had never done before: they sought the services of a hired, professional "expert."[11]

This man of the hour was known simply as Robert C. Webb. As it happened, "Webb" was an assumed name belonging to a professional writer, defender of causes, and self-styled expert on numerous matters. (Once, under a different name, he had even written a book in defense of the liquor industry!) However, his background and credentials seemed to be unimportant to Church officials. What was important was his willingness and ability to defend the Church's position on the Book of Abraham — that, and the fact that he would be doing so as a gentile.

Webb's scholarly-sounding articles began appearing in Church publications in 1913. He also wrote a small book on the subject entitled, *The Case Against Mormonism*. Promoted as a definitive work by a "non-Mormon" author, Webb's book was anything but a case *against* Mormonism. Rather, it consisted of an impressive display of argumentation, and enough linguistic pseudo-scholarship to baffle the layman — apparently Webb's intention. It made no difference that the best "experts" criticized and ridiculed his writings as "full of errors," "its own refutation," and "ridiculous." The always innovative Webb had by this time tacked a bogus Ph.D. onto his name,[12] thus becoming — at least in the eyes of the Church officials who were willing to pay him for his writing — one of the "experts" himself.

Webb remained a shadowy "expert" at the Church's disposal for many years, his little book dusted off and appealed to whenever occasion required the strengthening of a member's testimony or the refuting of an antagonist's criticism. Decades later, when researcher and author Fawn M. Brodie revealed that Webb's real name had been J. E. Homans, and that he had never earned a Ph. D. in Egyptology or any other field, few people seemed to care. "Webb" had served his purpose during the time he was needed most, and in the meantime Spaulding's report had become as outdated to the current generation as Deveria's was in Spaulding's day.

The main LDS argument used throughout the controversy still stood: The facsimiles could "remind" the scholars of anything they wished, but no legitimate grounds existed to judge Joseph Smith's work, since none of the critics had ever had the Prophet's *original papyri* to examine. And that fact was not likely to change either, since the papyri collection had disappeared long ago, and was presumed destroyed in the great Chicago fire.[13] Without them, no test would ever be valid.

But Joseph Smith's original papyri had *not been destroyed.* Lost, yes — but not forever. They were one day to reappear.

CHAPTER FOUR

The Papyri Rediscovered:
A Timely Opportunity?

ONE DAY IN THE EARLY SPRING OF 1966, a professor of Arabic Studies from the University of Utah in Salt Lake City entered one of the vault rooms of New York's huge Metropolitan Museum of Art, seeking supplementary material for a book he was writing.

"I was in one of the dim rooms where everything was brought to me," Dr. Aziz S. Atiya would later recollect. "Something caught my eye, and I asked one of the assistants to take me behind the bars, into the storehouse of documents, so that I could look some more." Dr. Atiya soon located a file that contained an apparently forgotten collection of Egyptian Papyri — eleven tattered pieces, to be exact — which had been glued to stiff backing paper in the nineteenth-century in an effort to preserve them.

The crude preservation efforts had been remarkably successful. Nearly all the papyri contained beautifully clear and legible writing - mostly in black, with a small part in red — and many contained illustrations as well. But the vivid scene depicted on one fragment in particular was strikingly familiar to Professor Atiya, who, though not a Mormon himself, was well acquainted with the collection

ENG. BY R. HEDLOCK

Although the papyrus fragment from which Facsimile No. 3 (above) was copied is now missing, scholars agree that it would have come at the end (that is, to the left, since Egyptian reads from right to left) of the scroll which Joseph Smith identified as the Book of Abraham.

Facsimile No. 3 replicates a well known scene from the Egyptian *Book of the Dead,* and Egyptologists identify the "Book of Abraham" scroll as a late version of the pagan Egyptian *Book of the Dead,* known as the *Book of Breathings.*

Based on the writing style and other factors, Egyptologists date the "Book of Abraham" papyri about the time of Christ, or approximately 2,000 years later than the time of the biblical patriarch Abraham.

Papyrus Joseph Smith VI

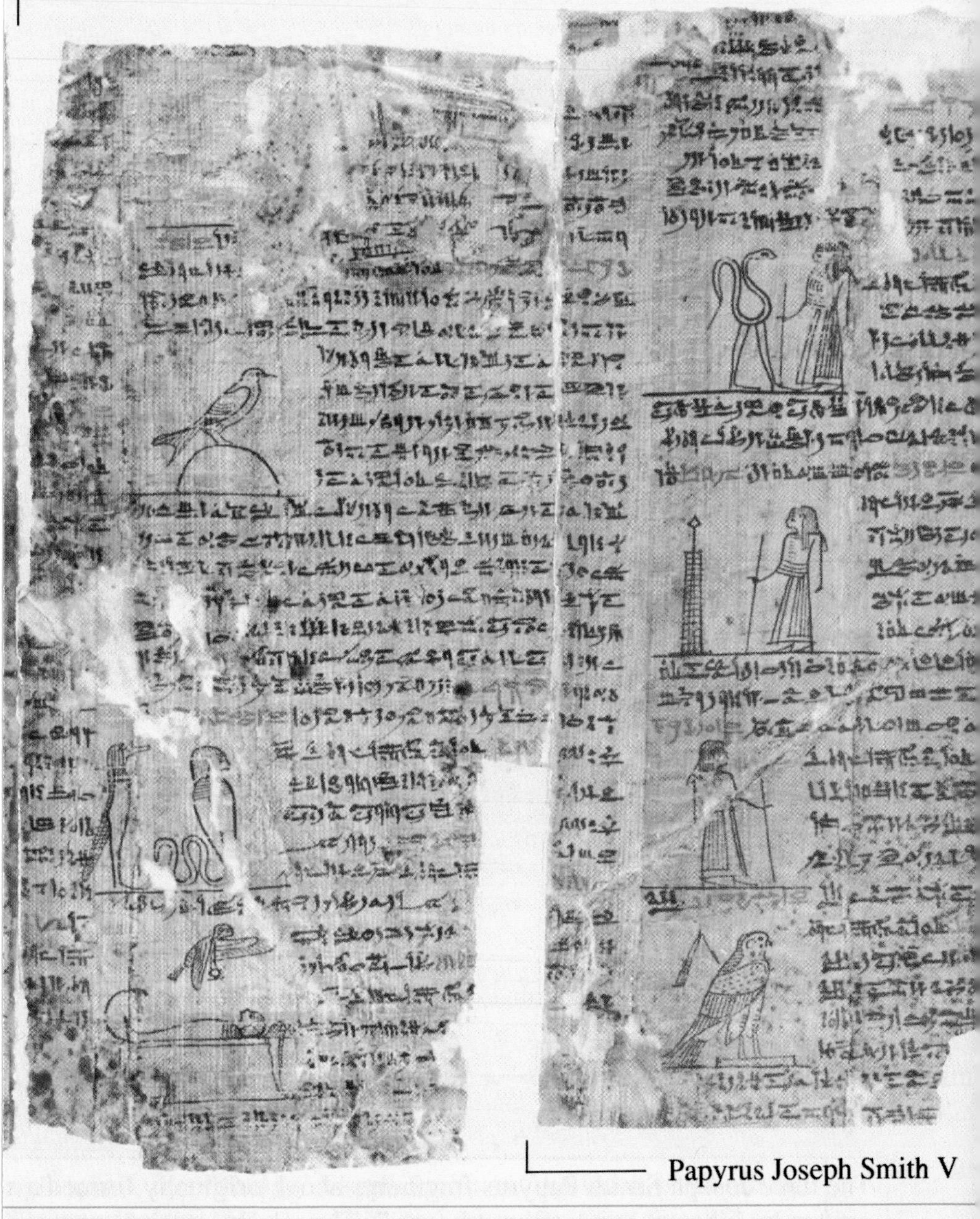

Papyrus Joseph Smith V

Papyrus Joseph Smith VII

Papyrus Joseph Smith VIII

Papyrus Joseph Smith IX, the "Church Historian's Fragment," was part of what Joseph Smith identified as the Book of Joseph. It would have come nearer the begining (that is, to the right, since Egyptian reads from right to left) of the scroll than the better preserved fragments on the foldout, at left.

Based on the writing style and other factors, Egyptologists identify this scroll as a copy of the pagan Egyptian *Book of the Dead* dating at least 1,500 years after the time of the biblical patriarch, Joseph.

of various writings his LDS friends and associates revered as scripture.

"When I saw this picture," Atiya would later explain to them," I knew it had appeared in the Pearl of Great Price."[1]

Thus began an extraordinary series of events which led, a year-and-a-half later, to what one prominent Mormon scholar has termed the most momentous transaction for the Church since the Angel Moroni retrieved from Joseph Smith the golden plates of the Book of Mormon.[2]   On November 27, 1967, the Salt Lake City *Deseret News* announced:

> NEW YORK — A collection of papyrus manuscripts, long believed to have been destroyed in the Chicago fire of 1871 was presented to The Church of Jesus Christ of Latter-day Saints here Monday by the Metropolitan Museum of Art . . .
>   Included in the papyri is a manuscript identified as the original document from which Joseph Smith had copied the drawing which he called "Facsimile No. 1" [see photograph on p. 33] and published with the Book of Abraham.

This startling news produced more than mere excitement within the Church. The sudden, unexpected reappearance of so large a portion of Joseph Smith's original papyrus collection caused feelings that could only be compared with those of the earlier Saints who had seen them that first time in Kirtland over a hundred and thirty years earlier.

And there could be no question that the Metropolitan papyri were indeed none other than the ones which Joseph Smith had once purchased and used. The reverse sides of the paper to which they were glued contained such things as architectural drawings of a temple and maps of the Kirtland, Ohio area.[3]

Several of the fragments contained Egyptian drawings, and while there was no sign among them of two of the facsimiles from the Book of Abraham, the original of Facsimile No. 1 stood out like a blazing banner. Two other fragments contained drawings that seemed to match perfectly Oliver Cowdery's descriptions of pictures in the Book of Joseph scroll. However, no one could be sure whether the Prophet had done more than simply identify that book during those last, hectic years of his life. In all, it was determined that about one-third of the entire papyrus collection once owned by Joseph Smith had been discovered in this dramatic find.[4] Wow !

Church members saw in this development a growing number of opportunities that could only have been foreordained of God. For one thing, the scholarly criticisms by Spalding and others of Joseph's explanation of Facsimile No. 1 could now be reviewed in light of modern scholarship and using the original document, and the Church would be able to prove, once and for all, that the arguments of the critics were faulty. In short, this discovery held out the possibility of dramatically vindicating before the world Joseph Smith's original identification of Facsimile No. 1 (along with the rest of the Book of Abraham and all the doctrines it represented).

There was also the tantalizing prospect of being able to demonstrate one of the Church's greatest gifts in the Latter-day dispensation: the gift of a *Seer,* the ability to translate by the gift and power of God just as Joseph Smith had done. As far back as 1878 Orson Pratt had seen fit to challenge the world on this subject, declaring in one of his sermons: "Have any of the other denominations got this gift among them? Go and inquire through all of Christendom . . . 'Can you translate ancient records written in a language that is lost to the knowledge of man?' No . . . the universal reply of the Christian denominations, numbering some 400,000,000, would be that they have not the power to do it . . . you must give us credit," he had chided, "of at least professing to have these great and important gifts."[5]

Nor was Apostle Pratt's point taken lightly by others in the Church; several decades later another Apostle, John A. Widtsoe, pointedly explained that if 'records appear needing translation, the President of the Church may at any time be called, through revelation, to the special labor of translation.'"[6]

And if ever there was a time when there were records needing translation, the Saints could reason, surely it was now — for who but Heavenly Father could have orchestrated such a glorious opportunity? And if these fragments turned out to contain any of the original Book of Abraham — well, who *then* could deny the truthfulness of the Restored Gospel?

There was an unfortunate complication within the Church at this time, however. The President of the Church at the time the papyri were rediscovered, David O. MacKay, was very old and had been ill for some time. He was simply in no condition to undertake such a calling to translate, no matter how divinely propitious or urgent. Though much of the membership understood the President's Counselors in the First Presidency to hold collectively all the necessary keys and authority to perform the duties of *Seer* to the Church,[7] the papyri were nevertheless turned over to some of the Church's top scholars at Brigham Young University in Provo, for evaluation and translation.

But while many Mormons were doubtless disappointed that the Church passed up this opportunity, such feelings were quickly brushed aside in anticipation of future developments. Would the arguments of the critics be overcome and silenced at last? Would Joseph's work finally be justified with devastating finality before the eyes of a skeptical world?

The Saints waited expectantly, and held their breath.

Part II

THE PAPYRI SPEAK
FOR THEMSELVES

CHAPTER FIVE

An Identification and the Critical Link

S EVERAL WEEKS AFTER THE LDS Church officially acquired the Joseph Smith papyri, it allowed sepia-toned photographs of all eleven fragments to be published in the *Improvement Era* magazine (February 1968). Though prior to this photographs of the papyri had been made available to selected Church scholars and some others,[1] this was the first real exposure of these historic documents to the general membership and the public at large. The effect of this public unveiling — for the members of the LDS Church at least — was spectacular. Readers were brought face-to-face with page after page of impressive documents, and an article that seemed to completely answer even the most persistent critic. Thus, the membership was reassured that the Mormon Church and all that it taught had to be true. Why else, Mormons could reason, would the Church be willing to lay these things out before the world, unless, as they had always believed, there was absolutely nothing to hide?

Recent events caused many Mormons to be grateful for this type of assurance from the Church. In what amounted to the latest round in the old "Could-Joseph-Smith-really-translate-ancient-Egyptian-or-was-he-just-faking" debate, an obscure document had come to light that had been nearly forgotten for a hundred and thirty years. Joseph had called it his "Grammar & Alphabet of the Egyptian Language."

Smith's "Egyptian Alphabet and Grammar," as it has come to be called, had never really been lost or missing. For a long time it was simply ignored, and more recently it had been considered *restricted*. It was among that portion of early Church records the Mormons managed to take with them when they left Nauvoo in 1846, and it was included in the list of materials recorded in the Church Historian's Office Journal as having been deposited in the Historian's fireproof vault in Salt Lake City in 1855. There the manuscript lay, apparently all but forgotten for eighty years, before being "rediscovered" in 1935 during the course of some historical research by Dr. Sidney B. Sperry of Brigham Young University, James R. Clark, a student of Sperry's, and A. William Lund, Assistant Church Historian at the time.[2]

These documents were not released for public examination or study, however. For the time being their discovery was not even announced.[3] It was not until 1938 that Dr. Sperry was allowed to publish a pair of rather indistinct photographs of two pages from the Alphabet and Grammar notebook which contained part of a translation manuscript from the Book of Abraham. The existence of the entire Grammar was still only hinted at for many years, and only a select handful of scholars and authorities within the LDS Church were allowed access to the material.[4] This, despite the great historical significance attached to it by LDS writers like William Berrett, who proudly described it as Joseph Smith's "most notable achievement . . . the development of a Grammar for the Egyptian hieroglyphic form of writing," and "the first Egyptian Grammar in America."[5]

Curiously, even as late as 1960 (by which time it had been known for some twenty-five years that the "Alphabet and Grammar" had survived and was in the Church's possession) Dr. Sperry remarked at BYU's *Pearl of Great Price Conference* that he did not know whether or not the Church authorities would yet allow it to be published, adding that he thought "it would be a little premature, perhaps, to do it now, until we can really do a good job of it."[6]

Others who had occasion to come into contact with the material apparently disagreed with the Church's reluctance in the matter. Late in 1965 a microfilm copy of the entire work was "leaked" to Jerald and Sandra Tanner of Modern Microfilm Company (now Utah Lighthouse Ministry). The Tanners were former Mormons who were rapidly gaining a reputation for printing documents relating to Mormonism that, though authentic, made Church officials uncomfortable. By 1966 the Tanners had produced the first complete photomechanical reprint and transcription of the entire *Egyptian Alphabet and Grammar.*[7]

But contrary to what most Mormons evidently expected, publication of the *Alphabet and Grammar* in no way substantiated Joseph Smith's ability to translate ancient Egyptian. Quite the opposite, for the book turned out to be nothing but page after page of nonsensical gibberish. Though it had apparently succeeded at one time in impressing unsophisticated minds, the work was unable to withstand the scrutiny of experts.

Professional Egyptologists to whom the *Alphabet and Grammar* was submitted for examination were quick to point out that the material in Joseph Smith's notebook bore no resemblance at all to any correct understanding of the ancient Egyptian language. As one of them, I. E. Edwards, put it, the whole work was, "largely a piece of imagination and lacking in any kind of scientific value." He added that it reminded him of "the writings of psychic practitioners which are sometimes sent to me."[8] There were many similar verdicts, all confirming that the person responsible for what Berrett had glowingly called "the first Egyptian grammar in America" could not possibly have understood the ancient Egyptian language.

Small wonder then that the timely appearance of the papyri (especially the one containing Facsimile No. 1), and the apparent willingness with which the Mormon Church displayed them to the world, helped to bolster the sagging confidence of those who were perhaps still shaken by the Grammar episode.

But things were not as simple as they used to be, and they were soon to become more confused.

Up to this point, a small number of people within the Church had for many years been intrigued by what were apparently Egyptian characters written on the margin of a number of the original Book of Abraham manuscripts.*

---

*At present there are four known original manuscripts of the Book of Abraham. Two

Speculation as to their significance occasionally surfaced,[9] but the figures were somewhat crudely drawn and it was apparently felt that little could be achieved by devoting much attention to them outside of scholarly circles. But with the growing number of people being exposed to the photographs of certain pages from the *Grammar*, it would now be only a matter of time before something startling was noticed: The figures on one of the Church's newly recovered papyrus fragments *matched — in order —* those found on the translation manuscripts! In other words, the *original source* (or at least part of it) from which Joseph Smith had translated the Book of Abraham had been identified![10]

But perhaps it was best to be cautious, for no one could say with certainty *who* had drawn what appeared to be Egyptian characters in the margin of the manuscripts, *when* they had done so, or *why* they had chosen the figures from this particular, unadorned scrap of papyrus

---

handwritten Book of Abraham manuscripts were included in Joseph Smith's Egyptian Alphabet & Grammar papers, and are referred to as "Manuscript No. 2" and "Manuscript No. 3." Both were penned simultaneously from dictation by two of Joseph's early scribes, William W. Phelps (Ms. No. 2) and Warren Parrish (Ms. No. 3). "Manuscript No. 2" is four pages in length and contains the text of the Book of Abraham from 1:4 - 2:6, and has Egyptian characters drawn in the left margin. "Manuscript No. 3" is six pages long and contains the text of the Book of Abraham from 1:1 - 2:2, also with Egyptian characters in the left margin.

A third manuscript, titled *Translation of the Book of Abraham written by his own hand upon papyrus and found in the catacombs of Egypt,* was located and purchased by LDS writer Wilford Wood in 1937, and has since been labeled "Manuscript No. 1," though it was actually produced shortly after manuscripts two and three. Ten pages in length and containing the text of the Book of Abraham 1:1 - 2:18, this manuscript was produced as follows: The first half of page one was written down from dictation in the hand of W. W. Phelps; the second half of page one through part of page seven was copied from "Ms. No. 3" in the hand of Warren Parrish; the remainder of page seven through page ten was recorded from dictation by Warren Parrish. This manuscript also contains Egyptian characters in the left margin of all pages.

One other manuscript, "Manuscript No. 4," is in the handwriting of Willard Richards, one of Joseph Smith's later scribes in Nauvoo. This is a copy of an earlier Book of Abraham manuscript, is fourteen pages in length, and contains the text of 1:1 - 2:18 and 3:18 - 3:26, only; there are no Egyptian characters accompanying this manuscript. It is believed that this was the copy used for the 1842 publication of the Book of Abraham in the *Times and Seasons.*

All four manuscripts are now located in the Historical Department of the LDS Church.

Translation of the Book of Abraham written
by his own hand upon papyrus and found
in the Catacombs of Egypt
In the land of the Chaldeans, at the residence of my
fathers, I, Abraham, saw, that it was needful
for me to obtain another place of residence, and seeing there was greater happiness and peace and rest
for me, I sought for the blessings of the fathers, and
the right whereunto I should be ordained to admin-
ister the same: having been a follower of righteousness;
desiring ~~to be~~ one who possessed great
knowledge, & a greater follower of righteous-
ness; a possessor of greater knowledge; a father of many nations; a prince
of peace; one who keeps the commandments of
God; a rightful heir; a high priest, holding
the right belonging to the fathers, from the beginning of time; even from the beginning, or
before the foundation of the earth, down to
the present time; even the right of the first
born, or the first man, who is Adam,
or first father, through the fathers, unto me.
I sought for mine appointment unto the
priesthood according to the appointment
of God, unto the fathers concerning the
seed.
my fathers having turned from their
righteousness, and from the holy commandments, which the Lord their
God had given unto them, unto the
worshiping of the gods of the heath-
ens.
utterly refused to hearken to my voice
for their hearts were set to do evil, and
were wholly turned to the god of Elkkener
and the god of Libnah and the god of

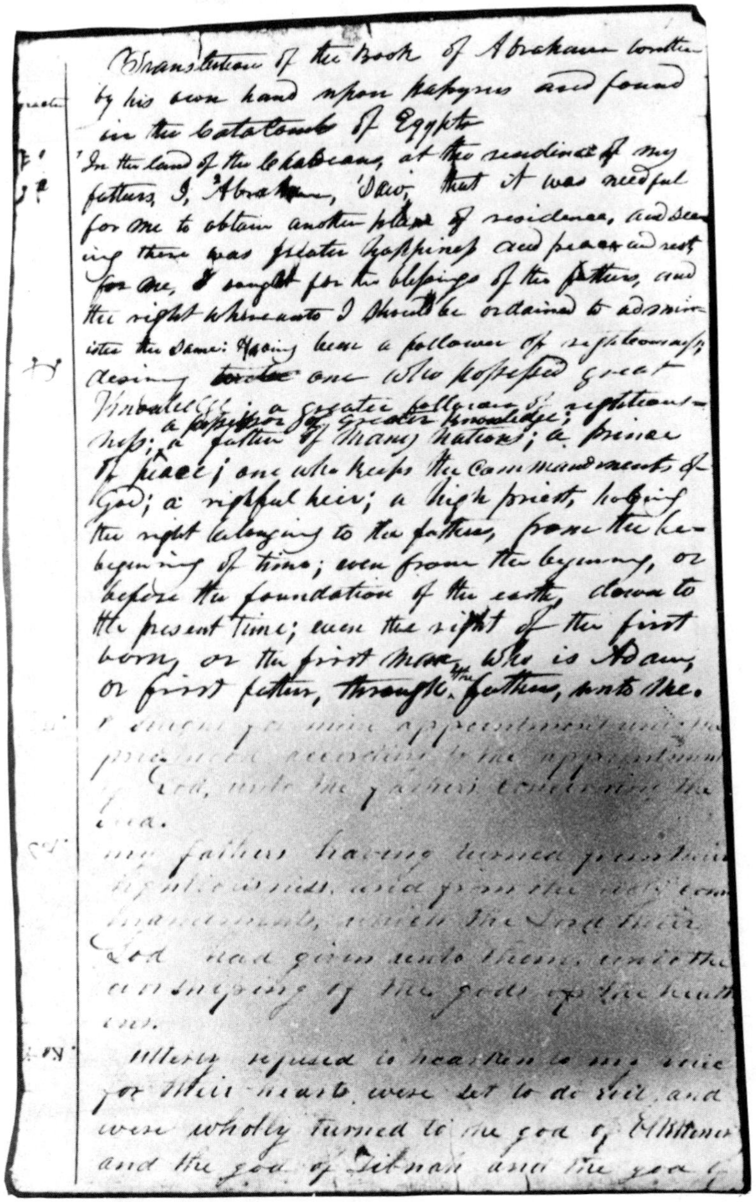

Page one of the ten-page Manuscript No. 1 (ca. 1835) in the handwriting of Joseph Smith's scribes, showing Book of Abraham material translated from Egyptian characters drawn on the left side of the page.

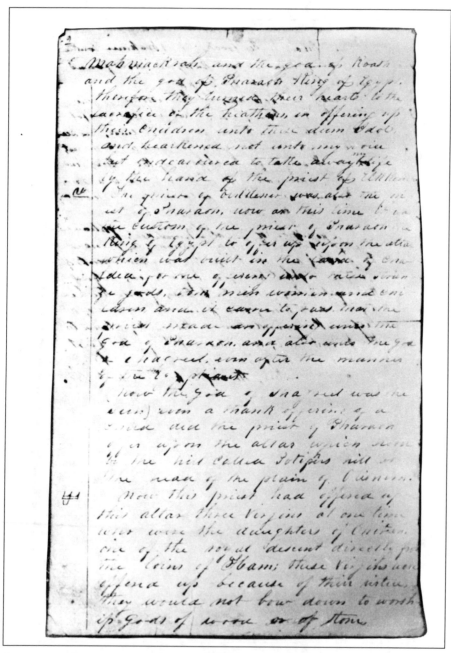

Page two of the ten-page Manuscript No. 1 (ca. 1835) in the handwriting of Joseph Smith's scribes, showing Book of Abraham material translated from Egyptian characters drawn on the left side of the page.

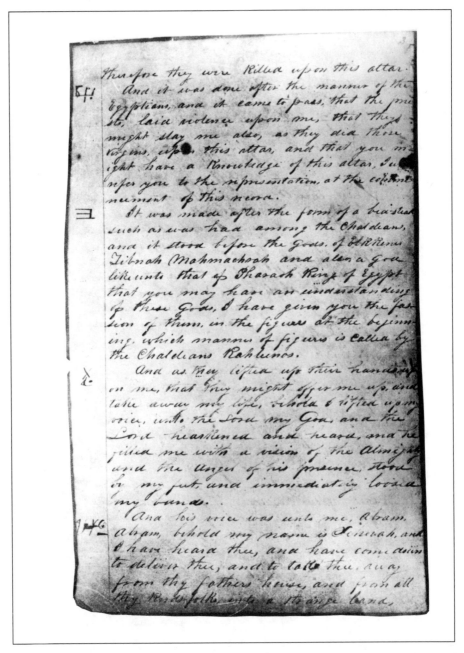

Page three of the ten-page Manuscript No. 1 (ca. 1835) in the handwriting of Joseph Smith's scribes, showing Book of Abraham material translated from Egyptian characters drawn on the left side of the page.

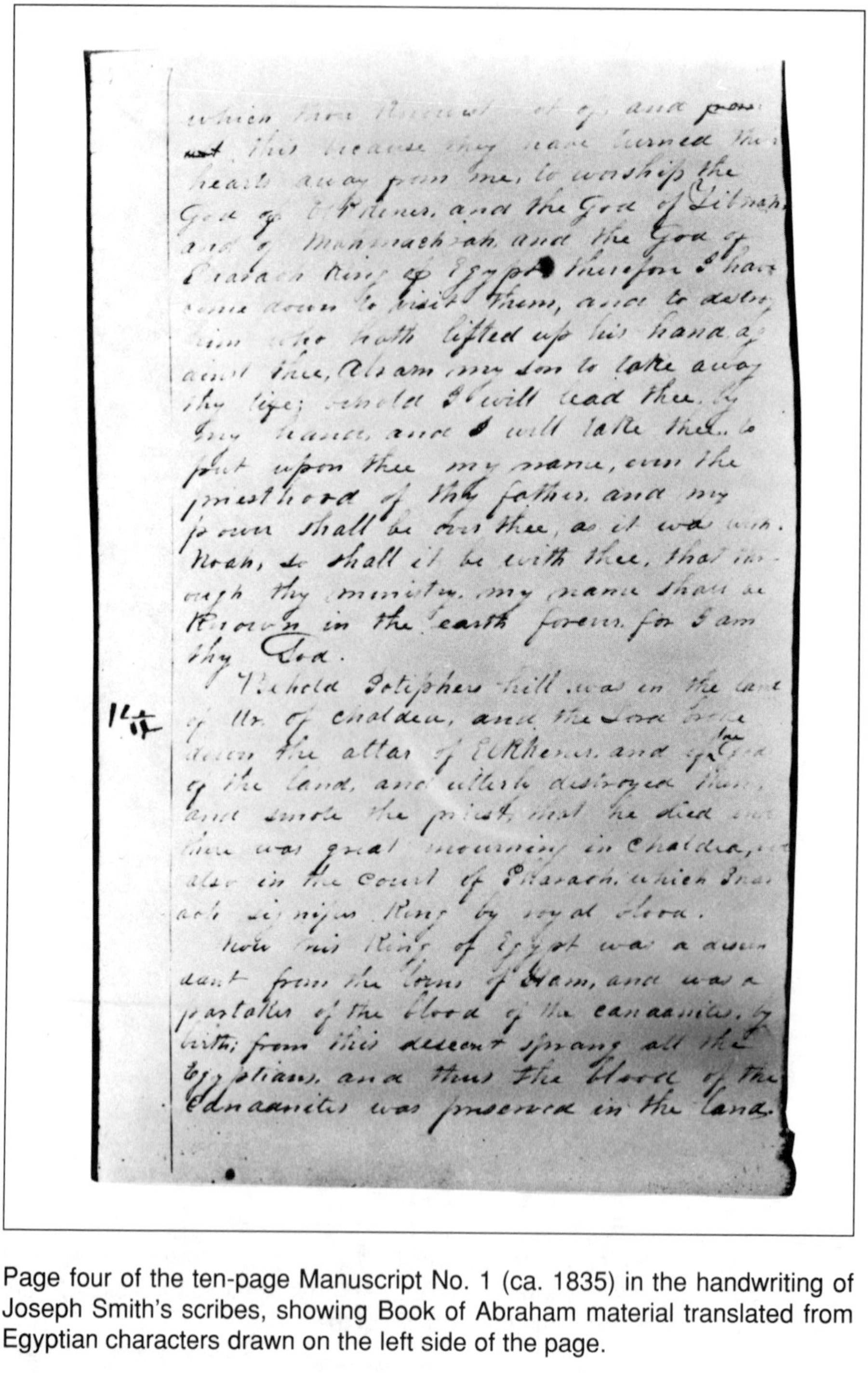

Page four of the ten-page Manuscript No. 1 (ca. 1835) in the handwriting of Joseph Smith's scribes, showing Book of Abraham material translated from Egyptian characters drawn on the left side of the page.

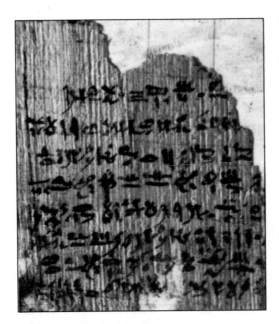

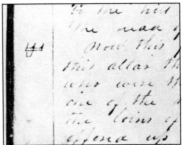

Page 2

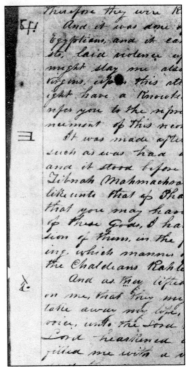

Page 3

These photographs show how the "Egyptian characters" on Manuscript No. 1 were derived from the first line of the "Small Sensen Papyrus" (Papyrus Joseph Smith XI). Manuscript No. 1 carried the figures from the first four lines of the papyrus; Manuscripts No. 2 and 3, which contain less text, carry the figures from only the first two lines. The same Egyptian characters in all three manuscripts correspond to identical passages of adjacent text, indicating a deliberate juxtaposition with the text of the translation manuscript.

over the other samples available.[11] Perhaps there was no real connection; if so, to proceed on such an assumption would invite a wild goose chase. Was there any *other* evidence to show that the fragment the *Improvement Era* article had labeled "Small Sensen Papyrus" could be unquestionably linked to the Book of Abraham?

As it happened, there was.

Papyrus Joseph Smith I — The original from which Facsimile No. 1 in the Book of Abraham was adapted.

Papyrus Joseph Smith XI ("Small Sensen Papyrus"), identified as the source from which the Egyptian characters on three Book of Abraham translation manuscripts were taken.

Of the eleven papyri fragments, only one *at first glance* had any apparent connection to the Book of Abraham (that is, the original from which Facsimile No. 1 was copied). But now, with attention drawn to the "Small Sensen" papyrus as well, it became obvious to at least one of the professional non-Mormon Egyptologists studying the material, Dr. Klaus Baer of the University of Chicago Oriental Institute, that the two fragments had once been joined to form a single, larger section of a scroll.

"They seem to have been cut apart after being mounted [on the backing paper]," Baer wrote after studying the photographs closely. Soon afterward he was able to confirm his theory by a physical examination of the fragments themselves. He found that the right edge of the "Small Sensen" papyrus (Papyrus Joseph Smith XI) had indeed originally been joined to the left edge of the fragment from which Facsimile No. 1 (Papyrus Joseph Smith I) had been copied.

Book of Abraham Scroll: This composite photograph shows how Papyrus Joseph Smith I and XI were once a single piece (see the color foldout on page 33 for a larger photo), glued to a common backing prior to being cut apart.

Dr. Klaus Baer of the University of Chicago said after examining them, "They clearly adjoin as proposed . . . matching upper and lower parts of handwriting are on the two pieces of paper with the cut going through the letters. The fiber patterns show that the papyri were adjoining parts of the same scroll and not simply mounted on adjoining pieces of paper. Papyrus fibers are always irregular and can be used (much like finger prints) to check whether fragments come from the same sheet; in this case, the horizontal fibers on the left and right edges of Papyrus Joseph Smith I and XI, respectively, match exactly." (From *Dialogue: A Journal of Mormon Thought,* Autumn 1968, pp. 133,134)

In fact, Dr. Baer's discovery fits perfectly with descriptions of the Book of Abraham papyrus scroll that occur in the Book of Abraham, itself:

> . . . and that you may have a knowledge of this altar, I will refer you to *the representation* [picture] *at the commencement of this record* (Book of Abraham 1:12).

A similar reference to Facsimile No. 1 is found two verses later:

> That you may have an understanding of these gods [before which stood the altar just mentioned], I have given you the fashion of them in the figures at the beginning [of the book] (Book of Abraham 1:14).

To appreciate the significance of these statements one must keep in mind that, in contrast to English, ancient Hieratic Egyptian (like Hebrew) was written from right to left, so that the story or message in a scroll begins at the right end and moves toward the left. Thus, the above statements tell us that a "representation," or drawing, of an Egyptian altar and gods occurs at the of beginning, or right edge of the Book of Abraham scroll (the "commencement of the record"), with the story then proceeding from right to left across the piece of papyrus material.

A look at the composite photographs of the Book of Abraham papyrus scroll on pages 33 and 51 shows that fragments I and XI of the Joseph Smith Papyri do in fact dovetail perfectly, as Dr. Baer discovered, and that piecing them back together results in just such an arrangement as is described in the Book of Abraham quotations above, with a drawing at the beginning, or right end, of the scroll.

Clearly Papyrus Joseph Smith XI — the "Small Sensen" papyrus — was as much a part of the Book of Abraham scroll as the Facsimile No. 1 fragment.

CHAPTER SIX

The Beginning of Disappointment

T HE STAGE WAS FINALLY SET for resolving the long, puzzling story of the Book of Abraham papyri: the ancient Egyptian hieroglyphic language had been deciphered by scholars, Joseph Smith's original papyri had been rediscovered and were available for study, and the three translation manuscripts pinpointed the specific fragment from which the Book of Abraham text had been taken, as well as providing a guide to how the Prophet related the Egyptian symbols to the English translation. All of the requirements for validation which both LDS Church apologists and the critics had insisted on for the last hundred years had been met. The question of whether or not Joseph Smith was telling the truth could at last be determined.

But more was at stake than Joseph Smith's reputation; more even than the validity of the Book of Abraham. Hanging in the balance was the entire religious system established by Joseph Smith. Mormonism could at last be *proven* to be either true or false.

Opinions within the Church were divided at this point as to the best direction in which to proceed. Since, unfortunately, there seemed to be no qualified Egyptologists within the Church, Dr. Sperry and Dr.

Clark from Brigham Young University both recommended a professional be consulted to work with the papyri. The University of Chicago's Dr. John A. Wilson, a brilliant man who had twice served as director of the University's Oriental Institute, was suggested, but LDS leaders were uncomfortable with allowing a non-Mormon scholar to do the translation. The papyri would remain under the Church's control at Brigham Young University, and by the end of 1967 the task of studying and translating them had fallen chiefly to BYU's Dr. Hugh Nibley.

From all appearances, the selection of Dr. Nibley for the project seemed an excellent one. An intense, deeply committed scholar, Nibley was perhaps more thoroughly versed in the study of ancient scripture than any of his LDS contemporaries. He was on familiar ground with the Latin, Greek, Hebrew, Syriac, Babylonian, Russian, French, German, Arabic, and Coptic languages. More importantly, he had produced a number of impressive books dealing with the interpretation of LDS scripture, doctrine, and responses to various "problem areas" raised by critics of the Church.[1]

However, Dr. Nibley was *not* an Egyptologist, as he himself was the first to admit. The ancient Egyptian language is a unique area of study that is extremely difficult to master. Nibley must have realized his expertise with other ancient languages would be of little help in working with the papyri, for shortly after learning of their existence (and long before their discovery was publicly announced) he had begun to study Egyptian in Chicago with Dr. John A. Wilson.[2] This "head start" in the ancient tongue was doubtless helpful to Nibley, but it was nevertheless quite inadequate, and he found himself unqualified to deal with the papyri on his own.

Fortunately, help was soon to appear from within the Church. Sometime early in 1967, Nibley had started corresponding with a Mormon elder named Dee Jay Nelson. Nelson explained that he had been involved in the study of Egyptology for some twenty years and that he had acquired an excellent functional knowledge of ancient Egyptian through years of field work under the late Egyptian Egyptologist Zakaria Goneim. For many years Goneim had been Keeper of Antiquities at the Necropolis of Saqqara. It was obvious to Nibley that Elder Nelson was probably the only available Latter-day Saint with sufficient exper-

BRIGHAM YOUNG UNIVERSITY
PROVO, UTAH

ERNEST L. WILKINSON, President

COLLEGE OF RELIGIOUS INSTRUCTION   June 27, 1967

Dear Bro. Nelson,

    Brother, you HAVE been around! But I am willing to bet you
that you have reach premature conclusions about the hypocephalus.
The Church has actually been able to procure some jars and other
artifacts from Qumran, and there MAY be some Ms fragments in the
collection: there are complications there that I can't go into. I
don't consider myself an Egyptologist at all, and don't intend to
get involved in the P.G.P. business unless I am forced into it—which
will probably be sooner than that. I actually don't know where the
original PG P Mss are, though I could find out easily enough; so far
my ignorance has served me well. I see no reason in the world why
you should not be taken into the confidence of the Brethren if this
thing ever comes out into the open; in fact, you should be enormously
useful to the Church. I have an colossal collection of notes which has
been building up through the years, and I think there is stuff in it
that would surprise and even conv ince you. As you know, this is a
happy hunting-ground for crackpots, and not being certified in anything
in particular I only rush in where fools fear to tread. I would like
very much to see you (I was in Billings last Thursday!) and hope that
we may collide before too long: this is the sort of thing that has to
be discussed makshufan wa maktuman. *in one place together* As you know, there are parties
in Salt Lake who are howling for a showdown on the P.G.P.; if they
have their way we may have to get together. Well, the nice thing about
discussion is that one never knows where it is going to lead—that is
why the experts are avoiding it as much as I am; what is even more wholesome,
all discussion quickly discloses interesting gaps and defects in the
knowledge of even the total authority. What have we to lose? Yours, Hugh Nibley

---

Hugh Nibley's letter to Dee Jay Nelson suggesting that Nelson could be
of assistance to the Church regarding the issue of the Joseph Smith
Papyri. This letter, though dated five months before the discovery of the
papyri was made public, was written at least a year after LDS authorities
were made aware of their existence. (Note Nibley's reference to "the
original PGP Mss" — that is, the original papyrus manuscripts used for
the Book of Abraham in the Pearl of Great Price). At the time this letter
was written, Dr. Nibley had had in his possession for at least a year the
photographs of the papyri which Dr. Atiya obtained from the Metropolitan
Museum.

tise to translate the papyri.[3]

In a letter dated June 27, 1967, Dr. Nibley told Nelson,

> I see no reason in the world why you should not be taken into the confidence
> of the Brethren if this thing ever comes out into the open; in fact, you should
> be enormously useful to the Church . . . As you know, there are parties in Salt
> Lake who are howling for a showdown on the P.G.P. [Pearl of Great Price,
> of which the Book of Abraham is a portion]; if they have their way we may
> have to get together . . . [4]

Which is just what they did, the two men finally meeting at BYU
early in January 1968, where they examined the original papyri. By
this time Dr. Nibley had probably been able to develop a sufficient
background knowledge in elementary Egyptian to be a fair judge of
Nelson's abilities. Apparently pleased and satisfied with Nelson, Nibley sent him, with a written recommendation, to meet with LDS Apostle
N. Eldon Tanner at Church headquarters in Salt Lake City. There
Nelson was to obtain one of the special sets of papyri photographs
which were then being selectively released for Church-related pur-
poses only.[5]

Confident that a translation would soon be forthcoming, the editors
of the Church's *Improvement Era* magazine prepared the February
1968 issue, complete with an impressive collection of photographs of
the Book of Abraham papyri, and the promise that in future articles Dr.
Nibley would reveal "the meaning of the hieroglyphics and illustrations on these valuable manuscripts."[6]

Meanwhile, two things were becoming clear to those working with
the papyri. First, two key papyri fragments belonged together to form
one piece. And second, these fragments could be linked to the Book of
Abraham. However, Nelson, who by now was close to finishing his
translations, was learning something which greatly disturbed him: not
only did the papyri (including Facsimile No. 1 and the Small Sensen
fragment) not contain the Book of Abraham, there was not even the
remotest connection between their contents and Abraham. They were
simply ordinary Egyptian funeral documents; nothing more and nothing less.

Nelson said as much when he submitted the results of his work to the LDS Church, sending copies by mail to both Nibley and Tanner.*

The church declined the offer to publish Nelson's findings, however, unless substantial revision or explanation of them was made beforehand, conditions Nelson felt he could not accept.[7]

Still, Dr. Nibley praised Nelson's work (and even quoted a portion of it) in the Spring 1968 issue of the publication *Brigham Young University Studies,* calling it a "conscientious and courageous piece of work," and pointing out that it supplied students with "a usable and reliable translation of the available papyri that once belonged to Joseph Smith." But when pressed as to why a translation was not forthcoming from the Church — indeed, why they had not proceeded with all haste to produce such a translation — Nibley puzzled his readers by admitting that "it is doubtful whether any translation could do as much good as harm."

Such comments from Nibley, and his remarks concerning Nelson, were probably prompted by the fact that Nelson's translation work had been in print since the first of April, despite the fact that the LDS Church had refused publication. When his own church had refused his work, Nelson offered his translation and conclusions to Jerald and Sandra Tanner, who were pleased to publish this work, as they had the *Egyptian Alphabet and Grammar*, earlier. While it would have been pointless for Nibley or anyone else to challenge a translation certain to be verified by others as time passed, it was still a sore spot among many LDS people that a press considered "hostile" to the Church had been the first to publish a translation of the papyri. Even publication by neutral, non-Mormon scholars would have been preferable to that!

It was at this point, and with this thought in mind, that the editors of *Dialogue: A Journal of Mormon Thought*, decided to approach a number of renowned Egyptologists, requesting *their* interpretations of the Joseph Smith papyri.[8] This was a dramatic and daring step, for *Dialogue* is not an official publication of the LDS Church. Rather, it is a

---

*Although Nelson's translation was considered correct and accurate by Nibley and others (though not suitable for publication by the LDS Church), both Nelson and his work soon came under attack by Church members when Nelson's association with the papyri eventually caused him and his family to lose faith in Mormonism and "resign" their membership in the LDS Church. (See Part III, LDS Reactions).

privately controlled magazine used as a vehicle by Mormon "intelligentsia" to discuss controversial topics not explored in depth by Church-controlled publications, such as the *Improvement Era*. On more than one occasion in the past *Dialogue* had presented articles dealing with "touchy" subjects such as polygamy and the Adam-God teachings of Brigham Young, and in doing so had focused the displeasure of various General Authorities on members of its editorial board. (One of *Dialogue's* editors later admitted that he had feared just such a confrontation with Church authorities over the plan to publish translations of the Joseph Smith papyri. As it turned out, the Church remained silent on the matter and the article was not opposed.[9])

Just the same, Nibley was quick to caution the Saints against attributing too much significance to the interpretations of the scholars. When the reports began to come in — from Dr. John A. Wilson (University of Chicago), confirming the identification of all the fragments as funerary texts, and from Dr. Klaus Baer (University of Chicago) and Professor Richard Parker (Brown University), each providing translations of the "Small Sensen" papyrus, they agreed in all essentials with Nelson's. At this point Nibley began to shift the focus of his own work. Instead of stressing an objective study of the papyri themselves, he began to develop various theories on how the Book of Abraham could have been produced other than as the result of "a 'translation' in any accepted sense of the word."[10]

After Wilson and Parker's translations and comments were published, Nibley wrote in an article in the Summer 1968 issue of *Dialogue,*

> Today nobody claims that Joseph Smith got his information through ordinary scholarly channels. In that case, one wonders how any amount of checking along ordinary scholarly channels is going to get us very far.

Nibley's articles in the *Improvement Era* ran for more than two years (January 1968 – May 1970). In them, his rather lavish display of scholarship portrayed him as confident and capable, and this created many favorable expectations within the Church. But contrary to what LDS readers were promised, Nibley never provided a translation of any of the papyri in these *Improvement Era* articles.

Meanwhile Nelson, armed with his published translations, a flair for public speaking, and a penchant for showmanship, began lecturing on his exclusive work with the Book of Abraham papyri. And the longer he lectured the more he embellished his list of credentials and past accomplishments.[11]

Thus, while Nibley and Nelson set out on very different courses, the actions of both men served to obscure the one vital issue in the controversy that mattered: the actual evidence of the papyri themselves.

CHAPTER SEVEN

The Evidence of the Papyri

W HEN THE OPPORTUNITY WAS extended to several Egyptologists to examine and comment on the eleven papyrus fragments from the Metropolitan Museum, the same papyri that once belonged to Joseph Smith and from which he claimed to have translated the Book of Abraham, each of them arrived at the same conclusion: the papyri were common funeral texts, all clearly dating after 500 B.C., fifteen-hundred years or more later than Abraham's time, and having no connection whatever with the biblical patriarch Abraham. Dr. Baer of Chicago's Oriental Institute identified the eleven fragments (and also an additional fragment from the Church Historian's office that had been included with Smith's Alphabet and Grammar material, for a total of twelve) as belonging to portions of three original papyrus volumes:[2]

1. *Book of Breathings* (also known as *Shait en Sensen*) "Breathing permit" for the priest Hor, son of the priest Osorwer and the lady Tikhebyt, as found on Papyrus Joseph Smith I, X and XI.

2. *Book of the Dead* belonging to the lady Amon-Re Neferirnub, as found on Papyrus Joseph Smith IIIA and IIIB.

3. *Book of the Dead* for the deceased Tshenmin (or Ta Shert Min; Ta-Shere-Min), daughter of Nes-Khensu, as found on Papyrus Joseph Smith II, IV, V, VI, VII, VIII, and IX (the fragment from the *Alphabet and Grammar*).

Photographs and examinations of all twelve of the Joseph Smith papyrus fragments appear on the following pages. The piece labeled Papyrus Joseph Smith I (the Facsimile No. 1 fragment) is given first, followed by Papyrus Joseph Smith XI (the "Small Sensen" text fragment), since the two were originally directly adjoining pieces of a single scroll, identified by Joseph Smith as "the writings of Abraham." Papyrus Joseph Smith X, another fragment from the same scroll, is given next. Next is Papyrus Joseph Smith IIIA and IIIB, and finally the remainder of the papyri. The numerical designations used are those which were originally given the papyri by Dr. Hugh Nibley in the February 1968 *Improvement Era.*

(The color foldout on pp. 33, 34 shows how a number of the fragments originally fit together to make up sections of two papyrus scrolls, identified by Joseph Smith as "the writings of Abraham," and "the writings of Joseph of Egypt," respectively. These are the first published, color photographs of the Joseph Smith papyri.)

Papyrus Joseph Smith I

This fragment (p. 64) bears a mortuary vignette, flanked by hieroglyphic writing. It is the opening portion of an Egyptian *Shait en Sensen,* or *Book of Breathings.* The *Book of Breathings,* a late and abbreviated funerary text that grew out of the earlier and more complex *Book of the Dead,* first appeared sometime near the beginning of the Ptolemaic (Greek) Period, in the late fourth or early third-century B.C. Written on a scroll, sealed with bitumen, and placed inside the coffin with the deceased, the *Book of Breathings* contained a series of magic spells to be recited by the spirit of the corpse after burial in order to teach itself to "breathe," and thus be prepared for its existence in the afterlife.

This particular scroll was prepared (as determined by handwriting, spelling, content, etc.) sometime during the late Ptolemaic or early Roman period (circa 50 B.C. to A.D. 50).[3] When it was originally unrolled in Kirtland in 1835, major portions of the book were damaged, as may be seen in the photograph. (Egyptologists have been critical of Joseph Smith's interpretation of this vignette, and have pointed out that there are serious errors in his reconstructions of missing portions. A professional reconstruction is compared to that of

Smith, on pp. 64, 65.)

The five vertical columns of hieroglyphic figures on the papyrus confirm the funeral nature of the vignette (see p. 102 for an explanation of the Egyptian mythology represented here), giving titles, name, and parentage of the man for whose benefit the scroll was originally prepared. Translated by Dr. Baer,[4] from right to left they read:

Lines 1 - 3 — ". . . the prophet of Amonrasonter, prophet [?] of Min Bull-of-his-Mother, prophet [?] of Khons the Governor . . . Hor, justified, son of the holder of the same titles, master of secrets, and purifier of the gods Osorwer, justified [?] . . . Tikhebyt, justified. May your ba live among them, and may you be buried in the West . . ."

Line 4 — too little remaining to translate.

Line 5 — "May you give him a good, splendid burial on the West of Thebes just like . . ."

The differences between these final two drawings are significant. In Smith's version, a human-headed figure holds a knife; in the professional reconstruction this is a jackal-headed figure without a knife. Also, in Smith's reconstruction the flying bird at the right has a bird's head, while in the professional reconstruction the bird has a man's head (notice the beard stroke coming down from the chin in front of the hair in the picture, and compare this with Smith's Facsimile No. 1). In Smith's the man lying down has both hands raised; in the other a bird is hovering over a man who has one hand raised, there being too many lines in the upper hand in the photograph to represent fingers. The man lying down is also shown as an *ithyphallic* figure in the professional reconstruction — this is explained further on page 102.

Before Joseph Smith's reconstruction of the drawing was published in the Mormon periodical *Times and Seasons,* he took special pains to insure that those portions missing from the papyrus itself were depicted exactly as he intended. He supervised the preparation of the woodcut,[5] approved the cut when it was completely finished, and provided the "inspired" explanation of the scene — including explanations of the parts he had restored. All this indicates the drawing of Facsimile No. 1 as it appears in the Book of Abraham is precisely as Joseph wanted it to be.

The rediscovery of the original papyrus has confirmed what

Egyptologists had long suspected — that Joseph Smith produced Facsimile No. 1 by copying a scene from a genuine but damaged Egyptian papyrus, and that the errors in Facsimile No. 1 correspond to the missing portions of the original, which Joseph

Right: Facsimile No. 1 from the Book of Abraham. Joseph Smith produced it by incorrectly restoring the damaged Papyrus Joseph Smith I.

TIMES AND SEASONS.

"Truth will prevail."

Vol. III. No. 9.]   CITY OF NAUVOO, ILL. MARCH, 1, 1842.   [Whole No. 45.

A FAC-SIMILE FROM THE BOOK OF ABRAHAM.
NO. 1.

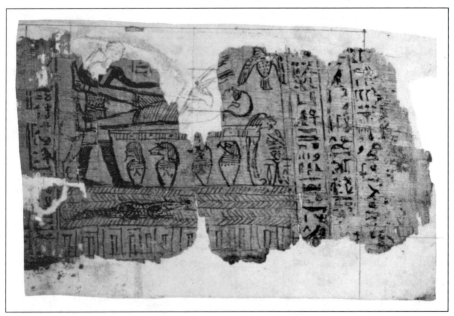

Above: The Facsimile No. 1 papyrus (Papyrus Joseph Smith I) — unretouched photograph as it appears glued to nineteenth-century backing paper, some sections slightly misaligned, with missing details crudely sketched in. Note the penciled-in head of standing figure, facing front, with a knife raised above his shoulder.

Above: As an intermediate step in producing a correct restoration of the above scene, a cleaned-up version must first be made.

Below: A restoration of the Facsimile No. 1 papyrus based on the modern study of Egyptology, and similar scenes in numerous existing papyri.

Smith incorrectly filled in. None of the reconstructions supplied by Smith are vindicated by the study of Egyptology. Instead, all of them have been shown to be erroneous.

Papyrus Joseph Smith XI

This single fragment is unquestionably the most significant of the eleven recovered by the LDS Church in 1967— more important than even the instantly recognizable "Facsimile No. 1" fragment. It was from the Egyptian characters on the right hand side of this "Small Sensen" papyrus that Joseph Smith claimed to derive the translated text of the Book of Abraham.

The right edge of this papyrus was once connected to the left edge of the "Facsimile No. 1" papyrus (see foldout, p. 33). The larger scroll section they formed was cut apart after it was glued to backing paper in the nineteenth century. A translation shows it to be the opening portion of a first-century A.D. *Book of Breathings* that had been prepared for Hor, a deceased priest of the Egyptian God Amon.

Divided into two columns, the figures on the right half give instructions to those embalming Hor's body on how to properly wrap up the collection of magic spells (that is, the *Book of Breathings)* so they are included in the mummy wrappings over his breast. (Translation by Richard A. Parker.)[6]

Line 1 — [. . . .] this great pool of Khonsu
Line 2 — [Osiris Hor, justified], born of Taykhebyt, a man
        likewise.
Line 3 — After (his) two arms are [fast]ened to his
        breast, one wraps the Book of Breathings, which is
Line 4 — with writing both inside and outside of it, with
        royal linen, it being placed [at] his left arm
Line 5 — near his heart, this having been done at his
Line 6 — wrapping and outside it. If this book be recited
        for him, then
Line 7 — he will breathe like the soul[s of gods] for ever
        and
Line 8 — ever.

The left side of the fragment begins the series of spells to be recited.

Papyrus Joseph Smith XI

Papyrus Joseph Smith X

Usually referred to as the "Large Sensen" papyrus, this fragment is a continuation of the same *Book of Breathings* scroll just examined (Papyri Joseph Smith I, XI; *see* foldout, p. 33). Prepared for a priest of the Egyptian god Amon, named Hor, son of the priest Osorwer and the lady Tikhebyt, it continues the spells begun in the second column of Papyrus Joseph Smith XI. The entire text deals with common themes from pagan Egyptian mythology and bears no similarity whatever to the subject of Joseph Smith's Book of Abraham.

Much of the right-hand portion of this brittle fragment has now flaked away from the backing paper to which it was mounted. There is, however, an impression of the papyrus that remains in the outline of glue, which allows us to see how much of it was originally present when it was unrolled. When all three fragments (Papyrus Joseph Smith X, XI and I) are lined up in order, an outline of their top edge shows a perfectly repeating pattern of dips and gouges, demonstrating that these missing portions once overlapped each other when the scroll was rolled up, and that they broke off and were lost together when the scroll was first unrolled. This point is particularly important since the major differences between Joseph Smith's version of the scene in Papyrus Joseph Smith I and the expert restoration are all found in the areas reconstructed by Smith. Joseph Smith could not have seen what was on those missing pieces, so that responsibility for the rendition of Facsimile No. 1 is entirely his own.

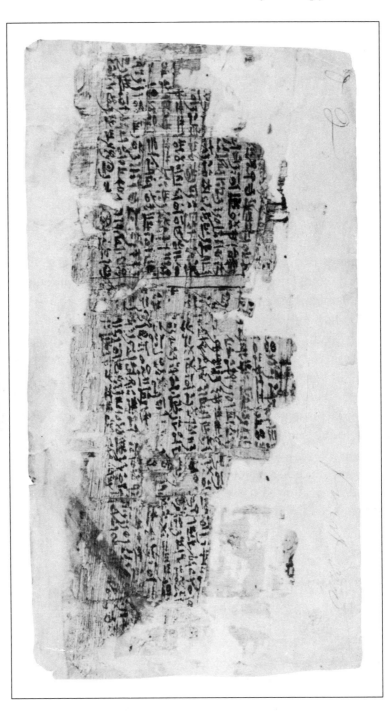

Papyrus Joseph Smith X

Papyrus Joseph Smith IIIA and IIIB

These two fragments are simply one scene cut into two pieces. Shown is an illustration from the Egyptian *Book of the Dead*, Chapter (or *Spell)* 125 — Osiris judging the dead. The deceased woman for whom this book was prepared, a female musician named Amon-Re Neferirnub,[7] is being led before the throne of Osiris, god of the underworld, by Maat, goddess of justice, while Toth (bottom center) is weighing her merit against her fault, on a balance. The deceased wears a perfumed cone and lotus flower on her head, in accordance with Egyptian festival attire. Osiris sits before a libation platform topped by a stylized papyrus plant and bearing jars of wines and oils, wearing the double-plumed crown and holding the royal flail and crook. This is a very common Egyptian funerary scene.

It is not known whether Joseph Smith ever made any particular identification of these fragments, or any other portions of this copy of the *Book of the Dead.*

Papyrus Joseph Smith III A   Papyrus Joseph Smith III B

Papyrus Joseph Smith IV

This fragment and the six remaining fragments which follow, are all part of a single scroll, an illustrated Egyptian *Book of the Dead* prepared for a woman named Ta-shert-Min, daughter of Nes-Khensu, sometime in the second half of the Ptolemaic period.[8] This was after hieratic writing had evolved from the more elaborate hieroglyphic form, but before the *Book of the Dead* was generally replaced by simpler funeral texts (such as the *Book of Breathings*). The book is divided into many short chapters, or "spells," which are readily identifiable and often accompanied by vignettes to illustrate them. The scenes contain the same basic material and occur in the same order typical of the *Book of the Dead* during this late period. For example, shown on this fragment are portions of Chapters 99, 100, 101, 103, 104, 105, and 106. In addition, several small fragments from a completely different work — the later *"Book of Breathings* for the priest Hor"* — have been glued haphazardly over stains and gaps that appear on the original fragment, apparently as a cosmetic measure to make the fragment appear more attractive. It is not known who may have done this or when, but it appears that whoever attached these additional flakes had more of the *Book of Breathings* scroll available to him than the three fragments from the Metropolitan Museum collection. While at least two major flakes can be traced to Papyrus Joseph Smith X and at least one to Papyrus Joseph Smith XI, the large flake in the upper left corner (which is upside down) comes from neither, though it unquestionably has its origin in the *Book of Breathings*. Also, a tiny flake atop the large flake directly in the center (also glued on upside down) appears to contain design elements similar to the upper border of "Facsimile No. 3 from the Book of Abraham" (the papyrus original of this scene has not been located).

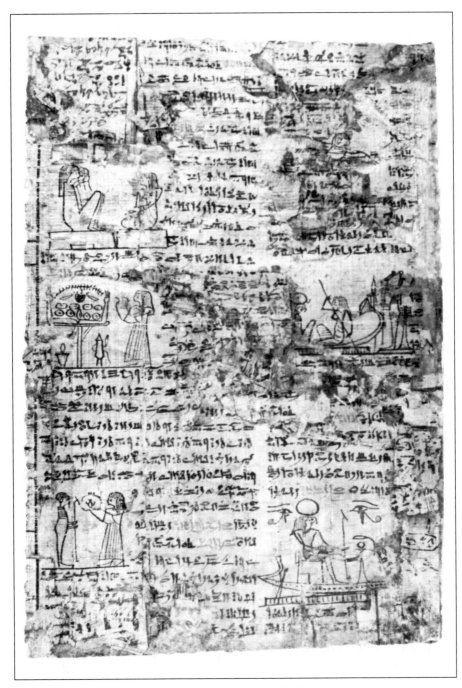

Papyrus Joseph Smith IV

Papyrus Joseph Smith VI

Another portion of the Egyptian *Book of the Dead* for Ta-shert-Min, this fragment contains chapters 83, 86, 87, 88, and 89. It fits between Papyrus Joseph Smith V on the right, and Papyrus Joseph Smith IV on the left, and contains several sets of rubrics, or writings in red. A large flake with writing from a different papyrus has been glued upside-down over a bare spot in the upper right corner of the backing paper.

Papyrus Joseph Smith V

Still another portion of the Egyptian *Book of the Dead* for the lady Ta-shert-Min. This one contains Chapters 72, 74, 75, 76, and 77. It also has numerous rubrics.

Certain features in this fragment and in Papyrus Joseph Smith IV have particular significance when compared with published statements made about them by Joseph Smith in 1835 (*see* chapter 8).

Papyrus Joseph Smith VII

This is actually two small, unconnected fragments, though they were once very close together on the original scroll. The fragment on the left attaches along the upper right-hand edge of Papyrus Joseph Smith V. Egyptian *Book of the Dead* for Ta-shert-Min, Chapters 53, 54, 63, and 65. Rubrics are visible on the left fragment only.

Papyrus Joseph Smith VIII

Egyptian *Book of the Dead* for Ta-shert-Min, Chapters 57, 67, 70, and 72. This fragment fits into the scroll on the lower right edge of Papyrus Joseph Smith V, immediately below the portion of Papyrus Joseph Smith VII. It also contains rubrics.

Papyrus Joseph Smith VII

Papyrus Joseph Smith VIII

Papyrus Joseph Smith IX

It is unclear how the LDS Church came to be in possession of this fragment, since no papyrus fragments were believed to have been taken west by the Mormons when they left Nauvoo. Some believe that this mounted fragment may have been given to an Indian chief as a token of respect by Joseph Smith while he was still living, and later returned to Brigham Young by the same Indian when the Mormons were moving west after Joseph's death.[9] In any case, it found its way long ago into the collection of notes and manuscripts that made up Joseph's Egyptian Alphabet and Grammar material in the Church Historian's Office. There its existence was known of at least since Sperry's "rediscovery" in 1935, though scholars coming across it were instructed by the Church Historian's office to keep it as "a matter of confidence." This they apparently did until a microfilm of the Grammar material reached the Tanners of Modern Microfilm Company (now called Utah Lighthouse Ministry) in 1965 and was published by them in 1966. The existence of this fragment was finally acknowledged by the LDS Church two years later in the February 1968 *Improvement Era.* The article announced as an "interesting development," the "locating of another fragment in the vaults at the Church Historian's Office."

Known as the "Church Historian's fragment," this badly damaged papyrus is also a part of the Egyptian *Book of the Dead* belonging to Ta-shert-Min, and was located on the original scroll somewhat nearer the beginning of the book (to the right) than the other, better preserved fragments recovered from the Metropolitan Museum (*see* p. 34).

Papyrus Joseph Smith IX — Church Historian's Fragment

Papyrus Joseph Smith II

With no text visible other than brief captions, this scene can still be identified as belonging to Chapter 110 of the Egyptian *Book of the Dead* for the Lady Ta-shert-Min. The right edge of this fragment connects to the upper third part of the left edge of Papyrus Joseph Smith IV. No rubrics are visible on this illustration.

Though no one copy of the *Book of the Dead* ever contains all the many known chapters (or *spells),* certain chapters are always shown in the same order in late scrolls such as this one. For instance, chapter 125 of the *Book of the Dead,* would follow shortly after this part of the book, with a typical depiction of the deceased being led before the throne of Osiris (basic elements similar to those found on Papyrus Joseph Smith IIIA and III B) being placed at the end (inside) of the scroll to conclude it. (The significance of the scene depicted in chapter 125 of the *Book of the Dead* is discussed in the following chapter.)

CHAPTER EIGHT

The Book of Joseph?

I T WILL BE REMEMBERED that when Joseph Smith first examined his new papyri collection in 1835, he reported that it included writings of the Hebrew patriarch Joseph:

> . . . I commenced the translation of some of the characters or hieroglyphics, and much to our joy found that one of the rolls contained the writings of Abraham, another *the writings of Joseph of Egypt,* etc., — a more full account of which will appear in its place, as I proceed to examine or unfold them.[1]

Recent discoveries have shown conclusively that the roll of papyrus Joseph had represented as the Book of Abraham was actually the *"Book of Breathings* for the priest Hor." But what of the "writings of Joseph of Egypt?" Is there any indication of what *that* scroll may have been?

The answer is yes. In fact, there is every indication that the scroll Joseph Smith identified as the "Book of Joseph," was in fact the "Egyptian *Book of the Dead* for the lady Ta-shert-Min, daughter of Nes-Khensu."

Joseph Smith apparently never produced any "translation" material for the "Book of Joseph" (as he did with his Book of Abraham),[2] but fortunately we do have Oliver Cowdery's observations on the scroll that the Prophet identified as the Book of Joseph. Cowdery, longtime associate of Joseph Smith and one of the principle scribes involved with the papyri, gave an excellent description of this scroll in a letter that appeared in a Mormon publication of the day. He writes:

> The language in which this record is written is very comprehensive, and many of the hieroglyphics exceedingly striking. The evidence is apparent upon the face that they were written by persons acquainted with the history of creation, the fall of man, and more or less the correct ideas or notions of Deity.
>
>   The representation of the god-head — three, yet in one, is curiously drawn to give simply, though impressively, the writer's views of that exalted personage.* The serpent, represented as walking, or formed in a manner to be able to walk, standing in front of, and near a female figure, is to me, one of the greatest representations I have ever seen upon paper, or a writing substance; and must go so far towards convincing the rational mind of the correctness and divine authority of the holy scriptures . . . as to carry away, with one mighty sweep, the whole atheistical fabric . . . Enoch's Pillar, as mentioned in Josephus, is upon the same roll . . . The inner end of the same roll, (Joseph's record,) presents a representation of the judgment: At one view you behold the Savior seated upon his throne, crowned, and holding the sceptres of righteousness and power; before him are assembled the twelve tribes of Israel and all the kingdoms of the world; while Michael the Archangel holds the keys to the bottomless pit in which Satan has been chained . . . (From a letter of Oliver Cowdery to William Frye, dated December 25, 1835, and published in the *Latter Day Saints' Messenger and Advocate* of the same month.)

A comparison of Cowdery's descriptions with scenes found on the recovered fragments of the *Book of the Dead* for Ta-shert-Min appears on the following pages. In addition, an important section of this scroll which is now missing, but which would surely have been included in the last part (inner end) of the *Book of the Dead,* is the scene from

---

*Notice here that Cowdery, in 1835, still maintains the then not uncommon concept among the LDS of the Trinitarian nature of God — ''three, yet in one . . . *that exalted personage.''* Mormon doctrine did not develop the concept of a godhead composed of three separate personages until several years later (see pages 21, 22 of this book).

Right: *"The representation of the god-head — three, yet one, is curiously drawn to give simply, though impressively, the writer's view of that exalted personage . . ."*

Detail from Papyrus Joseph Smith IV

Detail from Papyrus Joseph Smith V

Left: *"The serpent, represented as walking, or formed in a manner to be able to walk, standing in front of and near a female figure, is to me one of the greatest representations I have ever seen upon paper, or a writing substance . . ."*

Chapter 125, where the deceased is led into the presence of Osiris (compare photo and examination of Papyrus Joseph Smith IIIA and IIIB on pp. 70, 71; see also the color foldout on p. 34, which shows a large section of the Book of Joseph scroll). Cowdery's description of "the Savior seated upon his throne, crowned, and holding the scepters of righteousness and power," along with the other details he mentions associated with this scene, correspond very well to the major elements found in numerous similar scenes depicting the Court of Osiris.

It is quite apparent from the evidence Cowdery left us that he was indeed describing a typical scene from the Egyptian *Book of the Dead* rather than a story penned by the patriarch Joseph, as he had been led to believe. Still, Cowdery's interpretation should not be considered unusual for the period, as he was dealing with then indecipherable manuscripts of undetermined origin and date (there being no true understanding of Egyptian mythology or funerary texts available during Joseph Smith's lifetime). Cowdery's impressions are merely common-sense speculations by a person with no expertise regarding the esoteric subject matter at hand. Joseph's scribe could easily have been describing almost any *Book of the Dead* scroll. Joseph Smith's papyri collection included at least one other *Book of the Dead* manuscript

Detail from Papyrus Joseph Smith V. *"Enoch's Pillar, as mentioned in Josephus, is upon the same roll . . ."*

(that of Amon-Re Neferirnub)[3] and possibly still another (according to notes made in the Egyptian Alphabet and Grammar material). But he was most likely referring to one that had been made for Ta-shert-Min. The picture of the ''serpent with legs standing near a female figure,'' for example, that had so impressed Cowdery, had been copied from Papyrus Joseph Smith V into the pages of a small notebook (included among the Grammar material) bearing the handwritten title *"Valuable Discovery of hidden records that have been obtained from the ancient burying place of the Egyptians,"* followed by the signature of Joseph Smith, Jr.[4]

Also significant is the presence of rubrics on the Ta-shert-Min scroll. Again, it is Cowdery who identifies this feature for us in the article previously cited:

> Upon the subject of the Egyptian records, or rather the writings of Abraham and Joseph, I may say a few words. This record is beautifully *written on papyrus* with *black, and **a small part red,*** ink or paint, in *perfect preservation.* (emphasis added)

Cowdery's understanding that two of these "records" were the "writings of Abraham and Joseph" must be attributed to the fact that Joseph Smith identified them as such, since the Mormon leader never felt it was necessary to correct Cowdery's published descriptions. However, it should also be noted that some of the key phrases in Cowdery's description were derived from the published placard Michael Chandler used to help promote his traveling mummy exhibition. According to a statement by several prominent Philadelphia doctors who had viewed Chandler's exhibit, the placard read in part:

> The features of some of these Mummies are in perfect expression. The *papyrus*, covered with *black or red ink, or paint*, in *excellent preservation*, are very interesting.[5] (emphasis added)

It can be seen, then, that Cowdery's reference to "a small part red" does not mean to say that throughout the entire collection of papyri there was uniformly scattered a small number of rubrics, but rather, that of the two rolls, just one had this feature of writing in red. Regarding this *collection,* which did include some papyri with black and red writing, he believed *one* roll to contain the writings of Abraham, and a *different* roll the writings of Joseph. The crucial point is that of these *two rolls,* there was *only one* with black and red writing.*

Since the *"Book of Breathings* for the priest Hor" (the scroll identi-

---

*Some LDS apologists, in attempting to respond to the damaging implications raised by a connection between the *Book of Breathings* and the Book of Abraham, initially proposed the argument that Cowdery's description of "black and a small part red" writing must refer to *both* the Joseph *and* Abraham scrolls. Since the *Book of Breathings* fragments contained no rubrics, they insisted these could not be from the same roll identified by Cowdery; thus the original papyrus from which the Book of Abraham was produced must still be lost. In this way, Joseph Smith's credibility as a Seer and translator is not threatened. One Mormon writer (Nibley) even attributed Cowdery's description, verbatim, to Joseph Smith, indicating that it was Smith who gave the description found in *History of the Church*, vol. 2, p. 348. Nibley evidently ignored the footnote at the end of the same entry which clearly points out that the wording had been adapted from Cowdery's letter.

The growing realization that Cowdery's remarks had also been adapted from Chandler's earlier source has caused this particular approach to the problem to lose credibility. It has now been generally abandoned by most of those originally proposing it (including Nibley), though from time to time it is considered valid by novices who come across older, outdated, LDS writings which seek to defend the Pearl of Great Price. For a brief look at other explanations and defenses that have been offered, see *Part III — LDS Reactions.*

fied by Joseph Smith as "writings of Abraham") does not contain rubrics, the scroll identified by Smith as the "writings of Joseph" should. And, indeed, it does. The *"Book of the Dead* for Ta-shert-Min,"* which matches so perfectly Cowdery's detailed description of the Book of Joseph is the only text among the recovered papyri that has these rubrics.* (The rubrics are clearly visible in the color foldout picture of the Book of Joseph scroll on p. 34.)

Conclusions

As this chapter has demonstrated, the papyrus fragments which Joseph Smith identified as the writings of the biblical patriarch Joseph correspond perfectly to the six papyri in the Joseph Smith Papyrus collection rediscovered in 1967: Papyrus Joseph Smith II, IV, V, VI, VII, and VIII (shown together in the composite photograph on p. 34). In light of Joseph Smith's identification of these papyri as the writings of the Hebrew patriarch Joseph, it is remarkable that the Mormon Church has failed to translate them through its self-proclaimed gift of *Seer* — described by Apostle Orson Pratt as a unique sign of the One True Church, the ability to translate "ancient records in any language" by the gift and power of God, just as Joseph Smith had done (see p. 37). Surely any manuscript of such antiquity and authored by such an illustrious person would be of inestimable archeological and spiritual significance. In *Mormon Doctrine*, Apostle Bruce R. McConkie, writ-

---

*There is also contemporary evidence which may suggest that the Ta-shert-Min papyrus was the only one among Joseph Smith's entire collection that contained rubrics. Some months before Chandler's exhibit reached Kirtland, an article describing his offerings appeared in the Painesville, Ohio *Telegraph* — March 27, 1835, which included the following information:

"No.1 — 4 feet 11 inches, female — supposed age 60; arms extended, hands side by side in front; the head indicating motherly goodness. There was found with this person a roll or book, having a little resemblance to birch bark; language unknown. Some linguists however say they can decipher 1336, in what they term an epitaph; ink black and red; many female figures."

This description fits perfectly that of the Ta-shert-Min papyrus. Chandler's other mummies were then described, but no indication was given of any other scrolls containing both black and red writing upon them.

ing before the Joseph Smith Papyri were rediscovered, predicted that, "But the day shall come when the Book of Joseph shall be restored and its contents shall be known again."[6] Since the papyri which Joseph Smith identified as the Book of Joseph are now available, it is fair to ask, Why does the Book of Joseph remain *untranslated* through the gift of Seer which is claimed to reside in the First Presidency of the Mormon Church?

CHAPTER NINE

Translating Egyptian: A Comparison

A S MENTIONED EARLIER, the ancient Egyptian language was a virtually unbroken code to all but a handful of scholars in Joseph Smith's day. Half a continent and an ocean away from the Mormon prophet, a painstaking effort was underway that would unlock the secrets of the Rosetta Stone (a trilingual Egyptian-Greek inscription discovered in 1799 which played a key role in the deciphering of ancient Egyptian), and rediscover the grammatical elements of hieroglyphic language. As the decades passed and scholars persisted in their efforts, the understanding of the ancient Egyptian language took on more precise definition.

Before any comparison can be made between Joseph Smith's methods of translation and those used in the science of Egyptology, it will be helpful to understand a little about how the Egyptian language works.

Ancient Egyptian writing is composed of both *phonograms* ("sound-signs") and *ideagrams* (signs that convey their meaning pictorially). In this language a word was usually expressed by using one or more phonograms, followed by an ideagram. In this arrangement the ideagram is called a *determinative,* because it "determines" the meaning of the foregoing sound-signs and defines their meaning in a general way.[1]

To illustrate this, examine the word "sensen" as it appears in Papyrus Joseph Smith XI (picture below). To read this word one must start at the right side and read to the left.[2] The first letter that appears is a phonogram [⚏], and has the sound corresponding to the letter *"s"* The next letter, written below the first, is also a phonogram [ᗡ], and represents the sound of the letter *"n"*. These two letters are then repeated, resulting in *"snsn."* There are no written vowels in Egyptian, so Egyptologists usually insert the letter *"e"* when appropriate.[3] Thus, we have the word *sensen,* which means "breathe." (On this papyrus it is used as part of the name of the scroll, i.e., *Book of Breathings*). The last part of the word is an ideagram-determinative [⚵], in this case a picture of a sail. It does not enter into the sound of the word, but is supplied merely to show that the word has something to do with wind, breath, or air.

While some Egyptian words need no determinative, many have more than one; some words even require as many as three determinatives to express a single thought. Egyptian writing was thus cumbersome to use, and lacked any true depth of abstraction. That it was able to survive for more than three millennia was due more to its use within a stagnant society, than to any special merit of its own. Eventually its vast inferiority to other forms of writing, such as Greek or Hebrew, led to its disuse and ultimate disappearance.

But no one realized any of this in Joseph Smith's time. The whole

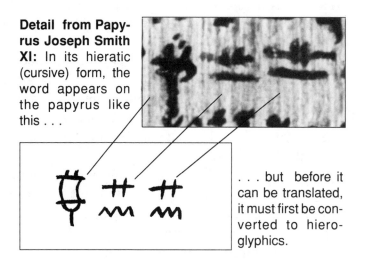

Detail from Papyrus Joseph Smith XI: In its hieratic (cursive) form, the word appears on the papyrus like this . . .

. . . but before it can be translated, it must first be converted to hieroglyphics.

matter of Eyptian language was a blank book, where one theory, speculation, or dogmatic pronouncement regarding the translation of an ancient Egyptian document would have seemed as valid as another.

In order to appreciatethe methods of "translating" Egyptian used by Joseph Smith, remember that this was not the first time he claimed experience in working with Egyptian writing. The golden plates of the Book of Mormon, wrote Smith in 1842, had been "filled with engravings, in Egyptian characters."[4] According to an account within the Book of Mormon (Mormon 9:32,33) the language which appeared upon the plates was more properly called "*reformed* Egyptian," for it had been modified somewhat by the Nephites "after their manner of speech." A man named Moroni explains in this passage that if their plates had been larger they would have preferred to write in Hebrew. From an LDS understanding, then, this passage,

> . . . suggests that it must have required less space to write reformed Egyptian than to write Hebrew. This helps us to better appreciate just how efficient the reformed Egyptian language must have been. Compared to English and many other Western languages, Hebrew is very compact. A typical English sentence of fifteen words will often translate into seven to ten Hebrew words . . . We have no indication of what size characters Mormon or Moroni wrote, but obviously if they rejected Hebrew because the plates were not 'sufficiently large' (Mormon 9:33), then reformed Egyptian must have been a language remarkable for its ability to convey much information with few words. (From *Book of Mormon Student Manual*, prepared by the Church Educational System, published by the LDS Church, 1979, pp. 13-14.)

Thus, "reformed Egyptian" has always been regarded among Latter-day Saints as a remarkably efficient and compact writing form, a kind of ancient shorthand.[5] But did Joseph Smith attribute this same characteristic of compactness to the older Egyptian of his papyri as he did to the "reformed Egyptian" of the gold plates from which he claimed to have translated the Book of Mormon?

At least two collections of early LDS documents — Smith's Egyptian Alphabet and Grammar material and his Book of Abraham translation manuscripts — illustrate that he definitely did.

First, consider briefly the Grammar material. The opening page bears the heading "Grammar & Alphabet of the Egyptian Language," and it begins by expounding a few of the basic "rules" for Egyptian, giving a symbol on the left side of the paper, with an explanation to the right, a format that is followed throughout the notebook.[6] With spelling and punctuation corrected, it reads:

1   This is called *Za Ki-oan hiash,* or *chaslidon hiash.* This character is in the fifth degree, independent and arbitrary. It may be present in the fifth degree while it stands independent

2   and arbitrary. That is, without a straight mark inserted above or below it. By inserting a straight mark over it thus, (2) it

3   increases its significance five degrees; by inserting two straight lines thus, (3) its signification is increased five more. By inserting three straight lines thus, (4) its signification is again

4   increased five more degrees than the last. By counting the number of straight lines, or considering them as qualifying adjectives, we have the degrees of comparison. There are five connecting parts of speech in the above character, called Za Ki-on hish. These five connecting parts of speech [are] for verbs, participles, prepositions, conjunctions, and adverbs.

In translating this character, the subject must be continued until there are as many of these connecting parts of speech used as there are connections, or connecting points, found in the character. But whenever the character is found with one horizontal line, as at (2), the subject must be continued until five times the number of connecting parts of speech are used, or the full sense of the writer is not conveyed. When two horizontal lines occur, the number of connecting parts of speech are continued five times further — or five degrees. And when three horizontal lines are found, the number of connections are to be increased five times further. The charac-

5   ter alone has 5 parts of speech increased by one straight line thus: 5 x 5 is 25; by two horizontal lines thus: 25 x 5 =125; and by three horizontal lines thus: 125 x 5 = 625. When this character has a horizontal line under it reduces it to the fourth degree, consequently it has but four connecting parts of speech.

6   When it has two horizontal lines, it is reduced into the third degree and has but three connecting parts of speech, and when

7   it has three horizontal lines it is reduced into the second degree and has but two connecting parts of speech.

As may be surmised from the above, almost any symbol could be (and was) given virtually any depth of interpretation, depending on which supposed "step," "degree," or "class" the translator decided the symbol belonged to. From this same notebook, consider the following figure with its five progressive "degrees" of meaning:

First Degree (p. 21)

> *Iota toues-Zip Zi:* "The land of Egypt"

Second Degree (p. 18)

> *Iota toues Zip Zi:* "The land which was discovered under water by a woman"

Third Degree (p. 14)

> *Iota toues Zip Zi:* "The womansought to settle her sons in that land. She being the daughter of Ham"

Fourth Degree (p. 1)

> *Iouta toues Zip Zi:* "The land of Egypt discovered by a woman who afterwards settled her sons in it"

Fifth Degree (p. 5)

> *Iota toues Zip Zi:* "The land of Egypt which first discovered by a woman while under water, and afterwards settled by her sons, she being a daughter of Ham — Any land over flown by water — A land seen when over flown by water - land over flown by the seasons, land enriched by being over flown — low marshy ground"

Compare this "fifth degree interpretation" with verses twenty-three and twenty-four of the first chapter of the Book of Abraham text. Joseph Smith actually incorporated many of the explanations of symbols as they appeared in his Grammar material into the text of the Book of Abraham. A number of the symbols appearing in the Grammar notebook were transcribed, in order, directly from the

The above "fifth degree" passage as it appears in the Book of Abraham (1:23,24).

23 The land of ªEgypt being first discovered by a woman, who was the daughter of Ham, and the daughter of Egyptus, which in the Chaldean signifies Egypt, which signifies that which is forbidden;
24 When this woman discovered the land it was under water, who afterward settled her sons in it; and thus, from Ham, sprang that race which preserved the curse in the land.

sides of the vignette on Papyrus Joseph Smith I (i.e., the "fifth part of the first degree," pages F and V*, is taken from column 5, Papyrus Joseph Smith I; the "fourth part of the first degree," pages E,O, and U*, is taken from column 1, Papyrus Joseph Smith I; the "third part of the first degree," page E, O, and U*, is taken from column 2, Papyrus Joseph Smith I, and so forth). In the same way, most of the symbols that appear in the translation manuscripts were taken from the first four lines of Papyrus Joseph Smith XI, column 1 (except for three or four symbols which occur where gaps are present in the papyrus, and which appear to be imaginary reconstructions — but which were translated, nevertheless).[7]

Joseph Smith clearly took his Egyptian Alphabet and Grammar material very seriously. His numerous diary entries (recorded in *History of the Church)* [8] mention the considerable labor he devoted to it, and he often quoted from it to demonstrate his understanding of Egyptian before various public and private audiences.[9] Also, Smith used many of the Egyptian "words" from the Grammar, along with their "interpretations," in his inspired explanations of the facsimiles in the Book of Abraham. Words such as *Kolob, Jah-oh-eh, Oliblish,* and *Enish-go-on-dosh,* were used, indicating that he presented such words and meanings to be equally as God-given and correct as the Book of Abraham text he produced. (In light of this clear evidence, a statement in the 1992 *Encyclopedia of Mormonism* that, "the purpose of the Alphabet and Grammar is obscure,"[10] is difficult to understand. See pp. 137, 138 for further comment on this point.)

Joseph Smith made it clear that the text of the Book of Abraham was to be considered an actual translation of the Egyptian writing contained in his papyrus collection, and not information he received by some supernatural, visionary means. This fact is established by many of his own diary entries from the latter half of 1835, later transcribed during his lifetime (1843) into the official *History of the Church.* It is further supported by personal remarks he made over a period of years to close associates, visiting dignitaries, and family members, which were recorded in letters, journals, newspapers, books, and magazines

---

*These page references are to Joseph Smith's Alphabet and Grammar, which used alphabetic rather than numeric pagination.

Line 1
Line 2
Line 3
Line 4

Upper right corner of Papyrus Joseph Smith XI

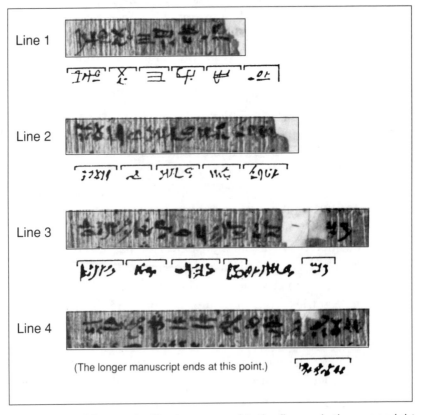

Line 1

Line 2

Line 3

Line 4

(The longer manuscript ends at this point.)

Figures from Manuscript No. 1 compared to the figures in the upper right corner of Papyrus Joseph Smith XI, from which they were derived.

(see examples on pp. 124-126), and even the published references to the first installment of the Book of Abraham as it appeared in *Times and Seasons* in 1842, edited by Joseph, himself. All of these records show that he intended the text of the Book of Abraham to be regarded as nothing less than a *direct, literal translation,* which he had taken from *Abraham's own papyrus record.*

On this crucial point the 1992 *Encyclopedia of Mormonism* apparently disagrees. It comments that,

> it was principally by divine inspiration rather than his knowledge of languages that [Joseph Smith] produced the English text of the book [sic]* of Abraham. His precise methodology remains unknown.[11]

This statement unfortunately deflects attention away from the clear implications of the evidence: namely, that while Joseph Smith presented himself as able to translate and understand ancient languages, and specifically, while he claimed to have produced the Book of Abraham by translating the ancient Egyptian text from one of his papyrus scrolls, we now know that the Joseph Smith papyri are in fact pagan Egyptian documents unrelated to the biblical Abraham (see pp. 137,138 for further comment on this point). Furthermore, if, as the 1992 *Encyclopedia of Mormonism* maintains, Joseph Smith received the Book of Abraham by revelation, not translation, why did he and his followers pay the then enormous sum of $2400[12] — over $28,000 in 1992 U.S. dollars[13] — for pagan Egyptian papyri that have nothing to do with the biblical Abraham?

For the papyrus record was in reality, according to the Book of Abraham translation manuscripts still in existence, the pagan *Book of Breathings* for the priest Hor. The photos on page 94 compare all the figures from translation Manuscript No. 1 with those found on Papyrus Joseph Smith XI.

It is impossible to ignore the decidedly different methods and results of Joseph Smith's approach to translating ancient Egyptian and that of the science of Egyptology. Fortunately, we can compare the

---

*For reasons that are unstated, the articles on the Book of Abraham in the *Encyclopedia of Mormonism* follow the unusual convention of not capitalizing the word 'Book' in the title 'Book of Abraham.'

results of both methods as regards a single Egyptian text, Papyrus Joseph Smith XI.

The charts on pages 97-99 show, on the left side, a number of figures taken from the margin of translation Manuscript No. 1, along with photographs of the characters they correspond to on Papyrus Joseph Smith XI to the right. The English translation of Egyptologists appears above them. The right side gives the text from the Book of Abraham, presented by Joseph Smith as a translation of the same characters.

As can be seen, on some occasions Joseph Smith separated a single Egyptian word to derive characters for his "translation," while at other times he combined more than one Egyptian word into a single set of characters. In all cases his translation attributes a far more complex explanation to the Egyptian letters and words of Papyrus Joseph Smith XI than do professional Egyptologists, and Smith ascribes meanings to words which are totally unrelated to their actual denotation. Thus, Joseph Smith's "translation" is completely incorrect in both method and content.

These results have obviously proved disappointing to those Latter-day Saints who had been expecting the vindication of their prophet. Perhaps the first great wave of frustration they felt was best expressed by Dr. Nibley, who, as soon as the results were in, wrote defensively:

> . . . Did he [Joseph Smith] really think he was translating? If so, he was acting in good faith. But was he really translating? If so, it was by a process which quite escapes the understanding of the specialists and lies in the realm of the imponderable . . .
>
> Today nobody claims that Joseph Smith got his information through ordinary scholarly channels. In that case one wonders how any amount of checking ordinary scholarly channels is going to get us very far (*Dialogue: A Journal of Mormon Thought,* Summer, 1968, p. 101).

TWO TRANSLATIONS OF PAPYRUS JOSEPH SMITH XI

CORRECT TRANSLATION	JOSEPH SMITH'S BOOK OF ABRAHAM TRANSLATION (1:11-15)
"the, this"	11. Now, this priest had offered upon this altar three virgins[r] at one time, who were the daughters of Onitah, one of the royal descent directly from the loins of Ham.[s] These virgins were offered up because of their virtue; they would not bow down to worship gods of wood or of stone, therefore they were killed upon this altar,
"pool"	and it was done after the manner of the Egyptians. 12. And it came to pass that the priests laid violence upon me, that they might slay me also,[t] as they did those virgins[u] upon this altar; and that you may have a knowledge of this altar, I will refer you to the representation at the commencement of this record.
"water" (determinative)	13. It was made after the form of a bedstead, such as was had among the Chaldeans,[v] and it stood before the gods of Elkenah, Libnah, Mahmackrah, Korash, and also a god like unto that of Pharaoh, king of Egypt.[w] 14. That you may have an understanding of these gods, I have given you the fashion of them in the figures at the beginning, which manner of the figures is called by the Chaldeans Rahleenos, which signifies hieroglyphics.
"great"	15. And as they lifted up their hands upon me, that they might offer me up and take away my life,[x] behold, I lifted up my voice unto my God,[y] and the Lord hearkened and heard, and he filled me with the vision of the Almighty, and the angel of his presence stood by me,[z] and immediately unloosed my bands;

TWO TRANSLATIONS OF PAPYRUS JOSEPH SMITH XI

CORRECT TRANSLATION	JOSEPH SMITH'S BOOK OF ABRAHAM TRANSLATION (1:16-31)
"Khonsu" (moon-god of Thebes)	16. And his voice was unto me: Abraham, Abraham, behold, my name is Jehovah,[2a] and I have heard thee, and have come down to deliver thee, and to take thee away from thy father's house, and from all thy kinsfolk, into a strange land which thou knowest not of;[2b] 17. And this because they have turned their hearts away from me, to worship the god[2c] of Elkenah, and the god of Libnah, and the god of Mahmackrah, and the god of Korash, and the god of Pharaoh, king of Egypt; therefore I have come down to destroy him who hath lifted up his hand against thee, Abraham, my son, to take away thy life.[2d] 18. Behold, I will lead thee by my hand, and I will take thee, to put upon thee my name, even the Priesthood[2e] of thy father, and my power shall be over thee.[2f] 19. As it was with Noah[2g] so shall it be with thee; but through thy ministry my name shall be known in the earth forever, for I am thy God.
"born of"	29. Now, after the priest of Elkehah was smitten that he died,[2t] there came a fulfilment of those things which were said unto me concerning the land of Chaldea,[2u] that there should be a famine in the land.[2v] 30. Accordingly a famine prevailed throughout all the land of Chaldea, and my father was sorely tormented because of the famine, and he repented of the evil which he had determined against me, to take away my life.[2w] 31. But the records of the fathers,[2x] even the patriarchs, concerning the right of Priesthood,[2y] the Lord my God preserved in mine own hands; therefore a knowledge of the beginning of the creation, and also of the planets, and of the stars,[2z] as they were made known unto the fathers, have I kept even unto this day,
"Ti" - first part of name	and I shall endeavor to write some of these things upon this record, for the benefit of my posterity that shall come after me.

TWO TRANSLATIONS OF PAPYRUS JOSEPH SMITH XI

CORRECT TRANSLATION	JOSEPH SMITH'S BOOK OF ABRAHAM TRANSLATION (2:1-9)
"khebyt" -second half of name (lit., "dancer")	1. Now the Lord God caused the famine[a] to wax sore in the land of Ur, insomuch that Haran, my brother, died; but Terah, my father, yet lived in the land of Ur, of the Chaldees.[b] 2. And it came to pass that I, Abraham, took Sarai to wife, and Nehor, my brother, took Milcah to wife,
sign indicating a woman's name	who were daughters of Haran.[c]
"justified" and "likewise"	3. Now the Lord had said unto me: Abraham, get thee out of thy country, and from thy kindred, and from thy father's house, unto a land that I will show thee.[d] 4. Therefore I left the land of Ur, of the Chaldees,[e] to go into the land of Canaan;[f] and I took Lot, my brother's son, and his wife, and Sarai my wife; and also my father[g] followed after me, unto the land which we denominated Haran.[h] 5. And the famine abated; and my father tarried in Haran and dwelt there, as there were many flocks in Haran; and my father turned again unto his idolatry,[i] therefore he continued in Haran.
"after"	6. But I, Abraham, and Lot, my brother's son, prayed unto the Lord, and the Lord appeared unto me, and said unto me:[j] Arise, and take Lot with thee; for I have purposed to take thee away out of Haran,[k] and to make of thee a minister to bear my name in a strange land which I shall give thee for an everlasting possession, when they harken to my voice. 7. For I am the Lord thy God; I dwell in heaven; the earth is
"grasp"	my footstool;[l] I stretch my hand over the sea, and it obeys my voice; I cause the wind and the fire to be my chariot; I say to the mountains — Depart hence — and behold, they are taken away by a whirlwind, in an instant, suddenly. 8. My name is Jehovah,[m] and I know the end from the beginning;[n] therefore my hand shall be over thee. 9. And I will make thee a great nation,[o] and I will bless thee above measure,[p] and make thy name great among all nations,

CHAPTER TEN

A Close Look at the Facsimiles

T HE MORMON PEOPLE HAVE always had a high regard for scriptural writings, as well they should, for they have many of them. Besides recognizing the sixty-six books of the Bible, they also accept as inspired scripture the fifteen books within the Book of Mormon, the one hundred and thirty-eight sections now found in the Doctrine and Covenants, and the three books which make up the Pearl of Great Price. The ninth LDS article of faith states:

> We believe all that God has revealed, all that He does now reveal, and we believe that He will yet reveal many great and important things pertaining to the Kingdom of God.

Most Latter-day Saints interpret this as an "open door" to an ever-increasing supply of scripture, be it through new revelation, or the discovery of older writings. Many even consider some of the ancient apocryphal works, including portions of the Dead Sea Scrolls, to be scriptural in nature.

But among all of these various texts, one interesting feature sets the LDS Book of Abraham apart. It alone features illustrations, it alone has inspired *pictures*.

Facsimile No. 1

Right: Joseph Smith's explanation of Facsimile No. 1 as it appears in the Book of Abraham. The drawing was adapted from Papyrus Joseph Smith I.

EXPLANATION OF THE ABOVE CUT.

Fig. 1. The Angel of the Lord. 2. Abraham fastened upon an altar. 3. The idolatrous priest of Elkenah attempting to offer up Abraham as a sacrifice. 4. The altar for sacrifice by the idolatrous priests, standing before the gods of Elkenah, Libnah, Mahmackrah, Korash, and Pharaoh. 5. The idolatrous god of Elkenah. 6. The idolatrous god of Libnah. 7. The idolatrous god of Mahmackrah. 8. The idolatrous god of Korash. 9. The idolatrous god of Pharaoh. 10. Abraham in Egypt. 11. Designed to represent the pillars of heaven, as understood by the Egyptians. 12. Rau-keeyang, signifying expanse, or the firmament over our heads; but in this case, in relation to this subject, the Egyptians meant it to signify Shaumau, to be high, or the heavens, answering to the Hebrew word, Shaumahyeem.

Below: Reference to the scene in the Book of Abraham (1:12-15).

12 And it came to pass that the priests laid violence upon me, that they might slay me also, as they did those virgins upon this altar; and that you may have a knowledge of this altar, I will refer you to the representation at the commencement of this record.

13 It was made after the form of a bedstead, such as was had among the Chaldeans, and it stood before the gods of Elkenah, Libnah, Mahmackrah, Korash, and also a god like unto that of Pharaoh, king of Egypt.

14 That you may have an understanding of these gods, I have given you the fashion of them in the figures at the beginning, which manner of figures is called by the Chaldeans Rahleenos, which signifies hieroglyphics.

15 And as they lifted up their hands upon me, that they might offer me up and take away my life, behold, I lifted up my voice unto the Lord my God, and the Lord ªhearkened and heard, and he filled me with the vision of the Almighty, and the angel of his presence stood by me, and immediately ᵇunloosed my bands;

The above scene from Egyptian mythology explained from the perspective of the science of Egyptology:[1] This picture depicts the mythical embalming and resurrection of Osiris, Egyptian god of the underworld. Osiris was slain by his jealous brother Set, who cut up his body into 16 pieces and scattered them. But Isis, beloved wife of Osiris, patiently gathered up the pieces and reassembled them. The jackal-headed god Anubis is shown embalming the body of Osiris on the traditional lion-headed embalming couch so that he might come back to life. Osiris holds one hand above his head, palm down, in a sign of grief, while his soul, or *ba*, is shown as a human-headed bird about to enter his body. Isis, meanwhile, has taken the form of a falcon and hovers over the groin of Osiris who holds his phallus (hence this is known as an *ithyphallic* drawing) in anticipation of the procreative act which will make Isis pregnant with their son Horus. (Horus will one day defeat Set in battle, thus avenging his father.) The four sons of Horus, grandsons of Osiris and Isis, are shown as the heads of the four canopic jars below the lion-couch — their names are Amset, Hapi, Duamutef, and Qebehsenuef. (Canopic jars were used to hold the soft viscera of a body being mummified.) Before the lion-couch is a libation platform bearing wines, oils, and a stylized papyrus plant. In the foreground is a pool of water, bordered at the front with stones, in which swims the crocodile god Sobek. In Egyptian funerary literature, the deceased person actually "becomes" Osiris, and would thus be referred to as "the *Osiris* Hor" (Hor being the actual person buried), much as we refer to a deceased person as "the *late* John Doe."

Facsimile No. 2

Joseph Smith's explanation of the Facsimile No. 2 drawing, as he reconstructed and published it as an inspired accompaniment to the Book of Abraham.

The original from which this drawing was adapted was briefly rumored in 1985 to have been located and purchased by an agent representing the interests of the LDS Church, though this has since been shown to be untrue. If the original hypocephalus does still exist, its location is unknown, and no photograph of it has ever been verified.

EXPLANATION

Fig. 1. Kolob, signifying the first creation, nearest to the celestial, or the residence of God. First in government, the last pertaining to the measurement of time. The measurement according to celestial time, which celestial time signifies one day to a cubit. One day in Kolob is equal to a thousand years according to the measurement of this earth, which is called by the Egyptians Jah-oh-eh.

Fig. 2. Stands next to Kolob, called by the Egyptians Oliblish, which is the next grand governing creation near to the celestial or the place where God resides; holding the key of power also, pertaining to other planets; as revealed from God to Abraham, as he offered sacrifice upon an altar, which he had built unto the Lord.

Fig. 3. Is made to represent God, sitting upon his throne, clothed with power and authority; with a crown of eternal light upon his head; representing also the grand Key-words of the Holy Priesthood, as revealed to Adam in the Garden of Eden, as also to Seth, Noah, Melchizedek, Abraham, and all to whom the Priesthood was revealed.

Fig. 4. Answers to the Hebrew word Raukeeyang, signifying expanse, or the firmament of the heavens; also a numerical figure, in Egyptian signifying one thousand; answering to the measuring of the time of Oliblish, which is equal with Kolob in its revolution and in its measuring of time.

Fig. 5. Is called in Egyptian Enish-go-on-dosh; this is one of the governing planets also, and is said by the Egyptians to be the Sun, and to borrow its light from Kolob through the medium of Kae-e-vanrash, which is the grand Key, or, in other words, the governing power, which governs fifteen other fixed planets or stars, as also Floeese or the Moon, the Earth and the Sun in their annual revolutions. This planet receives its power through the medium of Kli-flos-is-es, or Hah-ko-kau-beam, the stars represented by numbers 22 and 23, receiving light from the revolutions of Kolob.

Fig. 6. Represents this earth in its four quarters.

Fig. 7. Represents God sitting upon his throne, revealing through the heavens the grand Key-words of the Priesthood; as, also, the sign of the Holy Ghost unto Abraham, in the form of a dove.

Fig. 8. Contains writings that cannot be revealed unto the world; but is to be had in the Holy Temple of God.

Fig. 9. Ought not to be revealed at the present time.

Fig. 10. Also.

Fig. 11. Also. If the world can find out these numbers, so let it be. Amen.

Figures 12, 13, 14, 15, 16, 17, 18, 19, 20, and 21 will be given in the own due time of the Lord.

The above translation is given as far as we have any right to give at the present time.

These pictures were supposed to have accompanied the original manuscript, being intended by the ancient author to help clarify his writings.[2] Translated, the three pictures, known as "facsimiles," are considered an inspired portion of the Book of Abraham as a whole.

Scholars since Deveria's day (1856) have challenged Joseph Smith's "inspired" explanations of these drawings. This chapter gives some idea of just how much disagreement there is.

Joseph Smith identified the drawing shown on page 103 (Facsimile No. 2) as "Facsimile from the Book of Abraham," and offered with it the elaborate "inspired explanation" shown. It is actually a rather common funerary amulet termed a *hypocephalus,* so-called because it was placed under (*hypo*) a mummy's head (*cephalus*). Its purpose was to magically keep the deceased warm and to protect the body from desecration by grave robbers. According to Dr. Nibley, as of 1968 there were "about a hundred" such hypocephali known, a good many of which can be traced to the sun-worship cults centered around Heliopolis during the seventh century B.C. and later.

Egyptologists recognize Facsimile No. 2 as simply a hypocephalus, but there are also problems with that identification. *As with the drawing of Facsimile No. 1, the restored parts of the Mormon hypocephalus do not correspond to genuine ancient Egyptian hypocephali.[3]* Also, just as with Facsimile No. 1, an incorrect restoration (by Smith) of a damaged original was suspected as the explanation for the differences.

While no photograph of the original papyrus from which Facsimile No. 2 was taken is presently available, it is still possible to determine whether Joseph's hypocephalus was damaged at the time it came into his possession. This is so because when the collection of Smith's Egyptian Alphabet and Grammar papers was first published in 1966, one page was found to contain

Sketch included with *Grammar* material.

a fairly good pen and ink drawing of the Facsimile No. 2 hypocephalus. However, there was one important distinction, for this drawing showed a damaged, incomplete hypocephalus, with much of the right edge left blank, including a wedge-shaped empty space on the upper right that extended to the object's center. *Just as with Facsimile No. 1, those portions of Facsimile No. 2 which had long been questioned as being "wrong" or "suspicious" were found to match the areas of this sketch where the original papyrus was either damaged or missing.*

Some of these differences may seem minor to the inexperienced, but they are very noticeable to an expert. References to numbered "Figures" (i.e., Figure 1, Figure 2, etc.) correspond to the reproduction of Facsimile No. 2 found in the Pearl of Great Price. Joseph Smith numbered each section or figure to serve as a guide for his explanation (see caption of Facsimile No. 2 on p. 103).

The round faced creature in (upside-down) Figure 7 lacked a definable body, for instance, so the stylized body of a bird was innocently provided (it should have been an ithyphallic serpent with legs). The central seated figure (Figure 1) ordinarily has four rams heads, but perhaps only enough of the damaged papyrus flakes remained here to show Joseph that more than one head belonged, so it must have seemed logical for him to simply copy the profile of the two-headed Egyptian god Par (Figure 2) directly above it. Possibly a trace of a boat showed

Detail from Facsimile No. 2.

Detail from corner of Papyrus Joseph Smith IV.

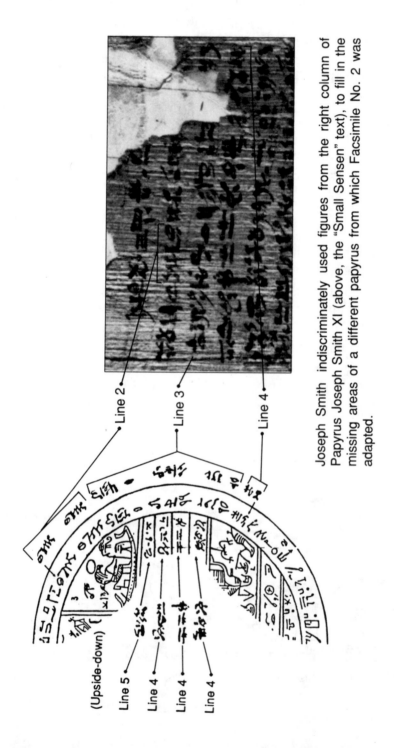

Line 2

Line 3

Line 4

Joseph Smith indiscriminately used figures from the right column of Papyrus Joseph Smith XI (above, the "Small Sensen" text), to fill in the missing areas of a different papyrus from which Facsimile No. 2 was adapted.

(Upside-down)

Line 5

Line 4

Line 4

Line 4

EVALUATION OF JOSEPH SMITH'S TRANSLATION OF FACSIMILE NO. 2 TEXT

SMITH'S TRANSLATION	CORRECT TRANSLATION [4]
"Fig. 8 — Contains writing that cannot be revealed unto the world; but is to be had in the Holy Temple of God."	Fig. 8 — "grant that the soul of the Osiris Sheshonk may live."
"Fig. 9 — Ought not to be revealed at the present time."	Figure 9 — "the netherworld (below the earth)and his great waters"
"Fig. 10 — Also."	Figure 10 — "O mighty god, lord of heaven and earth"
"Fig. 11 —Also. If the world can find out these numbers, so let it be. Amen."	Figure 11 — "O god of the sleeping ones from the time of creation" (Note: The above phrases make up a single message in the following order — 11,10,9,8.)
Figs. 12,13,14,15,	A trace of the original hieroglyphic writing from this hypocephalus is visible on the left edge of Figs. 12,13,14 and 15 (compare with photographs on p. 105), but only the phrase "his words" can be made out at the end of the line in Fig. 15. The remainder of these lines are filled with hieratic writing taken from lines 4 and 5 of Papyrus Joseph Smith XI: Fig. 12 — (upside down) "near" and "wrap" Fig.13 — (upside down) "which made by" Fig. 14 — (upside down) "breathings" Fig. 15 — (upside down) "this book"
16,	Fig. 16 —"and may this soul and its possessor never be desecrated in the netherworld."
17,	Fig. 17 — "May this tomb never be desecrated"
18,	Fig. 18 — Three-fourths of the original hieroglyphic inscription appears to have survived, and counterclockwise reads: "I am Djabty in the house of Benben in Heliopolis, so exalted and glorious. [I am] copulating bull without equal. [I am] that mighty god in the house of Benben in Heliopolis . . . that mighty god . . ."
19,20, and 21 "will be given in the own due time of the Lord."	Figs. 19,20,21 — "You shall be as that god, the Busirian."
"The translation is given as far as we have any right to give at this present time."	Fig. 22 — (to the left of the standing two-headed god): "The name of this mighty god."

Joseph Smith's interpretation of the writing found on Facsimile No. 2 is shown in the left column. The right column gives the actual translation of both the hieroglyphic characters original to this document, and of the hieratic characters from Papyrus Joseph Smith XI that were used to fill in the missing spaces.[4]

in the space where Figure 3 is. Two boats — a small one above a larger one — belong here; but not knowing this, Joseph copied the boat figure found at the bottom of Papyrus Joseph Smith IV (see comparison on p. 105). This, however, is a drawing of the sun-god in his solar bark, and is improper for a hypocephalus.

The most dramatic error found on Facsimile No. 2 though, is the restoration of the missing writing. While never offering an actual translation in his "explanation," Smith nevertheless implies that this writing contains great and mysterious secrets pertaining to God and the Temple (see caption of Facsimile No. 2, Figs. 8-10;12-21, on p. 103). *We now know the restored writing to be a mixture of two unrelated texts from different works written hundreds of years apart. The restored text includes different styles of handwritting, one being hieroglyphic, and the other hieratic, and some characters are even placed upside down in relation to one another!* In all cases figures from the right column of Papyrus Joseph Smith XI (the "Small Sensen" text) were used indiscriminately to fill in the missing area (see comparison on p. 106).

Variations of the scene shown on page 109 (Facsimile No. 3) are probably the single most common form of Egyptian funerary scene known — the deceased being led into the presence of the Court of Osiris, god of the underworld. Eventually the major elements became standardized into chapter 125 of the *Book of the Dead,* and the particular version in the Joseph Smith papyri is from a later, simplified text. The deceased, wearing the traditional perfumed cone and lotus flower on his head, is led by Maat, goddess of justice (identified by the plume within the orb on her head) into the presence of Osiris. He is supported from behind by Anubis, guide of the dead, who has helped him complete his journey (and assisted him in the use of the spells that were contained in his funeral book). Osiris wears his double-plumed crown, holds the royal flail and crook across his chest, and sits before the ever present libation platform that is common in nearly all drawings containing major god-figures. It is topped by the customary stylized papyrus blossom. Behind him stands his wife Isis, identified by her solar disc and cow horn. The object in her hand is probably an ankh, symbol of life and resurrection.

There are no glaring discrepancies or false reconstructions evident

Facsimile No. 3

ENG. BY R. HEDLOCK

EXPLANATION OF THE ABOVE CUT

1. Abraham sitting upon Pharaoh's throne, by the politeness of the king, with a crown upon his head, representing the Priesthood, as emblematical of the grand Presidency in Heaven; with the scepter of justice and judgment in his hand.

2. King Pharaoh, whose name is given in the characters above his head.

3. Signifies Abraham in Egypt—referring to Abraham, as given in the ninth number of the *Times and Seasons*. (Also as given in the first facsimile of this book.)

4. Prince of Pharaoh, King of Egypt, as written above the hand.

5. Shulem, one of the king's principal waiters, as represented by the characters above his hand.

6. Olimlah, a slave belonging to the prince.

Abraham is reasoning upon the principles of **Astronomy, in the king's court.**

Joseph Smith's explanation of Facsimile No. 3, included as an inspired insight, or perhaps a commentary at the end of the book. This particular scene is not referred to within the published text of the Book of Abraham, though it is represented as having been an integral part of the original scroll. The papyrus fragment from which this drawing was taken has not been found.

in this drawing. And, allowing for the slightly different style expressed by the person responsible for copying it, the scene is probably represented much as it originally was on the papyrus, indicating there was little damage to it. This could be expected, since it was located on the innermost end of the scroll where it would be the least likely to suffer damage.

Enough of the hieroglyphics depicted here are legible to determine that this scene comes from the same scroll as the Facsimile No. 1 drawing — the *Book of Breathings* for the priest Hor, son of the priest Osower and the lady Tikhebyt. The lines of characters below the scene read, as closely as can be made out: "O gods of . . . gods of the caverns, gods of the south, north, west, and east, grant well-being to Osiris Hor, justified . . . "[5]

As the preceeding pages have shown, when properly interpreted, none of the Book of Abraham facsimiles (or the papyrus drawings from which they were adapted) make any mention of Abraham, his life, travels, teachings, religion, or anything even remotely resembling the detailed explanations given of them by Joseph Smith. Instead, all three are common examples of well-known, late Egyptian funeral texts. The only points of difference are those portions of the facsimiles which Smith mistakenly reconstructed by guesswork, and inserted in places where the original papyri were already damaged when he obtained them.

Some LDS writers[6] have recently attempted to lay blame for these differences or errors on Reuben Hedlock, the Latter-day Saint who prepared the original woodcut engravings of the scenes in 1842. (His hallmark — ENG. BY R HEDLOCK — appears on two of the three drawings as they were originally published in *Times and Seasons*; this signature was absent from all editions of the Pearl of Great Price until quite recently, when it was restored.) Such reasoning is difficult to accept, however, in light of Joseph Smith's own statements of responsibility for their accuracy:

Thursday, March 1, 1842 - During the forenoon I was at my office and the printing office, correcting the first plate or cut [note: this would be "Facsimile No. 1"] of the Records of Father Abraham prepared by Reuben Hedlock, for the *Times and Seasons* . . . (*History of the Church*, Vol. 4, p.

519)

Friday, March 4, 1842 — At my office exhibiting the Book of Abraham in the original to Brother Reuben Hedlock, so that he might take the size of the several plates or cuts, and prepare the blocks for the *Times and Seasons;* and also gave instructions concerning the arrangements of the writing on the large cut, illustrating the principles of astronomy [this would be Facsimile No. 2] (*Ibid.,* p. 543).

The three Facsimiles from the Book of Abraham — errors included — and their interpretations, appear in the Pearl of Great Price exactly as Joseph Smith directed.

Part III

LDS REACTIONS

CHAPTER ELEVEN

The Intellectual Approaches

P RIOR TO THE REDISCOVERY of the Joseph Smith papyri in
1967, the LDS Church's official position regarding the Book of
Abraham was consistent and straightforward: Abraham, the
biblical patriarch, had personally written a record of his experiences in
Egypt, and had even illustrated it for clarity. This same record had
been hidden up, preserved through time, and eventually delivered into
the hands of Joseph Smith in the year 1835. Smith then translated the
papyri by the gift and power of God, producing what is now known as
the Book of Abraham. Prior to 1967, it seemed unlikely there would
ever be reason for any Latter-day Saint to question this position.

But the rediscovery of the papyri has changed this picture for thoughtful Mormons. As they encounter information about the Book of
Abraham, it becomes apparent that the official version of its origin is
hopelessly inadequate. This chapter examines a number of alternate
"intellectual" explanations devised by LDS apologists to salvage some
measure of credibility for the Book of Abraham and Mormonism in
light of this contradictory evidence.

Efforts by Latter-day Saints to reconcile the findings of Egyptology
with the claims of the Book of Abraham are nothing new. The first
serious attempt of this kind was probably that of George Reynolds in
about 1879. His efforts were followed in the early years of the present

century by the work of John Henry Evans and B. H. Roberts, and eventually the shadowy " 'Dr.' Robert C. Webb" (see pp. 29, 30).

These early arguments, though now recognized as dated and flawed, formed the groundwork for much of the first series of responses made by present day LDS apologists attempting to answer difficulties raised by the rediscovery of the Joseph Smith Papyri. Hugh Nibley, for instance, who at one point was the chief agent designated by the LDS leadership to defend the Book of Abraham during the papyri controversy, started out by devoting a considerable amount of space in his *Improvement Era* articles to attacking the motives of past critics such as the Episcopal bishop, Rev. Franklin S. Spalding. In article after article, Nibley hotly challenged the findings of Spalding's panel of scholars, in the process making repeated favorable references to the supposed expert he referred to as "the outsider, R. C. Webb."

Though Dr. Nibley much later admitted that he had "frankly skirmished and sparred for time" during this period in order to gain further expertise,[1] it is nevertheless interesting to follow the progress of his views as they develop, maneuvering back and forth from one theory to another, as quickly as they were suggested.

The "Hidden Meaning" Theory

Initially, Dr. Nibley appears to have had little difficulty accepting the idea that the papyrus Joseph Smith used to produce the text of the Book of Abraham was the "Small Sensen" fragment. This conclusion was demanded by three facts: (1) the Facsimile No. 1 fragment (Papyrus Joseph Smith I) belonged to the Book of Abraham, (2) the "Small Sensen" fragment adjoined the Facsimile No. 1 fragment, and (3) the characters from the "Small Sensen" fragment (Papyrus Joseph Smith XI) appeared, in order, on three translation transcripts of the Book of Abraham text penned by Joseph Smith's scribes. But this raised a major problem for those Latter-day Saints aware that a competent translation of the "Small Sensen" text did *not* produce anything like the Book of Abraham. How was this fact to be reconciled with the Church's claims? Could it be reconciled?

The first avenue that appeared to be open was the one Reynolds had proposed 90 years earlier — that the Egyptian text Joseph Smith had worked with had more than one meaning. There was a *literal* meaning which scholars could determine by direct translation, but there was also a *secret* meaning which perhaps could only be unlocked with something like the *Urim and Thummim,* or perhaps Joseph's *seer stone.* Nibley reported in an article for *BYU Studies* (Spring 1968),

> It has long been known that the characters 'interpreted' by Joseph Smith in his Egyptian Alphabet and Grammar are treated by him as super-crypto-grams, and now it is apparent that the source of those characters is the unillustrated fragment on which the word Sen-Sen appears repeatedly.

Nibley elaborated on this argument in a speech at the University of Utah on May 20 of the same year, stating,

> . . . you very often have texts of double meaning . . . it's quite possible, say, that this 'Sensen' papyrus, telling a straight forward innocent little story or something like that, should contain also a totally different text concealed within it . . . they (the Egyptians) know what they're doing, but we don't. We don't have the key.[2]

For a while Dr. Nibley made as strong a case as he could for this "hidden meaning" theory, and a number of Latter-day Saint authors were sufficiently impressed with it to lend it support in their own work. But the theory's one major weakness from the very first was simply its sheer improbability. The "Sensen" text did not come into use until about 400 B.C. and each copy of the text was adapted to the deceased person for whom it was prepared — incorporating his or her name, as well as the name of a parent. This means each copy of the text was different, which would muddle any supposed "hidden meaning."

No reputable Egyptologist anywhere was willing to support this theory,[3] and it soon fell into disuse. Still, it was felt there must be some connection that would allow, somehow, for the Book of Abraham to have come from the Sensen text.

The "Mnemonic Device" Theory

One of the most elaborate attempts to establish an indirect translation connection was proposed later in 1968 by two Mormon scholars named John Tvedtnes and Richley Crapo.[4] As they saw it, the two major objections of "non-member critics" to accepting the Book of Abraham as a translation of the Joseph Smith papyri were, (1) the implausibly high ratio of English words to Egyptian symbols, and (2) the lack of any clear connection between the Book of Abraham story and the contents of the Joseph Smith papyri.

"We should therefore reply to these objections if we wish to maintain that the Book of Abraham is scripture," they wrote candidly, "the more so because some respected members of the Church are beginning to accept the rationale behind the argument presented."

Tvedtnes and Crapo then pointed out that if the Book of Abraham was to be presented as "authentic," there were two possible approaches for the Church's scholars to take. They could either simply discount the implausibly high ratio of English to Egyptian symbols, and try to find a means of explaining how the Book of Abraham could have been derived from the Sensen text, or, they could try to demonstrate that there was some reason *other* than "translation" value for the Egyptian symbols to appear next to the Book of Abraham text on the translation manuscripts. If the first could be done successfully, Joseph Smith would be more or less vindicated as a true translator of the ancient document; if the second option was used, the troublesome Sensen text could be overlooked and a case could be made for a completely different papyrus — one still missing — as the *true* source of the Book of Abraham.

The first option offered perhaps the strongest support for the Church's traditional position in support of the authenticity of the Book of Abraham, and this was the one Tvedtnes and Crapo determined would be the most desirable to use.

Having decided on this approach, Tvedtnes and Crapo proposed that the hieratic Egyptian words appearing on the Sensen papyrus stood for "core concepts" that could be found within the English text next to which they appeared. For instance, on pages 97-99 of this book there are charts similar to the ones from which they worked. The first Egyptian symbol shown represents the word "the," or "this." Verse 11 Abraham I, shown next to it begins, "Now *this* priest had offered . . ." The two Mormon scholars felt that they had shown a parallel between the two works because the definite article "this" appeared in both.

The same procedure was used to construct parallels between as many words or portions of words as Tvedtnes and Crapo could find, all with equally unconvincing results. Probably their best connection was the hieratic symbol for a determinative indicating a woman's name (see p. 99) and the corresponding phrase from Abraham 2:2, "who were the daughters of Haran." Tvedtnes and Crapo went on to specu-late that, according to their model, the Sensen text was actually a "memory device" that could have been developed by either Abraham or his descendants. It was utilized to bring to mind "a set number of memorized phrases relating to Abraham's account of his life." Joseph Smith, reading these "core concept" words correctly by the gift and power of God, would then have received these phrases by revelation.[5]

This "mnemonic device" theory received favorable coverage in such papers as Brigham Young University's *Newsletter and Proceedings of the Society for Early Historic Archaeology*, and the *LDSSA Commentary*. In the February 24, 1969 edition the Newsletter reported that Tvedtnes and Crapo's approach was "quickly gaining support from LDS scholars." Even Dr. Nibley gave his tacit endorsement, explaining,

> . . . it seems that the idea is that if one takes the actual meaning of the hieratic signs in the order in which they occur, they can be roughly matched up with certain general themes of the Book of Abraham which occur in the same order . . . This would make the Sensen papyrus a sort of prompter's sheet . . . Far fetched as it may seem, there are many ancient examples of this sort of thing . . .[6]

Unfortunately, several serious flaws in the "mnemonic device" the-ory soon became evident. When Jay Todd, another popular Mormon writer, asked Klaus Baer his opinion of the theory, Dr. Baer replied that the English-to-Egyptian comparisons listed in the study were "re-lated by no visible principle."[7] There was really no consistent proce-dure employed at all, no governing rules of application that would make the proposed method useful as a genuine memory device by anyone; rather, all associations were haphazard, random, and chaotic, showing evidence of a strictly *forced* association. Furthermore, some of the "core concepts" were tied to the specific names of the deceased (Hor) and one of his parents (Tikhebyt), meaning that only *this par-ticular* "breathing permit" — and no other — was capable of carrying any intended code. Each time a *Book of Breathings* text was prepared over the centuries, different names would have been written in, making any transmission of "code" based on names impossible. Finally, the *Book of Breathings* had not even been composed (as a condensation of the earlier *Book of the Dead*) until sometime around 400 B.C., a dozen or more centuries after the time of Abraham.

Just the same, these objections were soon rationalized away, and although its impact had been blunted, the "mnemonic device" theory continued to be popular in some LDS circles for a number of years.

However, this was the final serious attempt to link the Sensen text with the text of the Book of Abraham.

The "Any Egyptian Connection" Theory

An Egyptian connection to the Book of Abraham was still desired and actively sought, however. Quite early in the game Dr. Nibley had given the impression that he felt the Mormon people ought to be willing to accept any association that could be found — even to pagan Egyptian mythology if need be — so long as it left open possibilities.

However, Nibley's approach in this regard is certainly in sharp conflict with the Bible, one of the four LDS standard works. Throughout the Old Testament it is abundantly clear that God took great pains to dissuade the children of Israel from any contact with the false gods and idolatrous practices of their pagan neighbors. He ordered the Israelites to destroy the inhabitants of Canaan when they conquered the land, lest they should mingle His holy name with pagan deities, and so pollute the truth of divine revelation (Deuteronomy 6:14; 7:2-4, 16, 25,26; 12:2-4). God specifically admonished His people to repudiate and completely forsake the gods of Egypt, to whom they had been exposed during their years of captivity there (Joshua 24:14). The Old Testament records that every time the children of Israel fell into pagan idolatry, they experienced God's chastening (Judges 2:2,3, 11-15). Later in Israel's history, the prophet Ezekiel traced Israel's fall into idolatry all the way back to her failure to completely forsake the pagan religion of Egypt (Ezekiel 20:7-9).

The New Testament likewise teaches the same principle that God does not use pagan or ungodly vessels to bear His truth. Acts 16:16-18 records the incident of a demon possessed girl who followed the

Apostle Paul and Silas, crying out that they were "servants of the most high God, which show unto us the way of salvation." Although this testimony was true, Paul completely repudiated any such association between the Gospel and pagan occultism. He rebuked the evil spirit and cast it out of the girl.

Since the Joseph Smith Papyri have been identified with absolute certainty as prayers to pagan Egyptian gods that, by biblical definition are ripe with occultism, it is inconceivable, given the holy character of God, that He would associate Himself or His revelation in any way with these pagan religious documents. This fact alone is ample grounds for totally rejecting the Book of Abraham as a revelation from the one True and Living God.

Nevertheless, regarding the actual subject matter of the Sensen papyrus, shortly after it was translated Nibley wrote,

> Even the casual reader can see that there is cosmological matter here, with the owner of the papyrus longing to shine in the heavens as some sort of physical entity along with the sun, moon, and Orion; also he places great importance on his patriarchal lineage and wants to be pure, nay baptized, so as to enter a higher kingdom, to achieve, in fact, resurrection and eternal life. And these teachings and expressions are secret, to be kept out of the hands of the uninitiated. And all these things have nothing to do with the subject matter of the Pearl of Great Price? . . . let's not get ahead of the game, or overlook any possibility that there might be something there after all — 'If it looks like an elephant,' Professor Popper used to say, 'call it an elephant!' (from *Dialogue: A Journal of Mormon Thought*, Summer 1968, pp. 103-104)

Of course, the above was written while Dr. Nibley was still proposing his "super-cryptogram" hypothesis, and considering the "mnemonic device" theory (and while also "skirmishing and sparring for time") before he and most others were finally forced to recognize that the Book of Abraham was simply too far off base to be considered a translation of the "Sensen" text.

But the idea of looking for Egyptian practices or beliefs that could be even loosely thought of as resembling those of Abraham was an intriguing subject to Dr. Nibley. Indeed, he has continued along this line, producing hundreds of printed pages of such speculations in the process. Then too, this approach became especially necessary in dealing with the facsimiles in the Book of Abraham. LDS Scholars discovered that the indisputable Egyptian identification of the *facsimiles* could not be so easily ignored or obscured as had the *text* of the Sensen papyrus.

Still, in giving up on the Sensen text, about the only viable alternative left to LDS scholars was the second approach Tvedtnes and Crapo had foreseen, that of trying to find an explanation other than "translation" for the appearance of the Sensen characters in Joseph Smith's manuscripts alongside the Book of Abraham text. If this could be done, the whole bothersome matter of the Sensen text could finally be disposed of, and the business of developing a new explanation for the origin of the Book of Abraham could move ahead.

The first obstacle to overcome was Joseph Smith's Egyptian Alphabet and Grammar material. Up to this time, it had been regarded by some as a kind of key to the Book of Abraham. As early as 1938, Dr. Sidney B. Sperry had written (without revealing that he had seen the Grammar in the Historian's Office) that he had for "many years" been "intrigued by the statement of the Prophet that he was 'translating an alphabet to the Book of Abraham.'"[8] He proposed that the Grammar had been a translating aid of sorts for Joseph, in which he had listed each Egyptian symbol with its meaning in English. Smith would have employed this procedure, speculated Sperry, because the meaning of the symbols, having been revealed once by divine aid, would perhaps not be revealed in the future.[9] Other scholars, (such as Dr. James R. Clark and Hyrum L. Andrus) even went so far as to suggest that the document had originally been formulated by an ancient writer — "probably Abraham" — to assist the eventual translator in deciphering the language.[10] However, such notions only strengthened the ties between the Sensen symbols and the Book of Abraham text, which in turn brought Joseph's abilities as a translator into question. This result was not faith promoting, and therefore, not even a viable option to LDS authorities. No, the Egyptian Alphabet and Grammar had to be discounted, and somehow separated from Joseph Smith.

The "Scribes Did It" Theory

Ultimately, it was Dr. Nibley who was more influential than anyone else in his attempts to break the link between the Prophet and his

Alphabet and Grammar. Challenging the traditional attitude of respect for the Grammar material and Joseph Smith's involvement in producing it, he argued that the "Kirtland Egyptian Papers" (a term coined by Nibley to use in place of the awkward "Alphabet" and/or "Grammar") had been a "purely speculative and exploratory" effort initiated by Joseph's *scribes* during the time of the translation of the Book of Abraham, and quickly abandoned when they saw it was getting them nowhere.[11]

These "men of Kirtland," Dr. Nibley proposed, were simply trying to see if they could learn Egyptian on their own through "studying it out in their own minds," by matching up symbols and words, formulating grammatical rules through trial and error, and making *guesses*, as it were. Nibley saw such trial and error practice by Smith's scribes as "not [any] more fantastic than the speculations of some eminent scholars of the world in their early efforts to decipher Egyptian."[12] It was *Smith's scribes*, he stressed, who placed the characters from the "Small Sensen" text next to the Book of Abraham text on the three manuscripts. Nibley insisted they did not do this as an exercise in "translation," and he pointed out that the "absurd disproportion" between one simple symbol and "a whole paragraph of English text including parenthetical remarks and at least a dozen proper names" would tend to "[w]ipe out even the remotest possibility of such a thing."[13] Rather, he claimed that this was merely evidence of an "exploratory exercise"[14] undertaken "in the process of trying out possible clues to help in the composing of an Egyptian Grammar."[15]

Dr. Nibley admitted that in their attempt to prepare this grammar, Smith's scribes were often encouraged and at times even assisted in their efforts by the Prophet (four pages of the Egyptian Alphabet material is in Joseph Smith's own handwriting). But Nibley felt that this ought not to reflect unfavorably on the seership of the Prophet Joseph Smith, since "his translation of the Book of Abraham was one thing; while his discussions and speculations and intellectual flights with the brethren in Kirtland were again something else."[16] He explained that Smith "would very much have liked to [write an Egyptian Grammar], as the subject intrigued him to the end of his life when he suggested the possibility of such an undertaking in the future."[17] But the *Kirtland Egyptian Papers* . . . ? Obviously they couldn't be taken seriously, since "nothing is more impressive than the promptness and finality with which the Alphabet, Grammar, and 'translation' projects were dropped the moment it became apparent they were leading up a blind alley."[18]

"Equally significant," Nibley continued, "was the care that was taken to avoid misleading anyone, raising false hopes, or giving false impressions. The whole business was strictly confidential in nature; these speculations and probings never got out of a closed academic circle." [19]

This was one of Nibley's most insistent points, for it not only indicated to him that Joseph Smith had regarded the Kirtland Egyptian Papers as having no value, but it also addressed the critics' charge that the material had for years been deliberately suppressed by the LDS Church:

> No claims were ever given for them. It was not the Prophet's habit to suppress anything he felt was true and relevant to the Gospel. On the contrary, his calling was to make everything known . . . He was not one to hold anything back.* *If the Kirtland papers were thought of as inspired or even reasonably helpful they would have been expanded, used, and their worth announced to the world.* The strictly confidential nature of the work tells us just what kind of an exercise it was — never circulated, never given out to the members of the church or the general public — no one was corrupted by it.[20]

Hugh Nibley's "Scribes Did It" theory immediately became a popular success. It offered LDS members a portrayal of events that distanced Joseph Smith from the embarrassing Kirtland Egyptian Papers, and evoked that confident authority and seemingly thorough appeal to evidence for which Nibley had become famous. To many it looked like a way had been found to close forever the door on the whole nest of troublesome questions brought up by the Sensen papyrus.

There were some problems with the theory though. For one thing, it

---

*This is not necessarily a correct assumption on Dr. Nibley's part. Joseph Smith is known to have suppressed information supposedly given by divine revelation. One well documented example is Smith's denial of the Church's involvement in polygamy at a time when it was being both taught and practiced secretly. Another concerns the Council of Fifty.

was built almost entirely on speculation. To many, it seemed simplistic to blame both the creation of the Grammar material and the placement of the Sensen symbols beside the Book of Abraham text in three separate manuscripts, entirely on the well-meaning but uninspired efforts of Joseph Smith's scribes. In going over the same evidence used by Nibley — the same notes, the same journal entries, the same references in the *Church History* and elsewhere — no LDS writer had ever felt compelled by the facts to reach such conclusions, even though the subject had been explored for years. Of course, other Mormon scholars had not been trying to discount Joseph Smith's involvement with these items. That Dr. Nibley should be able to do so, now that it had become necessary, seemed highly suspect.

In some ways the "Scribes Did It" theory was very much like the "Mnemonic Device" theory, for it bore all the marks of a totally contrived set of conditions where only very narrowly limited "evidence" was ever used. Even then, the interpretation of the evidence had to be strained to the limit in order to obtain the desired conclusion.

Actually, about the only way the theory could be developed at all was by overlooking a great deal of other evidence which linked the Prophet directly to the production of the Book of Abraham and the Grammar. Consider, for instance, Joseph Smith's own words as recorded in B. H. Roberts' *History of the Church:*

> *[July, 1835]* — The remainder of this month I was continually engaged in translating an alphabet to the Book of Abraham, and arranging a grammar of the Egyptian language as practiced by the ancients. (*History of the Church,* Vol. 2, p. 238)

Notice that Joseph is not saying he would some day *like* to put together an alphabet and grammar of the Egyptian language, as Nibley's writings imply, but that he claims that he actually *is*, in 1835, *"engaged in translating an alphabet"* and *"arranging a grammar."* Again, from Smith's diary account:

> *October 1 [; 1835]* — This afternoon labored on the Egyptian alphabet, in company with Brothers O. Cowdery and W. W. Phelps, and during the research, the principles of astronomy as understood by Father Abraham and the ancients unfolded to our understanding, the particulars of which will

appear hereafter. (*Ibid*, p. 286)

Notice also that the "astronomy" Smith describes (a significant factor within both the Grammar material and the Book of Abraham subject matter) was "*unfolded . . .* during the research" — not "received by inspiration" or as the result of "speculations," "probings," or "intellectual flights."

Another significant entry states,

> *November 17, 1835* — Exhibited the alphabet of the ancient records, to Mr. Holmes, and some others" (*Ibid*, p. 316).

Recall that, according to Dr. Nibley's theory, this material was "strictly confidential in nature" and "never got out of a closed academic circle" in order to "avoid misleading anyone, raising false hopes, or giving false impressions" so that no one would be "corrupted by it."

Given the early date of these citations, some argue that Joseph was still involved in the half-serious "speculations and probings" described by Nibley. This raised the question, did Smith in later years *continue* to exhibit and use the Egyptian Alphabet and Grammar material? Or, as time went on, was it "quickly dropped" with "impressive finality" and forgotten, as Nibley contends?

Evidently Joseph Smith continued to desire that people believe in the value of his Grammar, since all the previously cited references to it were transcribed from his 1835 diary during his lifetime, and placed in the official *Manuscript History of the Church* which was being compiled in 1843. If Smith had abandoned those Grammar writings several years earlier as "worthless," he would not have allowed such potentially misleading references to be copied (even expanded) during his supervision of the *Manuscript History*.

Additional evidence shows that Joseph Smith consistently represented the Egyptian Alphabet and Grammar and all the material related to it as a serious matter. A good example of this is found in a small pamphlet published in 1844 entitled *The Voice of Truth*.[21] In it, Smith was quoted at length as he demonstrated his linguistic prowess by quoting brief phrases from seventeen different languages, in quick succession:

Were I a Chaldean I would exclaim, *Keed'nauh to-me-roon lehoam elauhayauh dey - ahemayana veh aur'hau lau gnaubadoo, yabadoo ma-ar'gnau comeen tehoat sheamyauh allah* (Thus shall ye say unto them: The gods that have not made the heaven and the earth, they shall perish from the earth, and from these heavens.) An Egyptian, *Su-e-eh-ni* (What other persons are those?) A Grecian, *Diabolos basileuei* (The Devil reigns.) A Frenchman, *Messieurs sans Dieu* (Gentlemen without God.) . . .

And on Smith goes, quoting brief clips of Turkish, German, Syrian, Spanish, Italian, Hebrew, Danish, Latin, and other languages. It is notable that the phrases Smith uses from various languages do not constitute the related thoughts of a single message, but appear to be randomly selected phrases from various dictionaries. Even the Chaldean quoted is no more than an approximate translation of the Hebrew of Jeremiah 10:11, apparently copied from Smith's Hebrew Bible. The "Egyptian" he quotes, however, comes directly from the Egyptian Alphabet and Grammar, page A: *Sue-e-eh-ni* "What other person is that? Who?"[22]

Of course, a skeptic might question whether Joseph Smith actually uttered such strange words. Did he really write or talk in this manner?

Yes, the evidence shows that he definitely did. On November 13, 1843, Smith wrote a letter that appeared in the newspaper *Times and Seasons* (of which he had served as editor) which stated in part:

Were I an Egyptian, I would exclaim *Jah-oh-eh, Enish-go-on-dosh, Flo-ees-Flos-is-is*; [O the earth! the power of attraction, and the moon passing between her and the sun.]

These words were taken directly from pages 29 and 30 of the Grammar material:

Jah-oh-eh: The earth under the government of another or the second of the fixed stars, which is called
Enish-go-on-dosh or in other words the power of attra[c]tion it has with the earth.
Flo-ees: The moon — signifying its revolutions, also going between, thereby forming an eclipse.
Flos-is-is: The sun in its affinity with Earth and moon — signifying their revolutions showing the power the one has with the other.[23]

It is also interesting that the words *Jah-oh-eh, Enish-go-on-dosh, Floeese, and Kli-flos-is-is* occur in the "Explanation" of Facsimile No. 2 in the Book of Abraham (see p. 103 of this book).

And what of the appearance of the Sensen symbols in the three translation manuscripts next to the English Book of Abraham text?

Dr. Nibley saw this as the product of an "exploratory exercise" in which Joseph's scribes were simply "placing two completed texts [the Sensen and the Book of Abraham] side by side for comparison."[24] He defended this viewpoint by explaining,

> You cannot make a grammar or alphabet of any language if you don't have at least one example of a translation — without a Rosetta Stone you will get nowhere. And the Book of Abraham offered the brethren the only exemplar of a sure translation from the Egyptian. They compared it with various texts, trying it on for size.[25]

Taken at face value, Nibley's argument *could* perhaps be considered barely plausible, though it must be noted that there are no known examples of Egyptian characters from "various texts" appearing along-side Book of Abraham passages. Still, the random placing of two texts alongside each other without even the slightest idea of what the symbols from one of the languages means is hardly a rational way to begin to "make a grammar or alphabet." Smith's followers would, at the very least, have needed some reason to believe that the English text had somehow been derived from the *particular* papyrus at hand in order for their "exercise" to have had meaning. Only Joseph Smith could have provided them with such a belief.

But there is still more evidence against Nibley's theory here, for a number of figures on the three Book of Abraham translation manuscripts do not even come from the Sensen (or any other) papyrus! These characters occur in the places where there are missing sections in the Sensen papyrus, and do not resemble any form of Egyptian at all. Instead, these figures, which appear to be simply contrived, are based on (though with slight variations) similar non-Egyptian figures found in the Grammar material. They are placed next to portions of the English Book of Abraham text that closely match the subject matter of the "definitions" given for them in the Grammar.

An example of this can be seen on pages 92, 93 of this book. *Iota toues Zip zi* is an imaginary, non-Egyptian character; its counterpart is found at the top of page 5 of Manuscript No. 1, next to what would be Abraham 1:22,23 (the passage that the Mormon Church used, until 1978, as the sole scriptural basis for the exclusion of blacks from the priesthood). A hole occurs in the Sensen papyrus at the place where this character would have appeared (see photos on pp. 130,131).

So consider: if the "brethren at Kirtland" were merely placing two completed texts side by side for comparison, as Nibley proposes, why would they also have invented nonsense symbols to fill in the holes? This would have compounded error with chaos!

Furthermore, it goes against the claim made during and since Joseph Smith's lifetime that it was he, the Prophet, who filled in by divine inspiration the missing portions:

> These records were torn by being taken from the roll of embalming salve which contained them, and some parts entirely lost, but Smith is to translate the whole by divine inspiration and that which is lost, like Nebuchadnezzar's dream, can be interpreted as well as that which is preserved. (From *A Few Interesting Facts Respecting the Rise, Progress, and Pretensions of the Mormons,* a pamphlet published in 1837 by William S. West)

While many LDS writers in the past have confidently referenced this quotation, Dr. Nibley has chosen to ignore it. A number of the more serious LDS scholars have found it difficult to endorse Dr. Nibley's "Scribes Did It" theory, primarily for the reasons discussed above. Their position has been tactfully spelled out by Edward H. Ashment, a respected LDS Egyptologist, who wrote that the available evidence all points to the fact that "the Prophet has some positive connection with the production of the Joseph Smith Egyptian Papers [that is, Kirtland Egyptian Papers — author]. Therefore, even though involvement with them on his part has been disputed, thoughtful reexamination of the evidence leads us to the conclusion that the Prophet was connected with the entire project" (*Sunstone,* December 1979, p. 42).

But despite its serious weaknesses, many Latter-day Saints continue to rely on the "Scribes Did It" theory as means of defending the integrity of Joseph Smith.[26]

However, even with the frustrating Sensen papyrus finally out of the way, LDS scholars were still faced with the daunting task of looking for another explanation for how the Book of Abraham could have been legitimately produced.

The "Missing Black and Red Scroll" Theory

It is not surprising that the idea of a "missing scroll" — one that had not yet been recovered by the Church — would eventually be proposed as the *true* source of the Book of Abraham. For, if the goal was to rule out the Sensen papyrus, there would have to be an alternative Egyptian scroll from which the Book of Abraham was produced. However, making a case for a missing scroll would require reasons solid enough to counteract the convincing evidence that the ''Sensen'' papyrus was once attached to the Facsimile No. 1 fragment. It was clear that some sort of documentation to support the claim of a different scroll would be very helpful.

The documentation for this theory of a different source scroll appeared to exist in the *History of the Church,* Vol. 2, p. 348:

> The record of Abraham and Joseph, found with the mummies, is beautifully written upon papyrus, with black, and a small part red, ink or paint, in perfect preservation.

This statement appears to be in the words of the Prophet Joseph Smith himself, and therefore it was considered conclusive. The poor Sensen papyrus was surely not "beautifully written," was not in "perfect preservation," and showed no traces of "red ink or paint." So, it was quickly pointed out, this must mean that the original scroll for the Book of Abraham was still missing.

In his article, "Judging and Prejudging the Book of Abraham," written at the time his book *The Message of the Joseph Smith Papyri: An Egyptian Endowment* was in preparation, Nibley had this to say:

> . . . The fact is that the manuscripts at present in the possession of the church represent only a fraction of the Joseph Smith papyri. As President Joseph F. Smith stood in the front doorway of the Nauvoo House with some of the brethren in 1906, the tears streamed down his face as he told how he remembered 'as if it were yesterday,' his 'Uncle Joseph,' down on his knees on the floor with Egyptian Manuscripts spread out all around him, peering at the

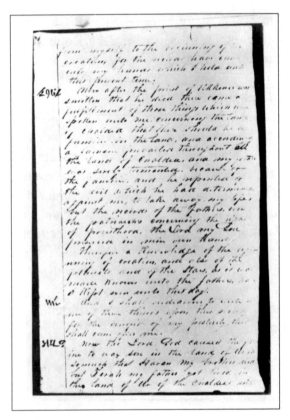

Above: Genuine Egyptian figures on page six of Manuscript No. 1 can be traced to line two of the "Small Sensen" fragment (**below:** Papyrus Joseph Smith XI), beginning just to the left of the large v-shaped hole. Joseph's imaginary characters on page five (see photo on next page) correspond to the part of the papyrus that is missing.

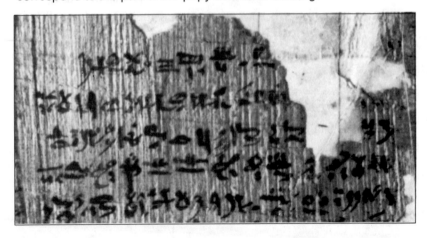

strange writings and jotting things down in a little green notebook with the stub of a pencil. When one considers that the eleven fragments now in our possession can easily be spread out on the top of a small desk, without the straining of the knees, back, and dignity, it would seem that what is missing is much more than what we have.

Thus, the "Missing Black and Red Scroll" theory was born, its

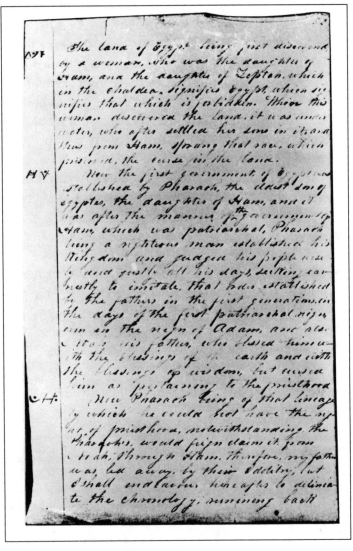

Page five of Manuscript No. 1 of the Book of Abraham translation material.

announcement being made in Hugh Nibley's 1975 book, *The Message of the Joseph Smith Papyri: An Egyptian Endowment.*[27]

Unfortunately, this new theory was a bit premature. Two pages later, in the *History of the Church,* at the end of the same entry in which "Joseph Smith's" description was given, a footnote by B. H. Roberts points out that the wording for the entire entry was not actually Joseph Smith's, it had only been written to *appear* so. Instead, the article had been adapted from a letter written by Oliver Cowdery published in the *Messenger and Advocate.* Cowdery, in turn, had developed his wording from a published placard provided by Michael Chandler. The placard quoted remarks made by persons in Philadelphia who were describing the appearance of the papyrus collection as a whole, and not any specific scroll that Joseph Smith would later identify as the Book of Abraham. (For more on this point, refer back to chapter 8, *The Book of Joseph?,* pp. 81-85.)

Moreover, through contemporary accounts it is very clear that the only papyri the LDS Church has ever possessed are the "two rolls of papyrus" (i.e. "the writings of Abraham and Joseph"), and "two or three other small pieces of papyrus, with astronomical calculations, epitaphs, &c."

Hugh Nibley's ideas have been examined; now consider the statements of Joseph Smith and Oliver Cowdery concerning the papyri:

> On the 3d of July, Michael H. Chandler came to Kirtland to exhibit some Egyptian mummies. There were four human figures, together with *some two or more rolls of papyrus* covered with hieroglyphic figures and devices. (*History of the Church,* Vol. 2, p. 235, emphasis added.)

And,

> Soon after this, some of the Saints at Kirtland purchased the mummies and papyrus . . . and with W. W. Phelps and Oliver Cowdery as scribes, I commenced the translation . . . and much to our joy found that *one of the rolls* contained the writings of Abraham, *another,* the writings of Joseph of Egypt . . . (*Ibid.,* p. 236, emphasis added.)

Before inferring that by the use of the words "two *or more* rolls of papyrus" Smith meant there were *other* rolls, we should carefully examine Oliver Cowdery's statements as they appeared (with Joseph Smith's direction and approval) in the *Messenger and Advocate*:

> Upon the subject of *the Egyptian records, or rather the writings of Abraham and Joseph*, I may say a few words. *This record* is beautifully written on papyrus with black, and a small part red, ink or paint, in perfect preservation. (Cowdery, *op. cit.*, emphasis added.)

Cowdery, thus, understands that *all* — not just a portion — of "the Egyptian records" are "the writings of Abraham and Joseph," which he then refers to as "this record."

But there is more. When giving an account of Chandler's receiving the mummies in New York (evidently supplied by Chandler) Cowdery goes on to say,

> On opening the coffins he discovered that in connection with two of the bodies, were something rolled up with the same kind of linen, saturated with the same bitumen, which, when examined proved to be *two rolls of papyrus, previously mentioned.* I may add that *two or three other small pieces of papyrus, with astronomical calculations, epitaphs, &c.* were found with *others of the mummies. (Ibid,* emphasis added)

Then in a postscript to the letter, he adds,

> You will understand from the foregoing, that eleven mummies were taken from the catacomb, at the time of which I have been speaking, and nothing definite having been said as to their disposal, I may, with propriety add a few words. Seven of the said eleven were purchased by gentlemen for private museums, previous to Mr. Chandler's visit to this place, *with a small quantity of papyrus*, similar, (as he says) *to the astronomical representation contained with the present two rolls, of which I previously spoke*, and the remaining four by gentlemen resident here [in Kirtland] (*Ibid*, emphasis added).

Cowdery proves that there were *two*, and *only two*, "rolls of papyrus," which he believed, because of Joseph Smith's identification of them, were "the writings of Abraham and Joseph," though there were also a few fragments "similar to the astronomical representation" [i.e. Facsimile No. 2] with the papyri. Together these make up what are referred to as "two *or more* rolls of papyrus." Portions of the only two reasonably complete rolls they had have been recovered: Hor's *Book of Breathings* and the *Book of the Dead* for Ta-shert-Min.

Despite the evidence that contradicts it, the "missing black and red scroll" theory has been widely popularized and heavily circulated by well-meaning Latter-day Saints. As recently as the July 1988 issue of the *Ensign* (p. 51), Michael D. Rhodes was still suggesting it, and the *Encyclopedia of Mormonism,* published in 1992, similarly implies that the papyri recovered in 1967 did not include the Egyptian source document from which Joseph Smith produced the Book of Abraham. However, a growing number of scholars, unable to accept the questionable advantage of such unreliable documentation as Nibley presents, have reluctantly felt compelled to abandon this theory.

The "Mistaken Identity" Theory

Meanwhile, some scholars and researchers within the Church were working on a completely different approach to the problem. They were seeking to show that — despite the many explicit remarks by Smith and his contemporaries to the contrary — a papyrus text in the hands of the Prophet would not have been essential for the production of any "translation." In other words, the Book of Abraham came to Joseph Smith through revelation alone.

As early as 1969, a Brigham Young University professor named James R. Harris felt he had uncovered, purely by accident, evidence to support such a view while reading the *Improvement Era.* In the second article in a series on the Three Witnesses, a chance quotation was given from a blessing believed to have been recorded by Oliver Cowdery on December 18, 1833. It read:

> . . . we sought for the right of the fathers, and the authority of the holy priesthood, and the power to administer in the same; for we desired to be followers of righteousness and the possessors of greater knowledge . . .

This was remarkably similar to the second verse found in the Book of Abraham:

> . . . I sought for the blessings of the fathers, and the right whereunto I should be ordained to administer the same; having been myself a follower of righteousness, desiring also to be one who possessed great knowledge. . .

That these remarkable parallel phrases from the Book of Abraham occurred in such brief passages in Cowdery's blessing was enough to convince Harris that one had most certainly been the basis for the other. Since Cowdery's comments were supposedly recorded at least a year and a half *before* the papyri collection came into Joseph Smith's hands[28] (and before any translation could be made from them), and since Prof. Harris apparently did not wish to consider the possibility that the Book of Abraham text was derived from a contemporary source, he believed this could only suggest that,

> The near identical wording of these passages would indicate that some of the text of the Book of Abraham was revealed and recorded before the Abraham papyri came into the possession of Joseph Smith. (*BYU Studies*, Autumn 1969, p. 127)

According to Harris, then, *Oliver Cowdery* had borrowed *his* phrases from the Book of Abraham — which must have been available to him well before the papyri were available to Joseph! (The blessing was not actually recorded by Oliver Cowdery with the similar wording until the fall of 1835, *after* the purchase of the papyri.)

At any rate, the point had been made that if *part* of the Book of Abraham had been written before the papyri appeared, then that portion did not *need* the papyri. It would have been received through *revelation* instead of "translation." And if *one* portion of the text was not dependent upon papyrus, perhaps the *rest* of it was not either.

This is how a young LDS writer named Kirk Holand Vestal saw it. Following Harris' lead, he wrote a paper (*Approaching the Book of Abraham*, unpublished) in 1980 in which he proposed the idea that Joseph Smith had first seen the original scroll containing the record of Abraham in a vision. This was theorized to have occurred as much as two years prior to receiving the papyri from Chandler. Later, when the pagan *Book of Breathings* was unrolled, it bore such a striking resemblance to what the Prophet had seen in his vision, that, as Vestal put it:

> It comes as little surprise that Joseph Smith may have indeed thought that what the papyri contained were the original Egyptian texts of the Book of Abraham . . . The striking similarity of the scenes in both documents would have led Joseph Smith to naturally assume that what he had in his hands in

July 1835 was in fact the very original manuscript of the Book of Abraham.

The next logical step in this "mistaken identity" theory, of course is to conclude that Joseph Smith continued to receive the text for the Book of Abraham through revelation, even though he may have actually believed (mistakenly) he was "translating from the papyrus."

Few Latter-day Saints seem willing to allow that Joseph Smith could have made such a silly mistake (or that God would have allowed his error to remain uncorrected). However, if one accepts the "mistaken identity" theory it does provide a solution to the major problem of relating the papyri to the text and facsimiles of the Book of Abraham. The solution is simply the assertion that the two are totally unrelated. This probably proved reassuring to some people.

Understandably, few people can accept the idea that the Book of Abraham text was written down prior to 1835. For one thing, there is a conspicuous lack of reference to Joseph Smith receiving the "writings of Abraham" by vision, revelation or any other means, prior to his obtaining the papyri. Another is Joseph Smith's own references to sitting down with the papyri and laboring at the translation.

Nevertheless, the idea of Joseph Smith having received his text by revelation alone was too appealing and practical a suggestion to ignore. The July 1988 *Ensign* article mentioned above provides this as an alternate theory.

The "Catalyst" Theory

By appealing to revelation, then, most of the papyrus fragments could be set aside. But if any of the Egyptian material simply *had* to be linked to the Book of Abraham, it would have to be those bearing the drawings associated with the facsimiles. Someone still needed to explain why Joseph Smith would have claimed that Egyptian burial scenes were in some way associated with the patriarch Abraham.

In a little booklet titled, *What Mormonism Isn't — A Response to the Research of Jerald and Sandra Tanner*, LDS writer Ian Barber made an interesting suggestion regarding the *Book of the Dead* and *Book of Breathings* illustrations used by Smith. He held that these scenes were correctly identified by modern Egyptologists in the context in which they appeared (that is, they were funerary documents), but went on to say, "there is absolutely no reason to preclude their existence in different contexts and at different times, certainly extending back to 2000 B. C."[29]

Barber strongly endorsed Hugh Nibley's long-standing comparisons between the Book of Abraham material and Egyptian mythology, apocryphal writings, and the like (see the "Any Egyptian Connection" theory), and he offered as his opinion that,

> Joseph Smith did not believe that he possessed Abraham's original writings, but rather reproductions that had been altered and perhaps placed in an entirely new context. The story that the Egyptologists . . . have given us describes this new context and not necessarily Abraham's world view some 4000 years ago . . .

While sounding much like the reasoning used in the "Hidden Meaning" theory, it is also the prelude to something new. The earlier "Hidden Meaning" theory was used primarily to support the concept of a *translation;* while this new approach, which can be termed the "Catalyst" theory, supports the *revelation* concept. As Barber explains,

> In my opinion the facsimiles and Egyptian material served as revelatory aids for the Prophet to prepare him intellectually and spiritually for the direct revelation of the Book of Abraham text.

The "Catalyst" theory also seems to have the blessing of Hugh Nibley and the 1992 *Encyclopedia of Mormonism.* Nibley comments in his book, *Abraham in Egypt* (1981), that Smith, "had already demonstrated at great length his power to translate ancient records *with or without possession of the original text.*"[30] And the *Encyclopedia of Mormonism* offers the vague hypothesis that in studying his papyri, Joseph Smith, "sought revelation from the Lord concerning them and received in the process the book of Abraham."[31] The papyri illustrations, in particular, it suggests, are somehow supposed to have served as a connecting link between the prophet's postulated Book of Abraham revelations and the Egyptian papyri. This disingenuous theory allows the *Encyclopedia of Mormonism* to conclude that,

> it was principally divine revelation rather than his [Joseph Smith's] knowledge

of languages that produced the English text of the book of Abraham. His precise methodology remains unknown.[32]

However, the "Catalyst" theory is fatally flawed in requiring us to believe that God would associate His sacred truth with a document consisting of prayers to pagan Egyptian gods, and ripe with occultism. As was noted earlier in connection with the "Any Egyptian Connection" theory (pp. 119,120), it is inconceivable, given God's holy character as revealed throughout the Bible, that He would associate Himself or His truth in any way with such pagan occultic documents.

Since the articles in the *Encyclopedia of Mormonism* were written by a committee of Brigham Young University professors working under the supervision of the University's broad of trustees and Elders Neal A. Maxwell and Dalin H. Oaks of the Quorum of the Twelve Apostles (*The Ensign,* March 1992, p. 79), its articles on the Book of Abraham are probably as close as one can get to an official LDS Church view of the Book of Abraham.

Of course, all of this is about as far as one can get from Joseph Smith's own words as he described his experience in July 1835:

> ... with W. W. Phelps and Oliver Cowdery as scribes, I commenced the translation of some of the characters or hieroglyphics, and much to our joy found that one of the rolls contained the writings of Abraham, another the writings of Joseph of Egypt, etc. — a more full account of which will appear in its place as I proceed to examine or unfold them (*History of the Church,* Vol. 2, p. 236).

The "Nobody Really Understands Egyptian Anyway" Theory

If the first five approaches mentioned in this chapter can be referred to as "translation" theories, and the last two as "revelation" theories, then perhaps this last approach should be called a "desperation" theory. Far-fetched as it seems, this final theory has been proposed by Dr. Hugh Nibley, who apparently is its only serious proponent.

Put simply, this theory tries to portray the entire scholarly field of Egyptology as being in such a constant state of flux and reappraisal that there is no reliable standard for interpreting ancient Egyptian. It holds that practically none of the established rules of Egyptology are valid, and that no interpretation can be trusted with any degree of certainty. This assumption also lies behind the "Any Egyptian Connection" theory, is the inspiration for the "Hidden Meaning" theory, and provides the reasoning for the "Mnemonic Device" theory. It implies that since nothing can be *fully* understood, nothing — especially the work done by Joseph Smith — can justifiably be challenged.

Nibley demonstrates this attitude in his 1975 book, *The Message of the Joseph Smith Papyri: An Egyptian Endowment,* where, after providing his own translation of the large and small Sensen fragments that essentially agrees with those that have been prepared by other scholars, he declares:

> To the often-asked question, 'Have the Joseph Smith Papyri been translated?' The answer is an emphatic no! What, then, is the foregoing? A mechanical transcription, no more . . . What we have is a transmission rather than a translation of the text . . . Though as correct and literal as we can make it, the translation in the preceding chapter is not a translation. It is nonsense (*op.cit.,* p. 47).

Nibley proceeds to give several examples in which noted Egyptologists have, over the years, expressed legitimate professional caution about basing any interpretations upon literal translations without an understanding of the context. And yet, it is exactly this *context* which Nibley evidently wants to disregard. In fact, his position becomes one of insisting that no context can be correctly determined despite careful scholarship:

> . . . translations into English are properly meant for English readers who know no other language — the Egyptologist may be expected to read the original; what the average reader has a right to is a flawless translation here and now, and through the years various Egyptologists, by pretending that they could supply such, have beguiled the public and exploited its restless impatience with devastating effect against Joseph Smith.
>
> The trouble is, in short, that the Egyptians just don't speak our language; every sentence of theirs from our point of view is a technical jargon, 'which,' as Santillana observes, 'can hardly be understood if it is not recognized. Nobody can interpret farther than he understands . . . The most refined philological method in the hands of expert philologists will yield only childish stuff out of them, if childish stuff is expected. Technical indications which would make clear sense to a scientist [or to a Latter-day Saint! —

Nibley] go unnoticed or mistranslated . . . It should be kept in mind that every translation is a mere function of the translator's expectations.' From which it would seem that no matter how well one knows one's *Gardiner*, or how many years one has spent in Egypt, one may still be totally excluded from the real meaning of any Egyptian text. Many scholars have known Greek better than any man alive knows Egyptian, yet to this day Greek Literature is full of texts that no scholar even pretends to understand; is Egyptian so much more obliging? (*ibid.*, p. 48)

But, if not by scholarship, then by what means *can* a proper interpretation of an ancient text be determined? Only by *inspiration*, Dr. Nibley goes on to explain. Thus, he finishes building his case for trusting Joseph Smith, no matter how compelling the evidence is against him.

Though Dr. Nibley frequently quotes from recognized authorities in order to give the appearance that his conclusions regarding the Book of Abraham are supportable, he actually stands virtually alone in his position. Even Professor Richard A. Parker of Brown University, who had provided Nibley with one of the first translations of the Sensen text and whom Nibley once described as "the best man in America for this particular period and style of writing,"[33] stated emphatically:

The ancient Egyptian language can be called completely decipherable. There are some words in the vocabulary whose specific meaning is still undetermined, but there are very few whose general meaning remains uncertain. We can read almost any text with a high degree of confidence.[34]

In spite of his professional isolation, Dr. Nibley has continued to develop and maintain his "Nobody Really Understands Egyptian Anyway" theory. Useful at first for obscuring the meaning of the Sensen text, and later helpful in attempting to reconstruct Egyptian mythology so that it resembled (as much as possible) Mormon doctrine, it has since become almost indispensable in rationalizing Joseph Smith's association of standard Egyptian funerary drawings with the history and religion of Abraham.

CHAPTER TWELVE

"All Is Well" —
Creating An Appearance

J UST AS THE LEVEL OF EXPOSURE to the subject of the
Joseph Smith Papyri varies among Latter-day Saints, so also do
their responses to the controversy. Most know little about it,
some have come across a few conflicts, yet choose not to investigate
them, and still others find themselves considering one or more of the
various "intellectual" approaches discussed previously. It is interesting
that it seems to matter little to Mormon belief which of these categories the individual member falls into.

Lack of awareness of the whole papyri issue helps perpetuate the
traditional understanding of the Book of Abraham's origins. *Confusion,* on the other hand, can be a highly effective means of preventing
questions from becoming too critical when problems are encountered.
A person who finds a topic very confusing will often suspend judgment and keep right on believing in whatever he hopes is true. Over
time, his questions lose urgency, and though not resolved, cease to
become bothersome. *Trust* in a system will also help sustain a person
through confusion until he reaches the point of no longer caring whether
an answer is reasonable or not, or indeed, whether an answer even
exists.

It is not surprising then, that the LDS Church heavily stresses the absolute necessity of trusting its system and leadership. Members are taught, for instance, that praying to know the truthfulness of a matter[1] is a more sure way of determining its validity than thoughtful examination of the evidence. *But in so doing, the very evidence God has provided to steer us to truth may be ignored.*

Contributing to the confusion is the fact that there is no "official" answer from the LDS Church that addresses the issues raised by the discovery of the Joseph Smith Papyri. Nor has there ever been. All approaches, theories, and defenses, including those proposed by Hugh Nibley and others in Church publications, have been offered solely at the author's own initiative, and as his own opinion. (In fact, the works of Mormon apologists almost universally include a disclaimer to the effect that the author does not write as an official spokesperson for the LDS Church.)

In the absence of official answers from LDS authorities, those with questions are left with only the efforts of the various apologists to provide solutions. Under these circumstances it is not surprising that occasional contradictions occur when a variety of approaches are used to give the impression that "all is well." A good case in point is the way the subject of the Joseph Smith Papyri have been treated in various LDS books and periodicals.

The "LDS Book"

It appears that the primary reason most LDS articles of an apologetic nature are written is to paint, at all costs, a favorable picture of the Mormon faith — one that is "faith promoting." Accuracy and credibility seem to be distinctly secondary matters.

The following examples illustrate three techniques typically found in LDS apologetic writings:

"Nothing has changed." This is the approach the casual reader of Mormon apologetic literature on the Book of Abraham is most likely to encounter. It is calculated to create the impression that the traditional viewpoint remains intact, almost as though the Metropolitan papyri collection had never come to light, and no questions or problems have ever arisen as a result.

This technique is especially common in the popular, non-academic books that are intended to present a favorable overview of Mormonism. These books generally contain a great deal of fluff, but little substance, and are often marked by serious inaccuracies and misrepresentations, as well as the omission of controversial details. Specific mention of newer material likely to challenge traditional perceptions is studiously avoided, and older works undergo only minor revisions, or none at all.

An excellent example of this is the book *The Latter-day Saints: A Contemporary History of the Church of Jesus Christ*, by William E. Berrett (Deseret Book Company, 1985). In Chapter 12, "Other Scriptures Come Forth," Berrett discusses "The origin of the Book of Abraham:"

> In July 1835 Joseph Smith came into possession of some ancient records, the value of which is not even yet fully appreciated.
>
> Sometime in 1828 a French explorer named Antonio Sebolo secured permission to make a certain excavation in Egypt. Three years later, having secured the proper license, he employed 433 men and began excavating a catacomb or tomb near the site of ancient Thebes. The tomb contained several hundred mummies, of which Sebolo took eleven, still encased. En route back to Paris, he put in at Trieste, where he died after a brief illness. The mummies were left by will to a nephew named Michael Chandler, who lived in Philadelphia, Pennsylvania. Some two years later Chandler took possession of them in New York. When he opened the caskets, he was disappointed to find no jewels or precious ornaments. But attached to two of the bodies were rolls of well-preserved linen, and within these coverings were rolls of papyrus bearing a perfectly preserved record in carefully formed black and red characters. When he could find no one in New York or Philadelphia who could translate the characters, Chandler began touring the country with the mummies. On July 3, 1835, he reached Kirtland, Ohio, where he sought an interview with Joseph Smith, who, he had been told, might be able to help translate the characters (*op.cit.*, p. 105).

Almost every statement of fact in the foregoing quotation is inaccurate, though adapted directly from the pages of Robert's History *of the Church.* This material is essentially unchanged from its appearance in Berrett's 1961 book *The Restored Church* (which for many years was used as an LDS high school Seminary textbook). This despite the fact that for nearly twenty years it has been well known among LDS researchers and historians that the explorer's name was *Lebolo*, not *Sebolo* (an error originally created long ago by someone mistaking a handwritten "L" for an "S"); that he was a Piedmontese (Italian) licensed through a French office, not a Frenchman; that he did his digging in Egypt in the early 1820's, not in 1831; and that he died not in Trieste, but at his home in Castellamonte in 1830.[2] LDS genealogical researchers have long admitted that no record of a family connection between Lebolo and Chandler seems to exist, and when BYU's H. Donl Peterson reported his discovery of Lebolo's will in 1985, it made no mention of either Chandler or the mummies.

Although these errors are peripheral and have no real bearing on the true identity of Joseph Smith's papyri, Berrett's failure to correct mistakes in his book when more accurate information became available does point out a tendency of some LDS writers to persist in maintaining a picture of things exactly as they have "always been," regardless of whether that picture is correct. About the only item here that seems to apply to present concerns is the reference to "rolls of papyrus bearing a perfectly preserved record in carefully formed black and red characters." Of the "Missing Black and Red Scroll" theory, though, we have said enough already. The article continues:

> When the Prophet was able to interpret some of the characters, Chandler responded with a letter of certification . . .
>
> Friends of the Prophet in Kirtland later purchased the four mummies together with the rolls of papyrus. Joseph Smith, assisted by W. W. Phelps and Oliver Cowdery as scribes, subsequently began to study ancient languages and to translate the papyrus . . . it would appear that considerable translating had been done before the end of 1835, but the difficulties that faced the Church and the Prophet during the years immediately following prevented him from completing the work. In addition, no grammar of the Egyptian language had appeared in America by 1835. Thus the results of his labor become the more remarkable . . .
>
> The Prophet completed only part of the scrolls dealing with the life of Abraham. One of the rolls of papyrus containing the writings of Joseph, who was sold into Egypt, was apparently never translated sufficiently for publication. Publication of the Book of Abraham began in the newspaper *Times and Seasons* in March 1842 at Nauvoo, Illinois, along with facsimi-

les of certain portions of the papyrus" (*Ibid.*, pp. 105-107).

All of this is a very *traditional* viewpoint in that it assumes a direct translation of a physical record that could actually be laid out on a table or held in the hand, not some intangible impressions received from seeing a scroll in a vision, or some such thing. And while the phrase "scrolls dealing with the life of Abraham" *can* be understood by the naive traditionalist to mean something that was actually penned by Abraham "by his own hand, upon papyrus," such an interpretation is not required. A reader knowing something of the theories that attempt to deal with the first-century date of Papyrus Joseph Smith I could interpret this as meaning something that was written on papyrus after Abraham's lifetime by someone else. The author provides no information that would clarify the matter or upset either view.

Berrett did make one concession to the 1967 rediscovery of the Joseph Smith papyri. Back in 1961, a statement in *The Restored Church* read:

> For years after the publication of the facsimiles, the original documents remained in existence. They were considered as the property of the Smith family and, after the Prophet's martyrdom, were retained by his wife, Emma. They were later sold by her to a museum at St. Louis, from whence they found their way into the Museum of Chicago. In the great Chicago fire, the museum was totally destroyed and with it the precious ancient manuscripts. (pp. 107, 1969 edition)

In the 1985 book, *The Latter-day Saints*, this material was placed in the back of the book as a footnote, and was changed to read:

> For years after the publication of the facsimiles, the original documents remained in the possession of the Joseph Smith family. After the Prophet's death, they were retained by his widow, Emma. She later sold them to a museum at St. Louis, and they were subsequently found in the Museum of Chicago. In the great Chicago fire of 1871 the museum was destroyed, as were most of the precious ancient manuscripts it housed (p. 395, 1985 edition).

It is remarkable what the author leaves unmentioned here. If his readers are to learn that some of Joseph Smith's papyri survived, have been discovered, and have since become a source of controversy, they will not do so through Berrett's book.[3]

The Latter-day Saints is by no means a unique example of this type of presentation, nor is the Church's recent heavy emphasis on promoting such literature incidental.

Not long ago certain General Authorities, in particular Apostle Boyd K. Packer, criticized a number of prominent Mormon writers and historians for what he termed an "exaggerated loyalty to the theory that everything must be told."[4] Packer felt that an objective approach to Church history "may unwittingly be giving 'equal time' to the adversary" since it "may be read by those not mature enough for 'advanced history,' and a testimony in seedling stage may be crushed."[5] Elder Packer went on to insist that the role of Mormon historians ought to be mainly to demonstrate and affirm that "the hand of the Lord [has been] in every hour and every moment of the Church from its beginning till now." In effect, LDS writers were being told that they should produce only an *accommodation history*[6] that would exclude anything not "faith promoting."

Even the late Apostle Bruce R. McConkie's widely respected *Mormon Doctrine* continues to withhold any information that might threaten the simplicity of a traditional view of the Book of Abraham, or lead to controversy. First published nearly a decade before the papyri were rediscovered, McConkie's Book of Abraham entry under the Pearl of Great Price heading still has not been revised or updated in the twenty years since their discovery.

And of course, this perpetuation of known inaccuracies can also be found in preface to the Book of Abraham, which still reads just as it has since 1878:

THE BOOK OF ABRAHAM
TRANSLATED FROM THE PAPYRUS, BY JOSEPH SMITH.
A translation of some ancient records, that have fallen into our hands from the catacombs of Egypt. — The writings of Abraham while he was in Egypt, called the Book of Abraham, written by his own hand, upon papyrus.

"Incredible New Insight."   This is a second available approach LDS apologists resort to in attempting to defend things like the Book of Abraham. Here writers feel quite free to admit as much information as they feel comfortable with in order to intimate that *now* the reader has been exposed to an understanding of matters that probably everyone should have realized in the first place. Exposures of this sort serve a two-fold purpose. First, by proposing a way in which this new information justifies belief in the LDS system; second, by laying to rest any fears among Latter-day Saints that anyone in the Church should be concerned about such information.[7] After all, many will reason, if the "best minds in the Church" have resolved matters and show no concern, why should the average member?

The best examples of this technique can be seen in the books and articles that have come about as a result of the "intellectual approaches" discussed earlier. As has been shown, these authors can take widely divergent and even contradictory positions, and yet each is equally dogmatic. In addition, many of these concepts are so elaborate and complex that many readers are probably unable to judge their worth or validity because they are so difficult to understand. Confused, the reader can only fall back on his trust in the system.

Many Latter-day Saints have an especially high regard for Hugh Nibley's writings, for example, and are impressed with his direct, pragmatic-sounding style. On the subject of the Joseph Smith Papyri Nibley has been especially prolific, setting forth his positions and pronouncements in the pages of *Improvement Era, Dialogue,* and *BYU Studies*, as well as authoring numerous other articles, books, and talks about them over a period of many years. There are probably few Latter-day Saints who would presume to question his conclusions — which were invariably favorable to the Church — yet this is exactly what Edward H. Ashment of the Church Translation Department finally did.

In a sixteen-page article in the December 1979 issue of *Sunstone* magazine, Ashment refuted, point by point, in scholarly detail, the greater part of Dr. Nibley's most basic contentions in defense of the Book of Abraham over the years. In a number of major areas, such as the question of the damaged condition of the papyri in Smith's day, the erroneously restored material on both Facsimile No. 1 (see pp. 101,102) and Facsimile No. 2 (see pp. 104-108), and Smith's involvement with the Egyptian Alphabet and Grammar material, Ashment's frank admissions sided squarely with the charges that critics of the Book of Abraham have leveled throughout the controversy.

In his response to Ashment's article in the same issue of *Sunstone*, Dr. Nibley was not only forced to admit that he had been in error, but stated, "I refuse to be held responsible for anything I wrote more than three years ago. For heaven's sake, I hope we are moving forward here. After all, the implication that one mistake and it is all over with — how flattering to think in forty years I have not made one slip and I am still in business! I would say that about four-fifths of everything I put down has changed, of course."[8]

Unfortunately, this tongue-in-cheek acknowledgement was probably read by only a fraction of those who read Nibley's *Improvement Era* articles. *Sunstone* magazine is one of only a handful of LDS-oriented publications that have attempted to discuss the Book of Abraham controversy in any depth. However, such publications are generally read only by the Church's intelligentsia. The controversial issues it raises are seldom encountered by the average Latter-day Saint because of its limited circulation.

The "Red Herring" technique. This is the third, and most widely used method apologists have employed in responding to papyri difficulties. It is a diversionary tactic which consists of focusing attention on peripheral matters in order to "draw the scent away" from the real issue (as a herring is dragged across the trail of a fox to distract the pursuing dogs).

Much of Dr. Nibley's writing on the subject of the Book of Abraham papyri employs the "red herring" strategy. Good examples include his early series of *Improvement Era* articles stressing the "Any Egyptian Connection" theory and more recently his emphasis on the "Nobody Really Understands Egyptian Anyway" theory. The basic intent of these articles is to lead the reader away from the damaging evidence and on to inconsequential matters. For the novice, his efforts appear to have been quite successful; toward professionals, somewhat less so.

Another good example of the "red herring" technique is found in the 1981 book by Robert L. and Rosemary Brown entitled, *They Lie in Wait to Deceive* (Brownsworth Publishing Co.). Within just a few years of its appearance it had become a veritable mainstay for bishops, missionaries, priesthood leaders, home teachers, and anyone else needing a quick, simple "answer" to the complicated problems of the papyri controversy.

Billed as "a study of anti-Mormon deception," *They Lie in Wait to Deceive* proposes to tell "the amazing story of how 'Dr.' or 'Prof.' Dee Jay Nelson, Jerald and Sandra Tanner, and other anti-Mormons work to obstruct and distort the truth."[9] Actually, the work focuses on the series of false claims and representations made by Dee Jay Nelson during the years he lectured against the authenticity of the Book of Abraham. It shows that he used fraudulent background information to promote himself, including a spurious Ph.D. (a certificate purchased from a "diploma mill" for one hundred and ninety-five dollars). Nelson is rightly portrayed as an opportunist of questionable character, bent on exploiting the LDS Church's vulnerability over the Metropolitan Museum papyri for his own profit. Others, especially the Tanners, are also condemned for their part in promoting Nelson's conclusions, and thus lending legitimacy to his reputation.

As an exposé of Nelson, this work appears to be both appropriate and commendable. It is now well established that Nelson made a number of false and misleading statements about himself over a period of several years. This was very unfortunate, for in doing so he not only exploited the weakness of the Mormon position for personal gain, but also took advantage of the good faith of a great many people who had come to respect him, including a large number of non-Mormons and former Mormons.

The Browns, however, did not stop with simply exposing an impostor. They went on to try to establish a kind of "anti-Mormon conspiracy," in which "lies, deception, partial truths, and misrepresentation" were the primary tools used whenever a challenge was made concerning the Book of Abraham's validity.[10] Moreover, (and here is the red herring) they make it appear that the entire case against the Book of Abraham is dependent on the work and claims of a phony Dee Jay Nelson, thereby drawing attention away from the true facts of the case. They write, for example:

Mormons and non-Mormons alike need to be aware of the tactics used by the adversary . . . This book contains a thorough investigation of the

fraudulent credentials of 'Dr.' and 'Prof.' Dee Jay Nelson, 'World Renowned Egyptologist' — this century's most outspoken foe of the Book
of Abraham (and thus Joseph Smith) . . . Nelson has long been the No. 1
witness against the Book of Abraham according to Jerald and Sandra
Tanner, Walter Martin, and other leaders in the anti-Mormon movement
(Preface, p. i).

And:

This man, Dee Jay Nelson . . . has been busily engaged perpetrating his
false credentials and a false story against the Book of Abraham . . .
His denunciation of the Book of Abraham is extensively quoted in nearly
all anti-Mormon books (Introduction, p. iii).

And:

It soon became obvious to this author that Jerald and Sandra Tanner had
the most to gain from pushing Dee Jay Nelson into the forefront with
regards to the Book of Abraham . . . [this is followed by some speculation
by Brown as to how much money the Tanners make]. Is this the reason
why the Tanners were not eager to expose Nelson, their No. 1 witness
against the Book of Abraham? (p. 162)

And:

Do you think you can find out the truth about the Mormon church by
asking people like Dee Jay Nelson or Jerald and Sandra Tanner? If you
do, you have missed the point of this whole book! (p. 172)

So, according to the Browns' thinking, if Dee Jay Nelson can be
discredited, then the entire file of evidence against the Book of Abraham should be stamped *"case closed"* as far as any Mormon is concerned. Since a disreputable man has attacked the Book of Abraham,
the Book of Abraham must therefore be a reputable work.

The faultiness of such reasoning is obvious.

To begin with, the "case against the Book of Abraham" is not
something "discovered" or "established" by Nelson. It was spelled
out long before the Metropolitan papyri ever surfaced, and the basic

direction of the charges have changed little since the criticism of Deveria's time, when the study of Egyptology first advanced to the level where Joseph Smith's own drawings could be read and shown to have no relation to his translation.

Furthermore, the actual findings concerning the papyri — what they were, when and why they had been written, and what they said — which Nelson reported on, were not simply his own opinions or guesses. *Whenever qualified people have studied the papyri, including such undisputed experts as Baer, Wilson, and Parker, they have always reached the same conclusions that Nelson did.* However he may have misrepresented himself, the fact remains that Nelson's identification of the papyri was quite correct, and his descriptions of them were reasonably accurate.

Nor was it Nelson who was responsible for applying the papyri information to the issue of the questionable authenticity of the Book of Abraham. This application was universal, and inevitable. Back during the 1912 controversy Dr. Albert Lythgoe had commented upon the desirability of examining the original papyrus,[11] and the following year LDS apologist John Henry Evans had insisted the original papyrus would have to be available before scholars or critics "would be warranted in saying that the entire Book of Abraham was not properly translated."[12]

Dee Jay Nelson, then, did not create the arguments being used to challenge the authenticity of the Book of Abraham, nor has his work ever, in any way, been an exclusive part of that challenge. What he did do was use the case against the Book of Abraham as a soapbox to gain attention for himself , and in the process made inflated and false claims about his credentials. This is quite different from what the Browns portray; they have tried to show him as using his false claims and credentials to give credibility to the case he presented against the Book of Abraham.

But what of the *real* issue, namely, the credibility of the Book of Abraham itself?

Only a minimal effort is made by the Browns in their book to deal with what they call "the truth about the Book of Abraham," and even this is done by merely falling back on a few of Hugh Nibley's more popular writings on the subject. Thus their "truth" turns out to be nothing more than an updated rehash of the "Scribes Did It" theory, followed by the "Missing Black and Red Scroll" theory.[13] Both of these views had already largely fallen into disrepute even before the Browns' book was published.

In some cases, in fact, the Browns have mentioned works in which at least one of the above theories has been clearly shown to be based on faulty assumptions, though they appear to be unaware of this. H. Michael Marquardt's *Book of Abraham Papyrus Found*, for example, which is listed on the back cover of the Browns' book among "some anti-Mormon publications which have been endorsing Dee Jay Nelson," contains a very plain refutation (pp. 1,2) of the premise upon which Dr. Nibley developed his "Missing Black and Red Scroll" theory (see pp. 129-134 of this book). Still, the Browns — who apparently failed to read the very books they list — have rather blindly followed Nibley into this error, accepting his writings as unqualified fact.

There are a surprising number of similar instances. At one point a list of five LDS works is provided in order to "enlighten the reader on the subject of the Book of Abraham:"

1. *Abraham in Egypt*, by Dr. Hugh Nibley.
2. *The Firm Foundation of Mormonism*, by Kirk Holland Vestal and Arthur Wallace.
3. *Improvement Era* articles from January 1968 — June 1970, by Dr. Hugh Nibley.
4. *The Message of the Joseph Smith Papyri: an Egyptian Endowment*, by Dr. Hugh Nibley.
5. *BYU Studies*, vol. 17, Spring 1977, article by Michael D. Rhodes.

The Browns caution the reader that the above "are scholarly books and are well-referenced. Scholars do not seem to write in easy, novel form. Therefore, the price for finding out the truth about the Book of Abraham may be to read and study these books more than once."[14]

This is good advice; but one could fairly ask if the Browns have followed it themselves. If they had, they would have known that Dr. Nibley's two books propose theories that contradict each other; that the Rhodes article confirms the identification of Facsimile No. 2 as a hypocephalus and makes no Abrahamic connection at all; that Hugh

Nibley's *Improvement Era* articles (prepared back when, he admits, he was "skirmishing and sparring for time") all contain an abundance of outdated concepts and disproven contentions; that the Vestal-Wallace book relies heavily upon the writings of Dee Jay Nelson as an "authority" to help support its views!

It is disappointing to find that people claiming to be responsible researchers are apparently not on a familiar basis with the books and articles to which they refer others. It is possible that the Browns were so convinced their position was correct that they felt such precautions would not be necessary.

Failing to check carefully into their sources has led the Browns to use faulty approaches and reach flawed conclusions. Much of this is probably due to the difficulty they have in being objective. Their writing expresses continuous and undisguised hostility toward anyone threatening their image of Mormonism, and this attitude often colors their understanding of the subject matter about which they write. Rather than presenting a reasonably thorough account of Dee Jay Nelson's use of false credentials and exaggerated claims, they go to extremes in attempting to discredit the man from every imaginable angle. As a result of this approach their contentions are often seriously flawed, even to the point of being refuted by their own arguments elsewhere in the book.

Though their efforts may be dismissed by some as generally uninformed or perhaps even intentionally deceitful, Robert and Rosemary Brown nevertheless appear to be motivated by a genuine sincerity in their desire to defend the Book of Abraham. However, they also demonstrate that they are not above using omissions, misrepresentations, errors, partial truths, and obscuring of facts to present their case — the very methods they accuse their "anti-Mormon conspiracy" of using.

Sadly, *They Lie in Wait to Deceive* amounts to little more than a superficial "defense of the faith" in which readers are expected to accept its statements at face value. It is this exploitation of the reader's *trust* which plays a major role in establishing the credibility of such works. The book is usually endorsed and recommended by Latter-day Saints who are unfamiliar with the actual facts behind the Book of Abraham controversy, a category of Mormons which seems to include even a great many in Church leadership positions, including bishops, stake Presidents, LDS Seminary and Institute Instructors, etc.[15]

Because of its widespread influence among Latter-day Saints, some of the charges and claims found in *They Lie in Wait to Deceive* deserve to be examined in more detail than can be done here. A review of these issues can be found in the *Appendix* of this book.

A Faith Promoting Display at BYU

Besides the use of published sources, other methods have also been used to lend the impression that "all is well" regarding the Book of Abraham-Joseph Smith Papyri matter, and that everything has been dealt with satisfactorily as far as the LDS Church is concerned.

Faith promoting displays, similar to the one shown below and on the following pages, are a common sight on the campus of Brigham Young University.

BYU's 1983 Pearl of Great Price exhibit consisted of a large, four-sectioned display case filled with mounted photographs, notes, and letters. A final section displayed several books on this subject pro-

A faith-promoting Pearl of Great Price exhibit in the lobby of the Joseph Smith Building at Brigham Young University (1983).

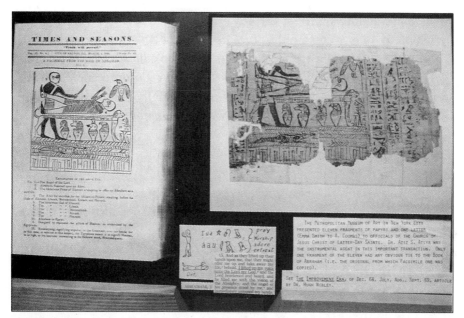

Detail from a 1983 Pearl of Great Price Display at Brigham Young University. This comparison failed to point out that the fundamental errors in Facsimile No. 1 correspond to the missing portions of Papyrus Joseph Smith I, which Joseph Smith incorrectly filled in (see chapter 10 of this book for further discussion).

duced by various LDS authors over a period of several years.

The most striking portion of this display can be seen in the center of the photograph above, a comparison of Facsimile No. 1 from the Book of Abraham to the Papyrus Joseph Smith I drawing from which it was adapted. A casual viewer — especially a young student — unfamiliar with what Papyrus Joseph Smith I actually represents (a standard pagan funeral text dating from about the time of Christ) cannot help but be impressed by the points of *superficial similarity.* There is no mention here at all of the *fundamental points of difference* between the two drawings due to Joseph Smith's incorrect restoration of the missing areas (see chapter 10 of this book).

As a matter of fact, in the photograph at the top of this page, the small drawing set between Facsimile No. 1 and Papyrus Joseph Smith I shows a hieroglyphic figure (standing man with both arms raised) that was taken directly from Alan Gardiner's *Egyptian Grammar,* and which can be interpreted as "pray." The character is then turned sideways so that it resembles the figure in Facsimile No.1, and is pasted beside an underlined portion of the Book of Abraham, chapter 1, verse 15, in which Abraham "lifts up his voice unto the Lord his God." This incorrectly (yet, it seems, intentionally) gives the impression that Joseph Smith's "translation" must be correct — in spite of the fact that the figure in Facsimile No.1 was never correct to begin with (see the discussion of Papyrus Joseph Smith I on pp. 62-65 for details of the discrepancies).

The most flagrant misrepresentation made here is found on the information card below Papyrus Joseph Smith I (see close-up photograph at the top of p. 157). The last sentence reads: "ONLY ONE FRAGMENT OF THE ELEVEN HAD ANY OBVIOUS TIE TO THE BOOK OF ABRAHAM (I.E. THE ORIGINAL FROM WHICH FACSIMILE ONE WAS COPIED)."

However, as was demonstrated in chapter seven, there is at least one other fragment from the Metropolitan Museum which has a very close tie to the Book of Abraham, namely, Papyrus Joseph Smith XI — the "Small Sensen" text. Not only does this fragment connect directly to Papyrus Joseph Smith I, as shown in the picture at the bottom of the next page (see also the color foldout on p. 33), but its characters were used to supply the "translated from" figures on three separate translation manuscripts when the Book of Abraham was initially produced by Joseph Smith and his scribes.

The fact of this connection between Papyrus Joseph Smith I and Papyrus Joseph Smith XI was not merely *overlooked* in this display; it was *deliberately obscured.* Papyrus Joseph Smith I (the Facsimile No. 1 papyrus) is shown standing alone (as can be seen in the photograph on p. 155) with a placard beneath it assuring the viewer that it is the "only" fragment of the eleven with "any obvious tie" to the Book of Abraham.

No hint is provided to suggest in any way that the "Small Sensen" fragment (Papyrus Joseph Smith XI) connects to, and is a part of the Facsimile No. 1 fragment (Papyrus Joseph Smith I); that in fact, it is the source of the Egyptian characters in the Book of Abraham translation manuscripts. Even if the originators of this display were to fall back on their use of the word "obvious" as a justification, such remarks

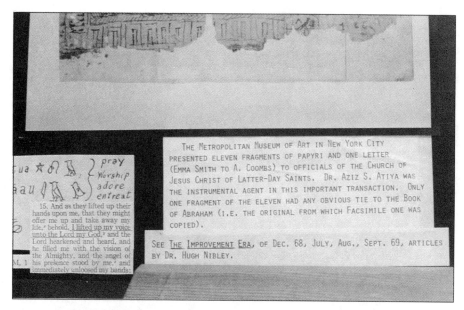

Above: Detail from the BYU Pearl of Great Price display: The last sentence of the caption describing Papyrus Joseph Smith I reads, "ONLY ONE FRAGMENT OF THE ELEVEN HAD ANY OBVIOUS TIE TO THE BOOK OF ABRAHAM (I.E., THE ORIGINAL FROM WHICH FACSIMILE ONE WAS COPIED)."

Below: This composite photograph — not a part of the BYU display — demonstrates that Papyrus Joseph Smith XI (left, the "Small Sensen" text) connects directly to Papyrus Joseph Smith I. The BYU display attempted to obscure this damaging association. (See the color foldout, p. 33, for a larger picture of the Book of Abraham papyrus scroll.)

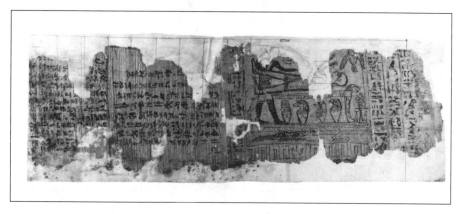

Above: Detail of the 1983 BYU Pearl of Great Price exhibit. Facsimile No. 1 and Papyrus Joseph Smith I are on the top shelf, right side; below on the right are the "Sensen Papyri."

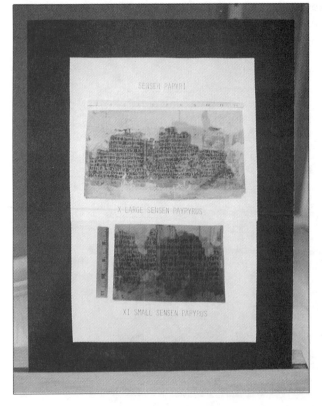

Left: Close-up of the "Sensen Papyri" fragments as they appeared in the BYU Pearl of Great Price exhibit. They are shown out of scale to each other and are inaccurately depicted as proportionately smaller than the Facsimile No. 1 fragment, of which they are in fact a part.

must still be regarded as intentionally misleading.

The "Small Sensen" fragment *is* shown in this exhibit, however. Look carefully at the photograph on the top of page 158: to the right, on a shelf just below the prominent, impressive Facsimile No. 1 display, is a plain card bearing two small photographs of papyri fragments. The close-up of these two fragments at the bottom of page 158 shows that they are labeled simply "SENSEN PAPYRI," with "X LARGE SENSEN PAPYRUS" and "XI SMALL SENSEN PAPYRUS" being the only identification or explanation offered for the two fragments.

Look carefully again at the photo on the top of page 158. The "Sensen Papyri" are not only out of scale to each other, but both are shown much smaller in proportion to the Facsimile No. 1 fragment than they actually are. Moreover, the photograph of the "Small Sensen" fragment used is overexposed, making its tone, shading, and overall appearance (as well as its size) very dissimilar to the Facsimile No. 1

Detail from a photo mural in BYU's Joseph Smith Building: Hugh Nibley examining Papyrus Joseph Smith I.

fragment.   It seems fair to conclude that producers of the display
deliberately masked the connection between Papyrus Joseph Smith I
and Papyrus Joseph Smith XI because it was known to be damaging to
the Mormon Church's version of how Joseph Smith produced the
Book of Abraham.

It has long been popular for Latter-day Saint writers to accuse the
Church's critics of resorting to "omissions, misrepresentations, partial
truths, and obscuring of facts" — yet these appear to be the very
methods used by Brigham Young University in this "faith promoting"
display.

CHAPTER THIRTEEN

The Criteria for Rationalization

A T THIS POINT ONE MIGHT wonder how Latter-day Saints can be aware of these things and still maintain belief and trust in the Book of Abraham, and through it, the entire Mormon belief system?

The key word here, of course, is *aware*. As has been noted earlier, many Mormons are relatively uninformed of any controversy concerning the validity of the Book of Abraham; or if they become aware controversy exists, will tend to fall back on the trust they have in their system, and avoid further investigation.

Of course, there are some LDS members who are more *active*, and there are various reasons why members become active. Commitment to *any* group or cause can be inspired by any number of personal factors which may have little or nothing to do with having a " testimony" that the cause is true. These factors usually come down to vested interests, such as cultural preference, a sense of appreciation for tradition, family relationships, economic advantage, a desire to exercise authority, or even a feeling of superiority brought on by being part of a select group (these are certainly significant values, but they should never cause us to compromise eternal truths). Given enough vested interests, we often simply do not *care* whether an objection is valid or not. They have what they want, are comfortable with it, and do not wish to be disturbed. This can hold true within any group; it is an altogether human condition.

One would hope, though, that the primary reason we are actively committed to something is because, above all else, we are *sincere*. In their commitment to Mormonism, Latter-day Saints may develop this sincerity in one of two ways: (1) there are those who, because they are convinced the LDS Church is true, feel a need to dedicate themselves to God, (2) there are others who, because they already feel a strong dedication to God and are Mormons, believe the LDS Church must therefore be true.

In the first case, confidence in the system leads to trust in God; in the second, trust in God causes faith in the system. Either will produce sincerity, but in both cases what makes this sincerity valid and vital is the person's trust in God. *This trust in God needs to be recognized as a matter that is separate from the issue of whether or not the LDS Church is true.* Until a Latter-day Saint grasps this distinction, he will usually be reluctant to question the validity of the Church as an organization, for fear of threatening his relationship with God.

But to respond constructively to issues that challenge our existing views, we must meet three conditions:

1. We must be *knowledgeable* of the objective evidence in the controversy. Fortunately, most of the topics dealing with Mormonism, including the Book of Abraham controversy, are not as complicated as they are made to appear by some apologists. A person does not need to become an Egyptologist to understand what a funeral papyrus is. Any person of average intelligence is capable of understanding such things without great difficulty. But since we sometimes allow feelings and emotions to overrule incontestable facts, a further quality is necessary.

2. We must be *reasonable* enough to consider the implications involved. God has given us the faculty of reason as a means of discerning truth and error. An examination of the facts is not a threat to true faith. A person who closes his mind to issues he is uncomfortable with and refuses to allow for the existence of any possibility other than his own attitude of "I am *right* — what I *want* to be so is so," is running roughshod over the God-given gift of human reason. Such a person cannot expect others to respect his position. More importantly,

he runs the risk of being deceived by counterfeit spiritual claims. But there is also a final ingredient.

3. We must be *honest* enough with ourselves to care about what the truth really is, even if it goes against what we want. The desire to accept and act upon this truth must outweigh any vested interests.

Those who do not apply these standards to investigating controversy must resort to rationalizing, rather than facing reality. Many Latter-day Saints seem willing to accept whatever rationalizations will permit their continued faith in the Book of Abraham.

So just what rationalizations are available? Stripped of all their excess verbiage, there remain only about a half dozen avenues open for the Latter-day Saint that will still allow Mormonism to be in some sense true. On a scale of the traditional to the increasingly radical, they are:

1. *Joseph Smith did just exactly as he said he did and as it has always been held: he obtained the actual, original writings of Abraham and did accurately translate them by the gift and power of God.* Either modern Egyptology is completely wrong, or else God has allowed Satan to alter the materials we now have, perhaps to separate the truly loyal Saints from among the less sincere.

2. *Joseph Smith did have Abraham's original writings and properly translated them, but the originals have not been recovered.* Either the *true* text of the Book of Abraham was from a different (lost) portion of the Book of Breathings scroll, or the Facsimiles were always on a different scroll, separate from Abraham's text, and Abraham's statements about them have been misunderstood. It is also possible that Satan has confused the world's scholars about Facsimile No. 1, and even altered the "Small Sensen" papyrus to make it look like it was once attached to it, though it never really was. Satan could also have altered the Egyptian Alphabet and Grammar to make Joseph Smith look bad, and done the same with Facsimile No. 2, Facsimile No. 3 and the rest of the material.

3. *The papyri we have, as well as the Facsimiles, are what the Egyptologists say they are, but they are also the Book of Abraham — technically speaking.* There is a deeper meaning to them, somewhat like a code, which has not yet been discovered by the world. Joseph Smith could determine this meaning by the gift and power of God, but

he did not know about or simply did not mention the other more "common" meaning of the papyri. Joseph Smith may have even been mistaken about them having been penned by Abraham himself, but that is all right because the important thing was the coming forth of the inspired text encrypted within the originals and handed down in them as they were copied over and over again through the ages.

4. *Joseph Smith only thought he was translating Abraham's record from the papyri. Actually, some ordinary funeral papyri from Egypt functioned as a sort of spiritual catalyst to Joseph Smith's mind, so that he received the Book of Abraham as a result of direct revelation — and God allowed him and everyone else to believe he was translating.* God also allowed Joseph Smith to believe his Egyptian Alphabet and Grammar was authentic and worthwhile, when actually it was useless. Or perhaps Joseph only considered it a hobby and all the statements he made concerning it have been misunderstood. And, though Joseph never said so, his clerks were the ones responsible for stupidly placing the characters from the "Small Sensen" fragment (Papyrus Joseph Smith XI) on three of his translation manuscripts.

5. *The Book of Abraham is not an ancient scriptural contribution, but a modern one that has simply been placed in an ancient setting.* As a modern revelation to Joseph Smith, its lessons, teachings, and values still apply, naturally, but it is a mistake to try to fit it into an historical context, such as the lifetime of Abraham. Better to just accept it for what it says, and not be concerned over what is said about it.

6. *The Book of Abraham is not really scripture at all, but merely the "speculative writing" of Joseph Smith.* Again, perhaps he thought he actually was translating and producing authentic scripture, perhaps not. If he did, he was mistaken. Joseph was still capable and worthy of being a prophet in other areas. (This is largely the view of the Reorganized LDS Church,[1] which is not affiliated with the larger, Utah-based LDS Church.)

It is remarkable that amid all the different suggestions proposed by LDS apologists (Nibley, Browns, Ashment, Crapo, Vestal, Barber, etc.) virtually *any* position is acceptable and yet *not one* of them is "official." A person can be considered a good Mormon and hold to practically any variation of the first five views mentioned — and even switch back and forth from one view to another — as long as the end result is *feeling good* about the Church. LDS authorities, meanwhile, remain silent about the entire controversy.

This same grasping for rationalizations is a typical response to many other problem areas within Mormonism, whether it be the Book of Abraham, discrepancies between archaeology and the Book of Mormon,[2] the Adam-God teachings of Brigham Young,[3] the historic origins of the LDS movement,[4] or the magic and occultic practices of Joseph Smith, Oliver Cowdery and others.[5] There always seems to be a superficial *popular* view, plus a range of increasingly radical approaches available to those who have come across things others do not know about yet. Gather a group of Latter-day Saints together and compare their respective views on any one of these subjects. It is disheartening to see the wide disparity that exists among the "true" positions offered to explain the "One True Church."

There is, of course, one other alternative explanation: that Joseph Smith did not produce legitimate scripture by translation through the gift and power of God or by any other means; he only *pretended* to do so. He *lied,* in other words, to justify the new doctrines and teachings he had been introducing among his people, and to uphold the image of a prophet of God he had created for himself. The methods of deception he used in doing this were more or less typical of all he professed to do in the name of God, for he never was a genuine prophet of God. Thus, the Mormon Church, which he founded on his calling as a prophet, is in reality a man-made organization; it cannot be God's "one true Church" restored to earth as it claims to be.

This conclusion is further reinforced when one considers the very essence of God's nature as revealed in the Bible. God took great pains throughout the Old Testament to dissuade the children of Israel from any contact with the false gods and idolatrous practices of their pagan neighbors. He ordered the Israelites to destroy the inhabitants of Canaan when they conquered the land, lest they should mingle His holy name with pagan deities, and so pollute the truth of divine revelation. Likewise, God admonished His people through Moses to repudiate and completely forsake the gods of Egypt, to whom they had been exposed during their years of captivity there. And the Old Testament records that every time the children of Israel fell into pagan idolatry, they experienced God's chastening.

Since the Joseph Smith Papyri have been identified with absolute certainty as prayers to pagan Egyptian gods, it is inconceivable, given God's holy nature and character as revealed throughout the Bible, that He would associate Himself or His revelation in any way with these pagan religious documents. Regardless of which of the above views of the Book of Abraham one holds, it is surely inconceivable that the God of the Bible would compromise his exclusivity as the one, true God by co-mingling His revelation with the idolatrous pagan teachings and rites of Egypt as expressed in the Joseph Smith Papyri.

Part IV

CONCLUSIONS AND DIRECTIONS

CHAPTER FOURTEEN

Facing the Truth

S OMETIME during the mid-1850s, shortly after the Latter-day Saints had left the open plains of the midwest, and the roots of Mormon culture had begun to take a firm hold in the isolated valleys of the Rocky Mountains, an LDS Apostle named Orson Pratt confidently laid a dramatic challenge before the world:

> . . . *convince us of our errors of doctrine, if we have any, by reason, by logical arguments, or by the Word of God, and we will be ever grateful for the information, and you ever will have the pleasing reflection that you have been instruments in the hands of God of redeeming your fellow beings from the darkness which you may see enveloping their minds.*[1]

Orson Pratt was no doubt confident that a successful case against the claims of Mormonism would never be presented because one simply did not exist. Over a century-and-a-half of close scrutiny, though, has proven the opposite to be the case. It is this fact which probably best explains why the contemporary LDS Church has shifted from the bold, confrontational stance of Pratt's day, to one of cautioning members to "rely on faith and not on historical fact" (see article on p. 170). The message coming from LDS spokesmen today appears to be more and more one of accommodation: If facts fail to justify faith (what one

Elder Decries Criticism of LDS Leaders

PROVO (UPI) — A Mormon apostle says church leaders should not be criticized because they are "the Lord's anointed" — even if that criticism is true — and he also warned members to rely on faith and not historical fact.

"Criticism is particularly objectionable when it is directed toward church authorities, general or local," Dallin Oaks, a member of the Quorum of the Twelve Apostles, said. "Evil speaking of the Lord's anointed is in a class by itself."

He said criticism of corporate or government leaders is one thing, but "it is quite another thing to criticize or depreciate a person for the performance of an office to which he or she has been called of God. It does not matter that the criticism is true."

Oaks spoke Friday to a symposium on the Mormon "Doctrine and Covenants." He also cautioned Mormons to rely not on historical facts but on faith in their beliefs in the authenticity of the church.

"Our individual, personal testimonies are based on the witness of the spirit, not on any combination or accumulation of historical facts," Oaks told the Brigham Young University audience. "If we are so grounded, no alteration of historical facts can shake our testimonies."

Oaks called his faith "the only true church" of believers who "persistently disdain the comfortable fraternity of ecumenical Christianity."

He cautioned members of the church — the Church of Jesus Christ of Latter-day Saints — to be wary of news media accounts of historical documents recently made public that give different accounts of critical parts of church history.

Oaks referred to a letter recently released by the church written by early member Martin Harris.

In the 1830 document, Harris says church founder Joseph Smith Jr. was at first prevented from obtaining gold plates, that the church says were the basis for the religion, by an "old spirit" that had transfigured itself into a "white salamander."

The official church version says an angel called Moroni and not a salamander appeared.

Oaks accused the news media of ignoring the context of the times in which the letter was written and other possible meanings of the word "salamander." He referred to one dictionary meaning of a salamander as "a mythical being thought to be able to live in fire."

"A being that is able to live in fire is a good approximation of the description Joseph Smith gave of the angel Moroni," Oaks said.

"The media should make more complete disclosures, but LDS readers should also be more sophisticated in their evaluation of what they read," he said.

Oaks also accused the news media of ignoring "scores of articles published in the last decade by respected scholars in many different fields that support the authenticity of the Book of Mormon."

Article from *The Salt Lake Tribune*, August 18, 1985, p. B-2

Faced with a growing awareness that Mormonism did not originate the way most Mormons have been taught to believe it did, LDS leaders have turned to bizarre and often embarrassing rationalizations in order to retain the confidence of their membership. General Authority Dalin Oak's advice, given to Latter-day Saints at a time when the notorious "White Salamander" letter was believed by most people (including Oaks) to be genuine, is a regrettable example of how Mormons are expected to deal with "facts" which challenge their beliefs.

Though the "White Salamander" letter was later exposed as a modern forgery, the Book of Abraham is an example of the many legitimate challenges to the authenticity of Mormonism. Yet, if LDS leaders must resort to such unlikely rationalizations as Oaks engages in above, in order to justify something that turns out to be a forgery, one must question whether they can objectively evaluate a genuine issue such as the evidence against the veracity of the Book of Abraham.

wishes to believe), *then faith should overrule facts.* This sort of thinking is evasive, and must be set aside if any real reckoning with the facts is to take place.

But going back to Pratt, the challenge he made is a valid one, and the tendency of contemporary LDS figures to rationalize away problems instead of confronting them only underlines the fact that serious problems do exist. If error or falsehood within a religious system exists, it *should* be exposed, and using reason and the Word of God to do so makes a great deal of sense. Exposing error is the *right* thing to do, as only good can be the ultimate result of people learning the truth.

We are not only justified, *then, in examining the evidences challenging the truth of the Book of Abraham which God has graciously allowed to come forth, we are firmly* obligated *to do so. And it is quite possible that the case against the Book of Abraham is the strongest evidence ever provided to test the truthfulness of Joseph Smith's claims.*

What are the facts of the matter, and how should they be applied?

Back in the year 1835, when Michael Chandler's small collection of Egyptian antiquities first found its way into the hands of Joseph Smith, very little was known or understood about such things by anyone. There was no known way to read, date, or accurately identify Egyptian artifacts and writings with any degree of reliability, and for all anyone knew, there never would be. Whatever representations Joseph Smith wanted to make concerning his ability to translate ancient Egyptian writing could be done quite safely, since there seemed to be little prospect of disproving such claims.

The Mormon people of that era were taught to trust and believe what their prophet told them, and seeing no reason at the time not to, did so. They believed he could translate ancient papyri, and (for the most part) willingly embraced the new doctrines he taught.

By the time scholars had reached the point where they could read Egyptian and Joseph Smith's claims could finally be tested, several important things had happened:

Joseph Smith had been killed, abruptly ending the production of the Book of Abraham in mid-story. It was never taken up by any of his successors, in spite of the LDS position that they hold whatever power and authority (keys) are supposedly necessary to do so.[2] Smith's death also brought an end to the series of specific claims, pronouncements, and identifications he had been in the habit of making about the Book of Abraham papyri, and other matters. People would now be able only to recall what had been said by him in the past about them.

The "Mormon Exodus" had occurred, placing the Mormon people in a condition of geographic isolation from the influence and controversies of most of the rest of the world. With immediate proximity gone, few non-Mormons knew or cared what Mormons regarded as scripture, and few Mormons cared about the opinions of non-Mormons.

The LDS Church lost control of the papyri. They were retained by Smith's widow, Emma, who refused to follow Brigham Young westward. Eventually they were dispersed, being either sold or given away to various parties, and were lost.

Other events overshadowed the importance of any Egyptian controversy, both to the Mormons and to the "gentiles." The western migration and gold rushes, the War Between the States, followed by the Reconstruction, the "Utah War" and Johnston's army, the Mountain Meadows Massacre, Indian wars, territorial colonization — all drew attention away from whatever the scholars might have had to say.

The Mormon people became culturally entrenched in their own Rocky Mountain Kingdom. Polygamy had become an accepted lifestyle for many,[3] and those who practiced it could not expect to find toleration for their families outside of Mormon society. In most instances virtually all of community life — be it social, economic, or legislative — was centered around the hierarchy of the Mormon priesthood authority.

All of these factors combined had the effect of causing the Mormon people (who had long since been conditioned to regard any criticism with suspicion) to become even less likely to be affected by any charges against Joseph Smith or the Book of Abraham. "Proof" of Joseph Smith's fraud offered by Egyptologists fell on deaf ears, for the most part.

As the criticism continued, becoming more developed, refined and widely known as time passed, the Mormon defense turned into an attack upon the competency and motives of their critics. No mere "outside opinions" could be considered valid by the Mormon people as long as no examination of their Prophet's *original papyri* (now missing and presumed lost forever) had ever been made. Without such a standard of comparison, it was argued, it was unfair for the critics to judge Joseph Smith wrong merely on the basis of the printed facsimiles. Meanwhile, Mormons staunchly maintained the divine nature and accuracy of Joseph Smith's work. If anything, the average Mormon was probably disappointed that the papyri were *not* available, being confident that the critics' charges would be refuted by the evidence. Indeed, this was the attitude which prevailed right up to the time the papyri were rediscovered.

However, prior to that rediscovery, LDS apologists enjoyed essentially the same position Joseph Smith had taken advantage of as he translated the papyri into the Book of Abraham, knowing the Egyptian language was not readable. By insisting upon comparisons that could not be made and demanding proof they believed did not exist, Mormon apologists could make almost any claim, advance any position, or deny any argument. As with Joseph Smith, there seemed little likelihood anything would happen to prove them wrong.

Then, quite unexpectedly, a major portion of Joseph Smith's original papyri collection reappeared. Suddenly, every condition that Latter-day Saints had been insisting on over the years was met. Every claim could be tested, every position examined, every argument answered.

As certain **facts** were established, a number of *beliefs* once thought safe from ever being proven false were shown to be wrong. Consider the following:

Belief: ". . . one of the rolls [of papyrus] contained the writings of Abraham, another the writings of Joseph of Egypt . . ." (July, 1835, *History of the Church,* Vol. 2, p. 236)

Belief: "The writings of Abraham while he was in Egypt, called the Book of Abraham, written by his own hand, upon papyrus . . ." (*Introduction* to the Book of Abraham)

Fact: Based on comparisons of the Metropolitan papyri to every available resource, including descriptions contemporary with Joseph Smith of the so-called Abraham and Joseph scrolls, as well as to a number of original translation manuscripts and other notes of the time, the papyrus scroll Joseph Smith represented as containing "the writings of Abraham" was shown to be merely a common pagan funeral papyrus of late date known as the *Book of Breathings*. The scroll thought to contain "the writings of Joseph of Egypt" was also identified as a typical late copy of the Egyptian *Book of the Dead*, which had been prepared for a woman named Ta-shert-Min. Neither scroll ever had anything to do with the biblical patriarchs Abraham or Joseph, except in the mind of Joseph Smith.

Belief: ". . . Joseph the Seer has presented to us (the Twelve) some of the Book of Abraham which was written by his own hand but hid from the knowledge of man for the last four thousand years but has now come to light . . ." (diary of Wilford Woodruff, Feb. 19, 1842)

Belief: "It is evident that the writings of Abraham while he was in Egypt, of which our printed Book of Abraham is a copy, must of necessity be older than the original text of Genesis. I say this in passing because some of our brethren have exhibited surprise when told that the text of the Book of Abraham is older than that of Genesis" (Dr. Sidney B. Sperry (of BYU) in his book, *Ancient Records Testify in Papyrus and Stone*, p. 83).

Fact: The *Book of Breathings* scroll that Joseph Smith represented as being the Book of Abraham was prepared between about 50 BC and AD 50 in Thebes for a man named Hor, who was a priest, or purifier, to the Egyptian god Amon at Karnak. It was written in hieratic script, a cursive adaptation of hieroglyphic writing that first appeared around 600 BC — at least a dozen centuries too late to have been used by Abraham. Moreover, the *Book of Breathings* itself had not even been composed until about the third or fourth-century before Christ.

Also proven wrong were Joseph Smith's claims to be able to translate Egyptian:

Belief: ". . . spent the day in translating the Egyptian records . . . " (Diary of Joseph Smith, Nov. 19, 1835)

Belief: ". . . spent the day in translating, and made rapid progress . . ." (*Ibid*, Nov. 20, 1835)

Belief: ". . . in the afternoon we translated some of the Egyptian records. . ."(*Ibid*, Nov. 24, 1835)

Belief: "The remainder of this month, I was continually engaged in translating an alphabet to the Book of Abraham, and arranging a grammar of the Egyptian language as practiced by the ancients" (Joseph Smith, July, 1835, *History of the Church*, Vol. 2, p. 238).

Belief: ". . . [Joseph Smith's] most notable achievement was the development at Kirtland of a grammar for the Egyptian hieroglyphic form of writing. This was used by him, as well as divine aid, in translating ancient writings of the patriarch Abraham (William E. Berrett in his book, *The Restored Church,* 1956 ed., p. 133).

Belief: "A study of the document [Joseph Smith's Egyptian Alphabet and Grammar] suggests that it was formulated by an ancient writer, probably Abraham, to assist a translator in deciphering the language in which the record was written. If this conclusion is correct, Joseph Smith literally translated an alphabet to the Book of Abraham" (Hyrum L. Andrus in his book *Doctrinal Commentary on the Pearl of Great Price,* 1967, 1970, p. 25).

Fact: Not a single word, thought, or concept from Joseph Smith's Book of Abraham, including his explanations of his three facsimiles, is in any way related to the subject matter of the common Egyptian funeral texts from which they were supposedly translated. Furthermore, modern examination of the "Egyptian Alphabet and Grammar" papers that had once so greatly enhanced the Mormon Prophet's claim to be a true translator has exposed them as a collection of gibberish, having no connection to genuine ancient Egyptian.

One by one, virtually every Mormon belief about the Book of Abraham once considered essential to its support and regarded as faith promoting, has been shattered by the facts.

Not one trace of reliable evidence has appeared that would support the LDS view of the Book of Abraham as an authentic scripture, while an enormous amount of evidence is available to show that it is a man-made production of the nineteenth century, created by Joseph Smith to support his claim among his people to be a "prophet, seer, and revelator."

The evidence against the Book of Abraham is so overwhelming, as earlier chapters of this book have enumerated and demonstrated in detail, that many consider it a God-given means to demonstrate the fraudulent nature of Joseph Smith's claim to be a prophet of God.

The Book of Abraham cannot possibly be what it is represented to be; and if it is not authentic, neither are the doctrines it teaches, nor the system to which it belongs.

CHAPTER FIFTEEN

Moving Beyond Rationalizations

"**I** BEAR YOU MY TESTIMONY," a Mormon will say, "that the LDS Church is true; I know that Joseph Smith was a true prophet, and that the Church is led by a prophet today. I know that the Book of Mormon is true, that it is the word of God, and that the Book of Abraham is likewise God's word . . ." and on it goes. Virtually every Latter-day Saint has "borne his testimony" at one time or another to family or friends, before the members of his ward, or for the benefit of someone he would like to see join the LDS Church. Mormons are encouraged to do so at every opportunity. In fact, one church service each month is regularly set aside for members to publicly share their testimonies with each other,[1] and at a very early age children are taught the basic pattern, such as using the positive term "I know" rather than what is regarded as the weaker expression "I believe."

However, is such a testimony a *valid* truth test? Is it a *biblical* truth test?

There is no reason to doubt that the majority of these testimonies are honest and sincere. But this in itself is no indication they are *reliable.* That portion of a testimony that pertains to things uniquely Mormon usually follows from the Latter-day Saint's exposure to an impressive presentation on a subject such as Joseph Smith's First Vision, the Book of Mormon, or the Book of Abraham. Once persuaded, Mormons learn to regard the conviction they feel as "the testimony of the Holy Ghost" that what they have accepted is true — and this is considered an absolute, unshakable proof.[2]

The real power of a Mormon testimony, then, can actually be a potential trap that a person falls into by failing to realize that we can literally talk ourselves into anything if we want to believe it badly enough.

It is a painful fact of life, though, that sincerity is not a guarantee against being wrong. Faith must have some basis in fact. For a testimony about anything to be valid, there must be something to support it, to serve as a witness for it. Conversely, there must be nothing that legitimately discredits it.

While spiritual insight or faith is one valid measure in spiritual matters, true spiritual insight never directly contradicts valid intellectual insight or facts in the physical world. Faith may go *beyond* reason, but does not go *against* it. It never blatantly contradicts the facts which we perceive with our God-given common sense. Faith and fact point in a single direction. When they do not, something is seriously wrong. This is why, in spiritual matters, we are admonished to "*believe not every spirit, but try the spirits whether they are of God*" (I John 4:1) and to "*prove all things; hold fast to that which is good*" (I Thessalonians 5:21). God does not usually create faith by first offering evidence, but at some point He does provide the evidence necessary to support true faith.

A Mormon believes his testimony about the Book of Abraham is supported by factual proofs, but a careful investigation shows that no such proofs exist, while there is overwhelming evidence against it. In the absence of valid evidence for the object of his faith, the Latter-day Saint is left with only *subjective feelings,* which are inconclusive. In order to be objective, one must be willing to examine the evidence both for and against religious claims.

Unfortunately, a Mormon testimony cannot be successfully maintained in this way, and many Mormons will refuse to attempt it. As a result, even the most well-meaning, hopeful LDS testimony is invalid because it fails to wholly address truth.

This is not to say that every part of a Mormon testimony is invalid, however.

Like all honest and sincere people, Latter-day Saints have firsthand knowledge of the value of such things as loyalty, integrity, patience, thrift, modesty, a desire to know God, and of course love. All of these things make up a major share of what Mormons believe in and try to stand for. However, high standards alone can only provide a system of partial truth at best. A willingness to accept facts as they exist, and to learn to use them to test the views one holds rather than falling back on subjective experience or rationalizations, is the first step towards discovering genuine truth.

CHAPTER SIXTEEN

Does It Really Matter?

I IN THE LONG RUN, does all this really *matter?* This is a very important question. To the person who doubts the existence of God or feels that God is not all that concerned with truth, probably not. The question of the authenticity of the Book of Abraham and the exclusive claims of the Mormon Church is, after all, primarily a religious one, and to those who have no real doctrine they hold dear, the issue must not seem all that important. One pleasant life-style may seem every bit as worthy as another, and if it is well-organized and impressive, so much the better.

However, the ultimate promise of a religious system lies not in its *life-style* — its buildings, programs, or fraternity — but in its ability to reconcile us to God. Mormonism's ability to meet this need stands or falls with the claim that its scriptures (including the Book of Abraham) are true revelations from God. If this claim is false, the system — no matter how admirable — is invalid and misleading. Its promises are empty; it cannot "deliver on them."

Again, this point may not matter to those who do not believe that there is a God, and that He has a plan for our lives. But it should matter very much to those who are genuinely trying to learn and obey God's will.

This book has dealt at some length in previous chapters with such subjects as accommodation, rationalization, and vested interests, and discussed ways in which each may have its own influence upon the Latter-day Saint who has been exposed to controversy. At this point, however, it might be helpful for the reader to gain an idea of the extent to which some people can be affected by such things.

On pages 182-187 there are photostatic reproductions of four letters, spanning an eight-year period, written by a man named Thomas Stuart Ferguson. Mr. Ferguson, now deceased, is often recalled by older Latter-day Saints as a stalwart defender of the faith who, among other things, established the New World Archaeological Foundation at Brigham Young University. Ferguson, once a general officer of BYU's Society for Early Historic Archaeology, wrote the popular LDS book *One Fold and One Shepherd,* and was co-author with Milton R. Hunter (of the First Council of the Seventy) of the book *Ancient America and the Book of Mormon.*

For many years Ferguson had attempted to uncover and present proofs for Mormon claims through the field of archaeology, and had even received substantial grants from the LDS Church to further these efforts. Then, in 1968 he was caught up in the Book of Abraham controversy.

Though excerpts from some of these letters have appeared from time to time in various printed works during the past several years, this is the first time these letters have been published in their entirety.[1]

One safety net which many Mormons fall back on when confronted with damaging evidence against their belief-system — such as that which the Book of Abraham case presents — is to reason along these lines: *"if there were really anything wrong, so-and-so (any of a number of well-known scholars and intellectuals in the Church) who understands much more about the subject than I ever will,would have discovered it and left the Church. But he has not."*

The letters of Thomas Stuart Ferguson illustrate the fallacy of such reasoning, for his study led him to reject Joseph Smith's claim to divine revelation, though Ferguson kept these conclusions private. His conclusions were shared with only a few during his lifetime, and when Ferguson died, it was as a member in full fellowship of the LDS Church, respected by many who thought he shared their religious beliefs.

It would be a serious mistake to assume that all, or even most intelligent Mormons must inevitably fall into Ferguson's category, for a great many are undeniably sincere in their beliefs. Still, Ferguson himself placed the number of those who "enjoy the good things and keep their mouths shut" in the "thousands."[2]

To be quite candid, it seems to have become almost fashionable for many to redefine their principles in a similar way, all in the high-sounding name of "charity" or "tolerance." Those who hold to this rather condescending attitude of "keeping up appearances for the sake of others" seem to feel they are doing their peers a great favor; protecting them, as it were, from "the chasm of death and extinction" which they perceive as being "the real truth."

Unfortunately, their actions run the risk of producing far more harm than the good they had originally intended. It is unrealistic to expect people to remain ignorant indefinitely. When an individual fails to respond openly and honestly to such a problem it only passes the problem — and the pain of dealing with it — to someone else, multiplying ignorance and hurt in the process. It is one thing for an insincere person to decide he enjoys being "comfortable," but quite another when he does so at the expense of others who *are* sincere, allowing them to one day discover they, too, have been deceived.

So much potential pain to loved ones and future generations could be avoided! How? By placing truth ahead of convenience, by being honest with ourselves and with others.

The question of meeting challenges to our faith really does matter, because truth matters. The Bible gives us the promise that "the truth shall make you free" (John 8:32) — and that includes being free from delusion.

There is another kind of freedom we can experience also, and that is the subject of the next and final chapter.

Law Office of

Thomas Stuart Ferguson
Robert R. Hall

23 Orinda Way
Orinda, California 94563
254-3030

3-13-71

Dear Jim:

This is in reply to yours of 3-10-71.

Nibley's Era articles on the Book of Abraham aren't worth a tinker -- first,
because he is not impartial, being the commissioned and paid defender of
the faith. Second, because he could not, he dared not, he did not, face
the true issue: "Could Joseph Smith translate Egyptian?" I clipped every one
of his articles, and have them in a single file -- and I have reviewed them--
looking in vain for that issue.

We have now published copies of Joseph Smith's working notebook that he
made up during his struggle with the Egyptian papyrus, the notebook
having been published under the title, JOSEPH SMITH'S EGYPTIAN ALPHABET
& GRAMMAR. This can be obtained, along with a lot of other published
things relevant to the Book of Abraham, from MODERN MICROFILM CO.,
BOX 1884, Salt Lake City (store at 1350 South West Temple, SLC). The price
is $5. and its a bargain.   By study of the GRAMMAR, the recovered
papyrus, and the illustrations, it is perfectly obvious that we now have
the oringinal manuscript material used by Jos. Smith in working up the Book
of Abraham. Prof. Klaus Baer of Univ. of Chicago, Prof. Lutz of U.C. (Berkeley),
Prof. Lesko (U.C. Berkeley) and Egyptologist Dee Jay Nelson, all agree
that the oxxix original manuscript Egyptian text translates into the Breathing
Permit of Hor (Egyptian God). Baer's translation was published by Dialogue.
Nelson"s was pb. by Modern Microfilm, SLC. The work of the two UC professors
was done at my request and is unpublished. All 4 agree with each other, and
without having conferred or collaborated. (My UC men did not, and still do
not, know that there is any relationship of the manuscript material to the
Mormon Church, Joseph Smith, Book of Abraham -- or whatever. I merely
asked them to tell me what the MS says -- and they did so. Didn't even
care enough to ask where I got the material. I had beautiful enlarged photos
received directly from Hugh B. Brown.)

Joseph Smith announced, in print (History of the Church, Vol. II, page 236)
that "one of the rolls contained the writings of Abraham, another the writings
of Joseph of Egypt. . ." Since 4 scholars, who have established that they
can read Egyptian, say that the manuscripts deal with neither Abraham nor
Joseph--and since the 4 reputable men tell us exactly what the manuscripts
do say -- I must conclude that Joseph Smith had not the remotest skill in
things Egyptian-hieroglyphics. To my surprise, one of the highest officials
in the Mormon Church agreed with that conclusion when I made that very
statement to him on Dec. 4, 1970 -- privately in one-to-one onversation.

First Ferguson letter, page 1.

– 2 –

If you haven't done so, I suggest you read, analyse, and even chart the very important data published by Brigham Young University in :

> BYU STUDIES
> (A Voice of the Community of LDS Scholars)
> Spring, 1969 number (Vol. IX, Number 3)
> PP. 275-300
> Article: Dean C. Jessee (Member of the staff at the LDS Church Historian,s Office, SLC, Utah), THE EARLY ACCOUNTS OF JOSEPH SMITH'S FIRST VISION.

Going back to ABRAHAM, for a moment, the Klaus Baer translation is in the Autumn, 1968 issue of DIALOGUE.

The attempts, including Nibley's, to explain away and dodge the trap into which Joseph Smith fell when he had the audacity to translate the Chandler texts, and keep the original Egyptian texts around, are absurd, in my view.

I have been trying to find a photostatic copy of a recently-discovered newspaper article published about 1830, I think in Palmyra, giving almost every detail of the 1826 trial and conviction of Joseph Smith -- on a charge of defrauding Josiah Stoal. It has been misplaced -- here in my office. In 1826 Joseph Smith was 21 and at this point was midway between the FIRST VISION and 1830. What a strange time to be convicted of fraud -- fraudulently getting money after convincing the victim that he could detect the whereabouts of hidden treasure on the victim's land. Wow. (Modern Microfilm furnished me this recently discovered data. It is as genuine and sound as can be -- published right in Joseph Smith's own camp.

My views are not for publication or spreading abroad. I am like you -- maintaining membership because of the many fine things the Church offers. But facts speak for themselves. I offered the data available to my Stake Pres. recently and he walked away without it -- saying he didn't want to read it. They can hardly execommunicate us when they won't look at the evidence.

Of course the dodge as to the Book of Abraham must be: "WE DON'T HAVE THE ORIGINAL MANUSCRIPT FROM XXXXXXX WHICH THE BOOK OF ABRAHAM WAS TRANSLATED." I conclude that we do have it and have translations of it.

Sincerely,

Tom Ferguson

First Ferguson letter, page 2

Law Office of
Thomas Stuart Ferguson
Robert R. Hall

23 Orinda Way
Orinda, California 94563
254-3930

February 9, 1976

Dear Mr. and Mrs. Lawrence:

This is in reply to your letter of February 6, 1976.

In the December issue of Reader's Digest is an article on the importance
of myths to the human family. People must believe in something. (Otherwise
we face the abyss of death and extinction.) Mormonism is probably
the best conceived myth-fraternity to which one can belong. It's
a refinement of Judaism (which would never have sold, had Moses
announced as his own ideas, the ideas he came up with on Sinai) and
a refinement of the Jesus story (which sold because of one supernatural
account after another--written down long after the events--creating
a story difficult to refute -- as in the case of Moses, who was alone).
Joseph Smith tried so hard he put himself out on a limb with the Book
of Abraham, and also with the Book of Mormon. He can be refuted --
but why bother when all religion is based on myth, and when must have
them, and his is one of the very best. It would be like wiping out placebos
in medicine, and that would make no sense when they do lots of good.
(I'm sure placebos and myths can do harm in some instances -- but I
also think, at this point, that they do far more good than harm.)

Why not say the right things and keep your membership in the great
fraternity, enjoying the good things you like and discarding the ones
you can't swallow (and keeping your mouths shut)? Hypocritical? Maybe.
But perhaps a realistic way of dealing with a very difficult problem. There
is lots left in the Church to enjoy-- and thousands of members have done,
and are doing, what I suggest you consider doing. Silence is golden -- etc.
Precious few believers will you change--no matter how the evidence mounts.
They believe because they want to believe -- and don't want to face the
chasm of death and extinction etc. etc. Rulers of the nations have used
religion since the dawn of civilization because of the good things religion
provides -- peace to the person and a measure of orderliness to family and
the nation. (One of the major reasons for the high degree of lawlessness in
the world today is the breakdown of the mythologies we call religions.
People that don't accept "divine law" are prone to make their own rules and
the going can get rough.) So why try to be heroic and fight the myths --
the Mormon one or any other that does more good than ill?

Perhaps you and I have been spoofed by Joseph Smith. Now that we
have the inside dope -- why not spoof a little back and stay aboard?

Second Ferguson letter, page 1

- 2 -

Please consider this letter confidential -- for obvious reasons.
I want to stay aboard the good ship, Mormonism -- for various reasons
that I think valid. First, several of my dearly loved family members
want desperately to believe it and do believe it and they each need it.
It does them far more good than harm. Belonging, with my eyes wide
open is actually fun, less expensive than formerly, and no strain at all.
I am now very selective in the meetings I attend, the functions I attend,
the amounts I contribute etc. etc. and I have a perfectly happy time.
I never get up and bear testimony -- but I don't mind listening to others
who do. I am much more tolerant of other religions and other thinking
and feel fine about things in general. You might give my suggestions
a trial run -- and if you find you have to burn all the bridges between
yourselves and the Church, then go ahead and ask for excommunication.
(The day will probably come--but it is far off--when the leadership of
the Church will change the excommunication rules and delete as grounds
non-belief in the 2 books mentioned and in Joseph Smith as a prophet etc...
but if you wait for that day, you probably will have died. It is a long way
off--tithing would drop too much for one thing. (And I wouldn't worry
about the tithing people pay -- almost all of it comes back to the people.
The Church is as free of graft and corruption regarding money as any
organization in the world.)

Reading:

> Mormonism, Shadow or Reality?
> Jerald & Sandra Tanner (1972)
>
> The True Believer
> Eric Hoffer (Non-LDS, found in good bookstores as paperback
> at cost of about 95 cents.)
>
> No Man Knows My History (1975 edition)
> Fawn Brodie
>
> The Early Accounts of Joseph Smith's First Vision
> by Dean C. Jesse (He is on the staff of the LDS Church
> Historian's Office, SLC.)
> Article appears in BRIGHAM YOUNG UNIVERSITY STUDIES,
> Vol. Ix, Number 5 (Spring, 1969), pp. 275 ff.

I recently wrote a paper concerning the big weak spots in the Book of Mormon,
from the archeological point of view and for $5 will make a photocopy of
it for you if you wish to read it.

Kindly do not quote this letter and please do not cite me. Your confidence
will be appreciated. I have tried to help you as best I can. If you are
out this way, come and see me. Kind regards.

Sincerely,

Thomas Stuart Ferguson

Second Ferguson letter, page 2

THOMAS STUART FERGUSON

ROBERT R. HALL
ATTORNEYS AT LAW
23 ORINDA WAY
ORINDA, CALIFORNIA 94563
254-5930

2-20/76

Dear Mr. and Mrs. Lawrence:

Thanks for your kind letter of 2-16-76. I'm pleased if my letter was helpful.

Herewith is a copy of my recent (1975) paper on Book of Mormon matters.
I will be pleased to have your response to it. It was one of several presented
in a written symposium on Book of Mormon georgraphy. (My thesis is that
Book of Mormon geography involves a lot more than playing with topography and
terrain.) The real implication of the paper is that you can't set Book of Mormon
geography down anywhere -- because it is fictional and will never meet the
requirements of the dirt-archeology. I should say -- what is in the ground will
never conform to what is in the book.

Best wishes in handling your difficult problem.

Sincerely,

Tom Ferguson

Third Ferguson letter.

Law Office of
Thomas Stuart Ferguson

23 Orinda Way
Orinda, California 94563
254-3930

12-3-79

Dear Jim:

Milton Hunter died a few years ago.

I lost faith in Joseph Smith as one having a pipeline to deity --
and have decided that there has never been a pipeline to deity--
with any man. However, I believe that judaism was an improvement
on polytheism; Christianity was an improvement on Judaism (to
some degree and in some departments only); that protestantism is
an improvement on Catholicism; that Mormonism is an improvement
on protestantism. So I give Joseph Smith credit as an innovator
and as a smart fellow. I attend, sing in the choir and enjoy my
friendhsips in the Church. In my opinion it is the best fraternity
that has come to my attention -- too good to try to shoot it down --
and it is too big and prosperous to shoot down anyway (as Tanner's
ought to figure out).

I think that Joseph Smith may have had Ixtlilxochitl and View of the
Hebrews from which to work. I don't agree with Mrs. Tanner
at all (your quote)... Hunter and I did not play around with the
translation to make it fit the Book of Mormon. The translation
from Spanish to English was done by a non-Mormon Mexican who
knew nothing whatsoever about the Book of Mormon when he did the
job. And we never changed a word of his translation. How Joseph Smith
got his hands on Ixtlil I don't know--Kingsborough had him in England
and Ireland -- but how Joseph Smith got hold of him I don't know.
I have tried to find out. Oliver Cowdery was in Ethan Smith's congregation
before he went from Vermont to New York to join Joseph Smith.
I have no copies of my books for sale. Sorry. You can borrow one
from anyone who has a copy, and have it xeroxed.

Best wishes.   Sincerely,

Tom

Fourth Ferguson letter. This is a different "Jim" than is mentioned in the first letter.

CHAPTER SEVENTEEN

The Alternative: Biblical Christianity

Charles Larson with Floyd McElveen

I WAS ONCE ASKED by a young Mormon whether I personally felt that Mormonism was "Christian." "I know that all individuals can be considered separate cases," he told me, "and that only God can truly judge what is in a person's heart — but I want to know if you consider *my* church to be 'Christian' on your terms, the same way you think of your church as being 'Christian.' "

What the young man apparently did not know was that I had once been a believing and dedicated Latter-day Saint myself. After considering for a moment, I told him that I felt the proportion of orthodox Christians who considered Mormonism to be Christian was probably about the same as that of Latter-day Saints who considered orthodox Christianity acceptable in God's sight.

There was a pause before he responded, and I suspected he was recalling, as I was, the memorized words of the popular account of Joseph Smith's First Vision —

... My object in going to inquire of the Lord was to know which of all the sects was right . . . I asked the Personages who stood above me in the light, which of all the sects was right (for at this time it had never entered into my heart that all were wrong) . . . I was answered that I must join none of them, for they were all wrong; and the Personages who addressed me said that all their creeds were an abomination in his sight; that all those professors were corrupt . . .(Pearl of Great Price, Joseph Smith — History 1:18,19)

"That was a very good answer," he finally responded, obviously surprised. So was I. I take no credit for the answer — I believe God gave it to me to use at that particular moment.

The fact remains that Latter-day Saints would like very much to be recognized as part of the Christian community and called by the label "Christian." This, despite the fact that they consider orthodox Christians (members of "the sects," as they call them) to be in an *apostate* condition; incomplete at best, corrupt at worst. The LDS Church holds that the "Apostasy" of Christendom was the whole reason for the "Restoration" which the teachings of Mormonism are supposed to represent. Every believing Latter-day Saint bases his or her acceptance of the Mormon Church on this premise.

Of course the Mormon charge that orthodox Christianity is apostate assumes that Mormonism is itself true. But as this book has demonstrated, the evidence overwhelmingly proves otherwise. However, the Latter-day Saint who discovers that his organization is not what he thought it was is not left with only the alternative of a "chasm of death and extinction," as Ferguson suggested. Biblical Christianity still remains, waiting to be examined and tested on its own terms.

However, some people are confused by the different Christian denominations. "Why are there so *many* churches," they ask? "And which is the *true* Church?" For want of a better analogy, this is like shopping for a vase in which to put some flowers, and, on seeing many different styles of vases, exclaiming, "But which is the *right* vase?"

The fact is that vases can differ a good deal in size and shape, and still share the essential requirements necessary to hold flowers. And so it is with the various denominations within orthodox Christianity. Though they differ a good deal in outward appearance (secondary doctrinal matters, worship style, etc.), they share the essentials of biblical Christianity. None of these denominations is the one true Church.

Instead, all true believers in these various churches are a part of what the New Testament calls the "Body of Christ" (1 Corinthians 12:27; Ephesians 5:25-32), the Church Universal.

Local Christian congregations are temporal vehicles for worship, fellowship, and the edification of believers. It is natural that a Christian will want to become a part of a local assembly of believers where he can find encouragement and edification, and Scripture commands us to seek such fellowship (Hebrews 10:25). However, the Bible makes it clear that a person's salvation is based on his relationship with Jesus Christ, not membership in a Christian congregation.

Following is a thumbnail outline of the essential doctrines of historic, biblical Christianity shared by all orthodox Christians regardless of denominational labels:

The Bible is God's unique, final, and infallible revelation. It is this solid foundation of the inspired writings of the apostles and prophets (Ephesians 2:20), on which the Christian Church was established, Christ himself being the cornerstone.

There is only one God (Isaiah 44:6,8) and He has eternally existed as God (Psalm 90:2). He is the Creator of all things, but is Himself self-existent and uncreated.

One biblical passage in which Jesus himself brings together the teaching of the Old and New Testaments on this point in Mark 12:28-34, where Christ is being questioned by Jewish religious leaders. One of them asks him, "Which is the greatest commandment of all?" The Lord Jesus responds by quoting the great Old Testament confession of faith found in Deuteronomy 6:4,5 — "The first of all the commandments is, Hear O Israel, *The Lord your God is one Lord.*" The scribe's response shows both that he fully endorsed Jesus' answer, and that the Jews understood the Old Testament passage Jesus had quoted to teach that there is only one God: "And the scribe said unto him, Well, Master, thou hast said the truth: for *there is one God, and there is none other but he.*" Jesus, in turn, gives his approval to the scribe's statement of faith: "And when Jesus saw that he *answered discreetly,* he said unto him, Thou art not far from the kingdom of God." (Other important Scriptures that emphasize that there is only one God include Isaiah 43:10,11; 44:6,8; 45:21,22; 46:9.)

All men are born in a fallen condition, separated from God in His holiness by the awful moral gulf of sin. God created man in a state of innocence and fellowship with Himself, but this fellowship was broken by the sinful disobedience of Adam and Eve. Their disobedience unleashed the power of sin and death in the world. All men are thus born with a sinful nature, and will be judged for the sins they commit (Ezekiel 18:20), unless they receive God's offer of grace through Jesus Christ. Romans 3:23,24 says that, "All have sinned and come short of the glory of God; Being freely justified by his grace through the redemption that is in Christ Jesus." God's Word describes us as "dead in our trespasses and sins" (Ephesians 2:1,5). We can do nothing through our own works or merit to remedy our separation from God — dead men are powerless to help themselves.

Holiness and love are equal attributes of God's character. God's holiness demands that He judge all sin. However, His love has moved Him to make a gracious provision to save lost mankind. God's attributes of holiness and love are reflected, respectively, in the Old Testament *moral law* (ten commandments) and *ceremonial law* (system of animal sacrifices). The moral law was given to make man aware of his inability to meet the perfect demands of God's holiness (Romans 5:20; 7:7; Galatians 3:19), and the ceremonial law was given to point to God's gracious provision of atonement and reconciliation that was ultimately accomplished in Jesus Christ, "the Lamb of God who taketh away the sin of the world" (John 1:29; see also, Hebrews 9:11-14; 10:1-14).

Jesus Christ is God, co-equal and co-eternal with the Father and the Holy Spirit; Father, Son, and Holy Spirit are not separate Gods, but are Persons within the one Tri-une Godhead. As we have seen, Jesus re-affirmed the Old Testament teaching that there is only one God. At the same time, the New Testament clarifies what is hinted at in the Old Testament (Genesis 1:26; 11:7), that there are three Persons within the one Godhead (Matthew 28:19,20; 2 Corinthians 13:14; 1 Peter 1:2). Therefore, we must reasonably understand that God is Tri-une.

While never ceasing to be God, at the appointed time the Son voluntarily laid aside the glory He shared with the Father and became flesh for our salvation (John 17:4, 5; Galatians 4:4,5; Philippians 2:6-11). His incarnation was accomplished through being conceived by the Holy Spirit and born of a virgin. On the cross He took the personal sins of all men — past, present and future — in His own body and bore the judgement of God in our place (1 Peter 2:24). *Jesus' atonement was first and foremost a solution for our sin problem.* His shed blood propitiated (satisfied) the demands of God's holiness (1 John 2:2) and is the only basis by which God can grant us forgiveness and eternal salvation.

God who is "rich in mercy" and "not willing that any should perish," came to reveal His love by identifying with us. Wonder of wonders, Jesus, the Creator of this universe and of all that is, fulfilled centuries of prophecy by word and picture. Millions of lambs were slain on Jewish altars pointing to Him, the Lamb of God. His blood shed on the cross as He bore your sins and mine in incredible pain and abandonment by God and man, forever paid the sin debt, and *sin* is all that ever has or could separate us from God. There is *nothing* left to be done, added or paid, for our complete and eternal salvation! To infer such is to cheapen the sacrifice of Jesus as if it were not all-sufficient (Galatians 2:21), and to minimize His great love.

He did not die just so we would be resurrected from the dead. All men are resurrected, some to eternal damnation in the Lake of Fire (John 5:29; Revelation 20:14-15). The brutal, bloody death of the Son of God on the cross is graphic testimony to the fact that we are already lost, a condemned race (John 3:18), in danger night and day of plunging into a lost eternity in Hell. To be in Hell is to be without hope, without God, in a place of torment, the Lake of Fire (Revelation 20:14-15). The Savior knows this, He wept for us, as He did over Jerusalem (Luke 19:41-44). He pleads with us to be saved '*now*' (2 Corinthians 6:2), as He knows the awfulness of Hell, the urgent need to be saved from our sinful 'going our own way,' acting as our own god.

The Savior also longs to dwell in us, to have sweet fellowship with us. For this we were created. He wants us to bring glory to Him and to bring others into His kingdom. He longs to shower His love upon us, but He cannot fellowship with us in our self-righteousness and sin. He wants us to have a new quality of life here, with peace, and certainty and joy in Him, and then to share the glory of Heaven with Him forever. He wants us to understand that we do not become new creatures by our own efforts, however 'good' and religious, and *then* invite Him into our lives. We are washed from our sins, and made children of God with a new nature, when He enters our life and we become "new creatures in Christ" (2 Corinthians 5:17). He wants us to be *absolutely sure* that we will go to Heaven, and not to Hell (1 John 5:9-13). No more sorrow, death, tears, parting, heartbreak, wickedness, war, sin, but instead, incomparable beauty, basking in His great love and sharing Heaven with Him and all the saved in His family forever. This is what He died for, shed his blood in agony for, rose again and conquered death for, to save people like you and me, now and forever. Oh, how He loves us! The cross proves that. He wants to give you new life in Him right now. That is what He wants. What do you want?

Dear reader, by a simple prayer of faith you can make the decision today to receive God's free offer of salvation. Recognizing your own helplessness and the precious provision of Jesus on the cross, you only need to confess your sin and ask God to forgive you and save you through the shed blood of Jesus Christ. The Word of God declares,

> That if thou shalt confess with thy mouth the Lord Jesus, and shalt believe in thine heart that God hath raised him from the dead, thou shalt be saved. For with the heart man believeth unto righteousness; and with the mouth confession is made unto salvation (Romans 10:9,10).

The promise of God's Word is clear and certain, "But as many as received him (Jesus Christ), to them gave he power to become sons (children) of God, even to them that believe on his name" (John 1:12).

If you agree with what God has said in His Word, that you are separated from Him by your sin, and you understand the good news that Jesus Christ died in your place so that you can be forgiven, why not bow your head right now and ask God to save you?

The following prayer may help you express your decision to place you faith completely in Jesus Christ and ask him to save you:

"Dear Lord , I acknowledge before you today that I am a sinner and fall short of your holy demands. I understand that I need to be reconciled to you, and that I cannot make myself acceptable to you through good works. I believe that you love me and sent Jesus Christ to die on the cross in my place so that through Him I can be forgiven and accepted by you. Here and now I ask you to forgive me and save me through Jesus Christ. I pray this in Jesus' name, amen.''

If you have prayed to receive Jesus Christ as your personal Savior, consider the words of John 6:47 carefully: "Verily, verily, I say unto you, He that believeth on me hath everlasting life." Believing, receiving, calling upon, and 'opening the door' (Revelation 3:20), are expressions used more or less interchangeably in the Bible. They mean that the kind of heart (not head) belief which saves is the kind that makes a definite decision at a point in time to accept, receive, believe in and call on Christ.

"He that believeth on the Son, hath (*already has*) everlasting life.'' So, what do you have right now, if you truly believed in Jesus Christ when you called on Him? What kind of life did he give you? Could anyone or anything ever take this 'everlasting' life from you? Where would you go if you were to die right now?

If you now realize that Jesus Christ has come into your life, saved you, and given you everlasting life, if you now *know*, based on the Word of God, that if you were to die you would go to Heaven to be with the Lord Jesus Christ, please bow your head and thank Him for saving your soul. Then tell others you have been saved by simply trusting Jesus Christ, and begin immediately a life of obedience to Him. This will demonstrate the reality of your salvation.

If you are still in doubt, you may not really be believing Him, and He only saves by *faith*. Or, you may not understand. Or, you may be clinging to some sin, or some false teaching that you are unwilling to turn over to Jesus.

Most likely, however, you are waiting for some 'feeling' to confirm your salvation. We are not saved by feelings, but by faith in Jesus, and in what God's Word says about saving us when we trust Him. Feelings come and go, but resting in God's Word is what gives permanent assurance of our salvation. To call on Jesus to save us, and then to wonder if He did, means we are doubting His integrity. In essence, this makes God a liar — 1 John 5:10. It also casts doubt on His love. Would He love you enough to die for you in sheer torture and blood, and then turn you down when you call on Him to save you?

Feeling are important — God gave us emotions, but never is our salvation to be based on feelings. They are too untrustworthy, deceitful at times, and fluctuate too much. Our salvation is based on the Word of God. The Spirit of God acts on the Word of God as we trust Jesus, to bring about the new birth in our hearts (1 Peter 1:23; Romans 10:17).

If an honest man promises us $1000 simply for the asking, and we *do* ask him for the $1000, he *must* give the money to us, regardless of how we feel or don't feel, or any other considerations. God is more honest than any man. If you asked Jesus to save you, you can know, based on His promise, that you have Jesus and His salvation.

Finally, knowing you are saved, because God said so, will time and again bring great joy and peace into your heart! You can memorize John 6:47 and Romans 10:13, and use them as a soft pillow for a tired head for the rest of your life, knowing, that if you were to die, you would go to heaven to be with Jesus Christ forever. Keep the order straight: Fact, faith, and feelings. Sometimes, God withdraws all feelings, so we can develop and walk by faith. Then the joy in Him eventually is increased.

Rejoice in Him and His salvation, and live obediently for Him the rest of your life. Read the Bible, pray, serve Him in church, and love Him with all your heart.

If you would like further counsel on this matter, or if you have questions about anything discussed in the book, you are cordially invited to contact the publisher:

Institute for Religious Research
1340 Monroe Ave., NW
Grand Rapids, MI 49505-4604
U.S.A.

Suggested further reading: John R. Stott, *Basic Christianity*, C. S. Lewis, *Mere Christianity* , J. I. Packer, *Knowing God.*

Reply Card

Please Evaluate This Book

Dear Reader:

It is our sincere prayer that this book has been helpful to you. We are interested in your comments. Please fill out this form and mail it to the address below.

In Christian Love,
Institute for Religious Research

My Church or Religious preference is (optional):

What did you find most helpful about this book?

What questions were left unanswered?

Please send more information about:

I made a decision for Jesus Christ as a result of reading this book
❑ Yes   ❑ No

Comments:

Name (optional) _____

Address _____

City _____ State _____ Zip _____

Phone (if you desire a call) Area (_____) _____

RETURN TO:

Institute for Religious Research
1340 Monroe Ave., N.W.
Grand Rapids, MI 49505-4604

APPENDIX

A Review and Discussion of
Robert and Rosemary Brown's Book
They Lie in Wait to Deceive
Mesa, Arizona: Brownsworth Publishing Company, 1981

As was discussed briefly in chapter 12 (p. 148-154), *They Lie in Wait to Deceive* is a work that relies primarily on the "red herring" technique. The authors, Robert and Rosemary Brown, attempt to "draw the scent away" from the damaging facts of the case against Joseph Smith's Book of Abraham. They do this by focusing upon an entirely separate issue — the personal integrity and credibility of a man who had been expounding that case, Dee Jay Nelson.

The Browns' basic conclusion is that since the Book of Abraham was attacked by a disreputable man, it must therefore be a reputable work. While this is their most fundamental error, the Browns' book is seriously flawed in other ways as well. The types of errors they have committed throughout its pages fall into three categories:

Simple Mistakes due to carelessness or lack of information. These are apparently honest mistakes, though their frequency is puzzling.

Faulty Conclusions due to flawed or biased judgement.

Deliberate Misrepresentations or Omissions apparently intended to portray their subject in the light they desire.

The purpose of this section is not to attempt a point-by-point examination of every error or misrepresentation the Browns have made in their book; such an undertaking would require far more effort than the results would be worth, and would make for extremely monotonous reading. Nor is this appendix intended to represent a "defense" of Nelson.

Still, if we are to make the claim that much of *They Lie in Wait to Deceive* is seriously flawed, it is appropriate to support that claim with specific examples. Here are a few to consider:

Brown's Claim No. 1: *Nelson was not asked by Dr. Nibley to help defend the LDS Church in the matter of the translation of the Joseph Smith Papyri* (pp. 106,

113-115, and various other places).

With the above statement, the Browns are attempting to respond to the issue of Hugh Nibley's letter to Nelson (shown on p. 53 of this book), in which he wrote that he saw no reason why Nelson "should not be taken into the confidence of the Brethren if this thing comes out into the open; in fact, you should be enormously useful to the Church." The Browns prefer to interpret this as follows:

> Notice that the letter is dated June 27, 1967 — *five months* before the church received the papyri. The papyri came into the church's possession in November, 1967. From the moment the church leaders learned that they may be the new owners of some of the original Joseph Smith papyri, it was a time of exciting speculation and anxious expectation — not an attitude of cover-up as Nelson would like everyone to surmise from the aforementioned letter.
>
> What, then, were they really discussing? It is certain that they were not referring to any translation as anti-Mormon writers would like to lead people to believe. The papyri had not even been received and translated yet!
>
> The letter by Nibley states: 'But I am willing to bet you that you have reached premature conclusions about the Hypocephalus (Facsimile #2).'
>
> *Dr. Nibley and Nelson were discussing the hypocephalus* — What were the facsimiles from the *Book of the Dead* doing in the *Book of Abraham?* At that point in time, they didn't know. They had questions, but no answers.
>
> From Dr. Nibley's comment, 'Brother, have you been around,' it appears that Nelson wasted no time giving his long list of phony credentials — professor, World's Greatest Egyptologist, author, lecturer, movie maker, etc. With credentials like that, why shouldn't Nelson be 'taken into the confidence of the brethren' and be 'enormously useful to the church' in helping to find out some answers? At the date of this letter, June, 1967, there was no papyri and no way to find a relationship.
>
> Providentially, the papyri came forth in November, 1967, *five months after* this correspondence with Nelson. The papyri tied everything together and explained the significance . . . The answer was simple. It contained important symbols clarifying the ancient apostate temple ceremony that Abraham participated in as mentioned in the first chapter of the Book of Abraham (p. 115).

In arriving at the above conclusion the Browns mistakenly assume that the Metropolitan papyri collection was unknown to Dr. Nibley (and to Mormon leaders) at the time of this correspondence simply because the LDS Church had not yet received the papyri. But according to the January 1968 issue of *Improvement Era* (which the Browns are apparently aware of, since they make reference to it), the papyri had already been discovered and recognized by Dr. Atiya in New York in May, 1966. This was *fourteen months before* Nibley wrote his letter to Nelson. Moreover, in the Winter, 1967 issue of *Dialogue* Glenn Wade reported the following:

> Dr. Atiya obtained photographs of the material in the file and returned to his home in Salt Lake City. He immediately got in touch with his good Mormon friend, Taza Peirce, and told her in confidence what he had discovered. A few days later the two of them met with President N. Eldon Tanner and the photographs were displayed. Later, the

photographs were sent to Brigham Young University for inspection by Professor Hugh Nibley, who confirmed that the papyri were from the Mormon collection (p. 53).

The Tanners also dealt with the entire subject in great detail in *Mormonism: Shadow or Reality.*

The fact is that Hugh Nibley was not only aware of the existence of the "original PGP manuscripts" (i.e., the Book of Abraham papyri) — though he claimed to not know their location — but that he even had pictures of them for a least a year before his letter to Nelson.*

Once it is understood that the existence of the papyri was already known within a very small, select circle of Latter-day Saints at the time of the Nibley-Nelson correspondence, and that any information about them was being withheld from the public until the Church could find a way to portray them favorably, the true meaning of Dr. Nibley's letter is quite easy to comprehend. Nibley was seeking Nelson's future cooperation if and when the existence of the original P.G.P. manuscripts were ever to become public knowledge, since there were "parties in Salt Lake (i.e., critics of the Book of Abraham) who are howling for a showdown on the P.G.P."

The existence of the manuscripts did, of course, become public knowledge in November 1967, as a result of which Nelson was evidently "taken into the confidence of the Brethren" so that he could be "enormously useful to the Church."

This brings up another contention the Browns make.

Brown's Claim No. 2: *Dee Jay Nelson was not commissioned by President N. Eldon Tanner to translate the Joseph Smith Papyri* (pp. 127ff, 147, and other places).

The Browns are very insistent about this point, but one can only speculate as to why they feel this issue is important. It may be a desire to hold on to their image of Nelson as a man who, in 1968, acted completely on his own initiative without any official encouragement from anyone in authority in LDS circles; or, perhaps they simply cannot accept the embarrassing thought that a prominent LDS leader, while supposedly possessing the gift of spiritual discernment, was taken in by Nelson's list of pretended accomplishments. Whatever their reasons, they report that the entire incident (as they heard Nelson relate it in a lecture) struck them as highly suspicious in a number of ways:

> . . . It was during this lecture that Nelson told how he first heard of the Joseph Smith Papyri, and how he went to Brigham Young University to see Dr. Hugh Nibley. After chatting with Dr. Nibley for a while, Nibley took Nelson to see the display of the papyri . . . Nelson then claimed that Nibley gave him a letter of introduction to President N.

---

*In a letter dated August 29, 1967, Dr. Klaus Baer also confirms that Dr. Nibley had possessed photographs of the Metropolitan papyri for a least a year prior to that time: "In the summer of 1966, Prof. Nibley showed me enlargements of the photographs; they had been obtained by a third party and passed on to Prof. Nibley, who was evidently interested in purchasing the papyri, which included the embalming scene reproduced . . . in the PGP." (as quoted in *Can the Browns Save Joseph Smith* by J. and S. Tanner, 1981, page 30)

Eldon Tanner of the First Presidency of the LDS Church. Nelson said that he spoke to President Tanner about fifteen minutes and then President Tanner said: 'I think you are the man to do the job; you are the one to translate the papyri.' Nelson said, 'We made a deal.' 'If I would just translate the hieroglyphics into their modern English equivalent, that the Church would publish the work.'

When Nelson made these statements, I knew that something was wrong! I have been in the Church long enough to know that no General Authority of the Church would make a decision like that by himself, especially that fast. I am sure that he would counsel with some of the other Authorities and most likely, would take the matter before the entire Quorum of the Twelve (Apostles) for a decision . . . (*Introduction*, p. vi)

Certain that Dee Jay Nelson had just been caught in a lie, Robert Brown writes that he decided the next morning to place a phone call to President Tanner in Salt Lake City in order to determine whether or not Nelson had received any such "commission" from him:

. . . President Tanner stated that it was not true, so I asked him if he would send me a

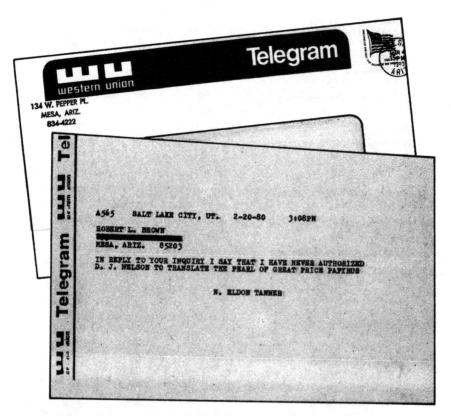

N. Eldon Tanner's telegram to Robert L. Brown, as shown on pages vii,108 in the Browns' book, *They Lie in Wait to Deceive.*

telegram to that effect.

The next day, I received the following telegram from him — 'IN REPLY TO YOUR INQUIRY, I SAY THAT I HAVE NEVER AUTHORIZED D. J. NELSON TO TRANSLATE THE PEARL OF GREAT PRICE PAPYRUS. SIGNED: N. ELDON TANNER.'

This reply was good enough for me . . . (*Ibid.*)

At this point the Browns appear convinced they have produced "proof" — through President Tanner's telegram — that the events Nelson had described could not possibly be true; even going so far as to conclude that no such meeting between Nelson and Tanner ever took place. Such a meeting, they point out, would have been totally unnecessary since "the papyri was [already at that time] available to the public and all were invited to try their hand in the translation." Their justification for such reasoning, though, turns out to be based on a rather weak chain of false assumptions.

To begin with, the Browns argue that Nelson would have to be "unfamiliar with LDS Church policy or he would know that 'commissions' are not given as he claims." To support this view they describe the elaborate series of review and decision making steps — all involving the highest governing bodies of the Church — that would have to take place before any formal commitment could be made to bind the money or services of the LDS Church to any important course of action. As to the question of Nelson's being "commissioned," then, they sum it up this way:

It is Church policy for leaders throughout the Church . . . to 'set apart' members who are called to do a specific work. This is done by two or more of the brethren holding the Priesthood placing their hands upon the head of the one called and delivering a blessing which asks for the Spirit of the Lord to guide and direct them in their work. Members are set apart for all jobs, whether teacher, camp director, clerk, Counselor, Bishop, Stake President, etc. Nelson claims he was 'commissioned', but makes no mention ever of being set apart to do the translation. He never mentions who the brethren were that set him apart. *Nelson is obviously not familiar with the LDS Church government!* (p. 108, emphasis in original)

Perhaps the confusion here arises over the use by both Nelson and the Browns of the term 'commission,' which suggests a formal arrangement, while Nelson's account of events indicates an understanding that was anything but formal. However, the Browns unnecessarily complicate the issue even further by confusing it with the term "calling," which describes an officially authorized job or position within the Church. This is formally and ceremonially bestowed upon members until such time as they are officially "released" from said job or position. This procedure of "setting apart" would hardly be used informally when a person is simply asked by one in authority to do something helpful, nor would it be necessary when a person offers to do something like produce a translation of some original Pearl of Great Price manuscripts that have finally "come out into the open." If it was with such a complicated impression of arrangements in mind that Robert Brown posed his questions over the telephone to N. Eldon Tanner, it is not surprising that President

Tanner could quite truthfully deny he had ever authorized or participated in any such thing.

Still, the Browns cannot seem to get away from their conviction that Nelson just could not have been sent by Hugh Nibley to President Tanner's office for a meeting in order to obtain a set of photographs of the papyri, since they do not believe the photographs had ever been restricted:

> When the LDS Church received the papyri, it was put on display for all to see and color reproductions were given upon request. Scholars were also invited to translate it. Nelson tries to make a big issue out of Dr. Nibley having given him a copy of the reproductions as if he was the only one able to get such secret inside information! (pp. 166-167)

Because of this belief, the Browns were suspicious of Nelson's mention in his lecture of having been given a note of introduction from Dr. Nibley to President Tanner, suggesting that he (Nelson) be given a set of photographs. They strongly disagree with what Nelson and other critics claim this note represents:

> This note purports to be a letter of introduction to President N. Eldon Tanner and is always shown in anti-Mormon literature to give credence to Nelson's claim that he met with President Tanner and obtained his commission to translate the papyri. Where on the note, then, is President Tanner's name? President Tanner's name does not appear anywhere on it! Who says this note was a letter of introduction? Nelson says, that's who! *This was merely a note instructing a secretary or clerk at the library to give Nelson copies of the papyri.* It was not necessary for Nelson to have a note because the papyri were available to the public, but Nelson insisted on having one so Dr. Nibley gave him one. (p. 113, emphasis by Browns; they make another statement almost identical to this again on p. 129)

If the Browns are correct about this, then they are also correct in pointing out that there would have been no reason at all for Nelson to see N. Eldon Tanner, or for President Tanner to personally provide Nelson with photographs, or for any sort of "commission," request, arrangement, or whatever, to be made between the two of them.

On the other hand, if they are *incorrect*, then what really did happen? The central question at issue here is whether or not Nelson really was sent to Tanner by Nibley, and if so, why?

Assuming for a moment that he was sent — or at least that he could have been — we will do a little "backward planning" and see what we come up with:

> If Nelson were not expected to do *something* with them that would be "enormously useful to the Church," he would not have been given copies of photographs that were still being restricted.
>
> And, if photographs of the complete set of papyrus fragments were not being restricted at that time, Nelson would not have needed to be sent to President Tanner to obtain them.

And, if Nelson was not sent to President Tanner to obtain the photographs, then Dr. Nibley's note was not intended as a "letter of introduction" for Nelson to Tanner.

And, if Nibley's note was not directed to N. Eldon Tanner, then that note should not be expected to turn up, along with one of Dee Jay Nelson's business cards, attached to a memorandum from President Tanner's office files which states that photographs of the papyri were there given to Nelson "at the suggestion of Dr. Hugh Nibley" on January 5, 1968.

But there is just such a memorandum. It was discovered, according to a letter by

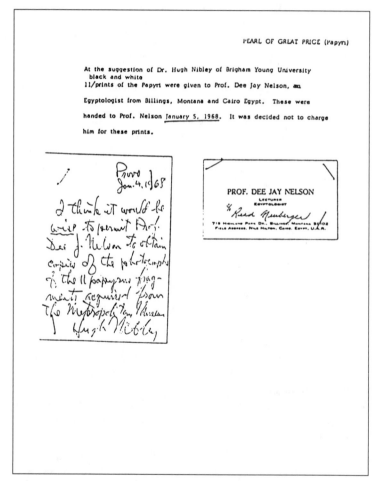

Photocopy of memorandum from President Eldon Tanner's office files, showing that Dee Jay Nelson visited him in early 1968 for the purpose of obtaining the papyri photographs.

N. Eldon Tanner to Wilbur Lingle dated May 18th, 1977, after an "extensive search" in a previously unsearched file in the Church's (or possibly Tanner's own) archives by the same secretary from President Tanner's office who had originally made the memorandum some nine years earlier (see picture on p. 199).

A copy of the memorandum, note, and business card was enclosed with the letter to Mr. Lingle, and has since been frequently reproduced and widely circulated, along with portions of President Tanner's letter.

What is incredible is that this memorandum was already fairly well known at the time the Browns were preparing the first edition of *They Lie in Wait to Deceive*. In fact, they even quoted Nelson's reference (several sentences long) to it when they transcribed their tape recording of his lecture on page 186 of their book. It seems remarkable that they would miss picking up on this, or fail to check into it before proposing their own version of things.

Obviously, then, the meeting between Nelson and Tanner did actually take place, and the purpose of the meeting was to provide Nelson with copies of the papyri upon Nibley's written recommendation. It is also obvious that these copies had to have been, at that time at least, restricted items in order for such precautions to be necessary to obtain them. And, while the question may remain unclear of whether or not a "commission," arrangement, agreement, request, offer, or favor was ever arrived at with the same understanding by both parties, it is also obvious that Nelson would not have had to meet with a General Authority of the LDS Church and present Dr. Nibley's recommendation in order to receive restricted photographs if he were not expected to do *something* with them that would benefit the LDS Church.

The only thing in this respect that Dee Jay Nelson could possibly have been expected to do, based on the representation he had given of himself and his abilities, was to produce a translation.

— Provided, of course, that the Church had not already made arrangements to obtain one, which leads us to yet another careless misimpression that the Browns create in their effort to discredit Nelson.

Brown's Claim No. 3: *Nelson's translation was not 'the first to be published' — Dr. Klaus Baer's, Dr. Richard A. Parker's, and Dr. John A. Wilson's translations preceded Nelson's!* (pp. 106, 110-111, 131, etc.)

In making the above statement, Robert and Rosemary Brown appear to be trying to strengthen their case for the claim we just discussed by attempting to "prove" that the LDS Church could not possibly have needed Nelson's services, since other "Egyptologists were invited to translate" the papyri just as soon as "the papyri were turned over to the Mormon Church." Another reason for taking this position seems to stem from some sort of desire on the Browns' part to imply Nelson must have been incapable of translating the papyri on his own. By portraying Nelson as being incompetent with Egyptian, they evidently hope to lessen the impact of the arguments he presented against the authenticity of the Book of Abraham. To demonstrate their point, the Browns state the following:

Nelson and his supporters, like to make it sound as if he was . . . the first to translate and publish the Egyptian document. In reality, the first scholarly publications were by Dr. Klaus Baer, Dr. Richard Parker, and Dr. John A. Wilson (p. 110).

On the next page they again repeat this point:

However, Nelson had the work of Baer, Parker, and Wilson available to him in preparing his own translation of the text of the papyri. The aforementioned three eminent Egyptologists had published their translations in *Dialogue: A Journal of Mormon Thought* before Nelson published his" (p. 111).

The Browns then go on to explain:

Dr. Baer published his translation, 'The Breathing Permit of Hor, a Translation of the Apparent Source of the Book of Abraham,' in *Dialogue* 3 (Autumn, 1968), pp. 109-134. After this time, Nelson asked Dr. Baer for help in his translation (*Ibid*).

According to the Browns' reasoning, then, Nelson's first published translation had to be based on the work of Baer, Parker, and Wilson. Their work did not appear until after the Summer and Autumn issues of *Dialogue* came out, so Nelson's work could not have preceded them.

Incredibly though, just prior to making the above statement, the Browns mention that Nelson's "preliminary work with the Facsimiles in the Papyri was praised by Hugh Nibley in *Brigham Young University Studies, Spring,* 1968, p. 247."

How could Hugh Nibley possibly have been praising Nelson's work in an article published in the *spring* of 1968, if Nelson's work had been based on articles that did not appear until the *summer* and *autumn* of 1968?

To lend whatever support they can to their claim, the Browns quote a portion of a letter written to them from Dr. Baer dated 22 October 1980 (shown on pp. 37-38, and elsewhere in their book) in which Baer writes that, after he had been asked to prepare his translation for *Dialogue:*

He [Nelson] wrote me on 19 August and included drawings for his pamphlet on the 'Eye of Ra' [note: this would be the Facsimile No. 2 drawing as it appears in the Book of Abraham — author]. I replied on August 22 with some general comments and annotations and corrections on the drawings. . . . There was some more correspondence during the remainder of 1968 regarding his next two pamphlets, again mainly concerned with the reading of the Hieratic; this was acknowledged, e.g. in 'Appendix 2' of THE JOSEPH SMITH PAPYRI, Part 2."

Robert and Rosemary Brown were evidently trying so hard to read their own interpretation into Dr. Baer's letter that they failed to understand what he was talking about. His meaning is perfectly clear if one simply considers what he says Nelson was working on in August of 1968 — his "Eye of Ra" booklet, and later his *Joseph Smith Papyri, Part 2.* The Browns could, and should, have known that Nelson published a total of four booklets on the subject:

1. *The Joseph Smith Papyri — A Translation and Preliminary Survey.*

This appeared in April 1968 and was advertised for sale in the Salt Lake Tribune on April 6, 1968. This is the work which Nibley praised that spring in *BYU Studies* as "a usable and reliable translation of the available papyri that once belonged to Joseph Smith."

2. *Joseph Smith's Eye of Ra.* This was a study and translation of the hypocephalus of Facsimile No. 2, and is the subject about which Dr. Baer says Nelson *first* contacted him in August of 1968. This booklet appeared in print the following month, September of 1968.

3. *The Joseph Smith Papyri, Part 2* . This booklet also came out in September, 1968, and dealt with what Nelson referred to as "additional and significant discoveries concerning the fragments."

4. *A Translation and Study of Facsimile No. 3 in the Book of Abraham.* This was the last of Nelson's booklets, and came out in February, 1969.

The reader will notice that Nelson's first booklet, which Nibley himself described as providing "a usable and reliable translation of the available papyri that once belonged to Joseph Smith" could not possibly have been what Nelson was conferring with Baer about in August — *four months after Nelson's own study was published,* and that Nelson could not possibly have "had the work of Baer, Parker, and Wilson available to him in preparing his own translation."

While one could conceivably argue that Nelson may have been able to use the *Dialogue* material in his later works (which would not be at all improper, provided the source was acknowledged), the Browns are completely out of line to insist, that "the work of Baer, Parker, and Wilson actually pre-dated that of Nelson" or that "Nelson's translation was not 'the first to be published'" when the material from their own book proves otherwise!

The Browns could have also caught their error if they had actually read Dr. Baer's article in the Autumn 1968 issue of *Dialogue.* On p. 118, n. 34, he commented:

> So far as I know, Nelson, *The Joseph Smith Papyri,* p. 42, was the first to point out that the bird above the head of Osiris clearly has a human head and therefore must be his ba [*soul* is the nearest English equivalent]. In 'Facsimile No. 1,' it is drawn with a falcon's head, and I must confess with some embarrassment that I also 'saw' the falcon's head before reading Nelson's study."

They should have also picked up on Baer's comment in the Ogden *Standard Examiner* article of March 29, 1980 (which they reproduced on p. 224 of their book):

> As to the papyri in question, Baer said Nelson's translation is 'essentially' correct. Baer said he prepared a translation of the same papyri, *after* being contacted by Nelson in 1968, and the translations say basically the same thing" (emphasis added).

And finally, in a footnote on page 152 of their book, the Browns mention one of Hugh Nibley's references for his 1975 book *The Message of the Joseph Smith*

Papyri as "Parker, Richard A. ' The Book of Breathings,' Mimeogr. or Xerox copy of typed mss. signed, April 26, 1968." This was the first translation that either Baer, Parker, or Wilson had provided, the first that Nibley received from any of them, and it was dated *20 days after* Nelson's translation was in print and first advertised!

Regardless of what the Browns may think of Nelson or what claims about himself Nelson may have invented, the facts bear out the position that Nelson *was* "the first to translate and publish the Egyptian document." The failure of the Browns to realize this (and other points) is evidence not only of sloppy research, but of a personal hostility that appears to have obscured their ability to evaluate matters accurately, or interpret them impartially.

Perhaps the best indication of this is expressed in their vague allusions to some sort of relentless "anti-Mormon" conspiracy that is out to "distort truth" at the expense of the Mormon Church.

The frequency of passages like, "Such a stand by the anti-Mormon element is devoid of truth (as usual) but makes such an exciting story that it keeps them in business! It is their 'bread and butter!'" — p.166, stand out throughout their book, and are as unconvincing in and of themselves as the occasional "evidence" they present in an attempt to support their paranoia. And, though all so-called "anti-Mormons" are thus lumped together under the Brown's scathing condemnation, they become particularly vitriolic when referring to specific individuals. Nelson is but one example, and Jerald and Sandra Tanner are another.

A good illustration of this can be seen in chapter nine of their book, entitled "Errors and Distortions By Dee Jay Nelson and Jerald and Sandra Tanner." On p. 154 (first ed.) a cartoon of an old-fashioned apothecary-type scale appears — the sort that has two trays on either end suspended from an arm that is balanced in the middle. On the left hand side (in the dark) the tray is labeled "LIES, DECEPTION, PARTIAL TRUTHS, MISQUOTATION, MISREPRESENTATION, ETC." On the right hand side (in the light) the tray is labeled "PRAYER, TRUTH, THE FACTS." Back on the left side is a smiling cartoon figure of Nelson sitting out on the far end of the balance arm, adding his weight to it, while a man and a woman (the Tanners) are pulling downward on a rope that is also tied to the left arm of the scale. Thus the "bad guys" (meaning the "anti-Mormons") are shown battling desperately, using every dirty trick in the book, to overcome all that is good, honest, virtuous, praise-worthy, and so forth (meaning the Mormon Church). On the next page, they begin:

> The founding fathers of our great country created a system of checks and balances in the hopes of promoting honesty. The leaders of the LDS church are occupied using their time and talents in building up the kingdom of God here on earth. For them to spend their time answering all the baseless charges that can be thought up against the Mormon church would be too time consuming and non-productive — especially when the truth can be found through prayer. Therefore, the church has done very little to check the lies and distortions of truth propagated by the anti-Mormon elements.

This particular chapter also shows the Browns arriving at a number of patently false and misleading conclusions which they could have easily avoided, had they not been so intent upon discrediting those they see as being "the enemy."

A prime example is the following charge which they make on page 159.

Brown's Charge No. 4: *"Dee Jay Nelson Confuses Identity of Canopic Jars."* This appears to strike the Browns as a very significant point, enough so that they seem to desire to impress it strongly upon their readers. By attempting to demonstrate that "Nelson has extreme difficulty trying to identify the four canopic jars correctly in his lectures and also in print," he is again made to appear incompetent with Egyptian in order to foster their erroneous belief that it is somehow Nelson, and Nelson alone, who has been responsible for "creating a false case against the Book of Abraham."

To do this, the Browns present a chart listing four instances in which Nelson named the canopic jars under the embalming table in Facsimile No. 1 (these are accurately identified and discussed on p. 102 of this book). When compared to an identification of them provided by Dr. Klaus Baer, it can be seen that only one of Nelson's identifications corresponds with Baer's. Of the other three instances, two have the second pair of names reversed from the order given by Baer, and the other has the first two names as well as the second two transposed.

Obviously, then, the Browns are correct — Nelson did mix up the names of the canopic jars! They write:

> You will note that Nelson cannot remember the names of the canopic jars! (Errors are in parenthesis.) His booklets were published by Jerald and Sandra Tanner, Modern Microfilm Co., Salt Lake City, Utah, in 1968, which means that he has been familiar with their identity for at least the last twelve years and still he can't remember their correct names! His answers weren't right in most of his publications, but he messed them up even worse in his Mesa lecture — *He was 100% wrong!* (p. 159, emphasis Browns')

Then, convinced they have just struck a fatal blow to whatever claim to credibility Nelson may have ever had, the Browns simply cannot resist the urge to twist the knife a little:

> It would seem that Nelson could make far better use of his time if he would spend his time studying Egyptian instead of running Joseph Smith down. However, studying Egyptian has not been as *lucrative* for him as his baseless anti-Mormon campaigns (p. 160, emphasis Browns').

But before we leap blindly to the same conclusions the Browns have drawn here, let us look into the issue a little bit closer, both from the standpoint of the significance of their data as well as from the accuracy of it.

To begin with, one should normally be able to expect any presentation of fact to be as accurate as possible, but everyone knows that even under ideal conditions this will not always happen. The realization that errors do occur — even though we are looking for accuracy — is a concession to our own humanness that a reasonable person is willing to make.

For the Browns to set up and demand such a standard of inerrancy as they do in this case for Nelson is unreasonable and unrealistic. *What if the Browns themselves were to be judged by the same standard?*

As it happens, in the midst of giving this example, the Browns have themselves unwittingly provided the means to demonstrate this point. Recall that, after they presented their chart of Nelson's identifications on page 159 of their book, they wrote, ". . . His answers were not right in most of his publications, but he confused them even worse in his Mesa lecture—*He was 100% wrong!"*

. . . In his *Mesa* lecture? Just above their chart, the Browns listed references indicating that the identification mentioned on line 2 of their chart (the one that they show as being "100% wrong,") was made during "Nelson's Bakersfield, Calif., lecture (see p. 157)." A quick flip of the page back to p. 157 confirms, if the Brown's transcript is accurate, and we have no reason to suppose that it is not, that Nelson made the identification listed on line 2 during "his Bakersfield, Calif. lecture on Feb. 29, 1980."

. . . During his *Bakersfield* lecture? The Browns mention elsewhere that they live in Mesa, and that they attended Nelson's lecture there at the Central Christian Church, 315 North Hobson, at 7:30 p.m. on the evening of February 22, 1980. They even included a transcription of this lecture in their book on pages 184-207 — but indicate that their "tape ran out" just as Nelson was beginning to discuss the Book of Abraham, leaving them with no canopic jar identification to quote. So, since the dates are also different, it would seem quite likely that the "Bakersfield CA lecture" mentioned on page 159 and quoted from on page 157 actually did take place in Bakersfield, California.

. . . But the Browns *said* Mesa . . . even though they must have *meant* Bakersfield.

If we were to judge the Browns (or their editor, or their proofreader, or their printer) by the same uncompromising standard which they are condemning an error made by Nelson, we would have to say these people must be so unable to recognize landmarks and buildings they cannot even tell the difference between the city of Bakersfield, California and their own home town of Mesa, Arizona!

Such a charge (based on a simple slip) would be ridiculous, of course. And so is the charge made by the Browns.

But that is not all. As it turns out, the standard by which they evaluated the accuracy of Nelson's identifications — the identification provided by Dr. Klaus Baer (*Dialogue,* Autumn 1968) — is itself in error. In the Summer 1968 issue of *Dialogue,* on page 86, Richard A. Parker (Chairman of the Department of Egyptology at Brown University) identified the canopic jars as: ". . . representative of the four sons of Horus, human-headed Imseti, baboon-headed Hapy, jackal-headed Duamutef, and falcon-headed Kebehsenuf." In the Browns' book, Baer identified the jackal-headed jar as the god "Qebehsenuef"* and the falcon-headed jar as the god "Duamutef," when they should have been named the other way around. Klaus

---

*Since the occidental spelling of Egyptian was influenced largely by French, German and English, it is apt to vary considerably.

Baer is recognized as one of the most competent Egyptian philologists living, and yet he is evidently not above occasionally mistaking one minor Egyptian deity for another. Questioned about this varied identification, Dr. Baer pointed out that in one Egyptian tomb, that of Nefretari, three different identifications occur. Dr. Baer adds, "even a queen of Egypt couldn't get consistent, careful decisions in such matters." (*Journal of Pastoral Practice*, V, No. 2, 1982, pp. 117-118) Would the Browns be as quick to condemn him in the same spirit as they condemn Nelson?

Or, for that matter, would they condemn a member of their own camp, such as Dr. Hugh Nibley? The Browns give a reference on page 154 to one of Nibley's *Improvement Era* articles (note: written back during his own admitted "skirmishing and sparring for time" period) in which Nibley is attempting to "open doors" to "possibilities" that would tie Joseph Smith's identifications of the canopic jars to geographic regions surrounding Egypt. The reference is to page 86 of the August 1969 issue, which happens to contain a chart by Nibley listing the canopic deities in an order identical to that which the Browns have supplied as "Dr. Klaus Baer's identification," with the jackal as "Kebhsenef" and the hawk as "Duamutef." Interestingly though, only four pages earlier in the same article (on p. 82), Nibley wrote:

> . . . The four children of Horus began as stars in the northern sky; their names *Imsty, Hpy, Dwamutf,* and *Qbhsnuf* designated the four stars of the Dipper bowl and seem to go back to the earliest times, when they are also identified with the major cosmic deities.

Here he identified the deities in their *correct* order.*

Now if Browns had been familiar with Nibley's article, and also with the *Dialogue* article by Parker, they would have been aware of this conflict of identifications; and even if they themselves were unsure which identification was correct, we would have expected them to be as concerned about these discrepancies as they were with Nelson's. Should the fact that they fail to mention it at all be taken to mean that they did not read the very material they are attempting to reassure questioning Latter-day Saints with; or is this a case of intentionally withholding unfavorable information — something the Browns themselves would categorize as "intended deception?"

They make use of the expression, "a clear case of intended deception" in this same chapter when they attempt to demonstrate an elaborate scheme on the part of both Nelson and the Tanners to obscure the fact that, in at least two of Nelson's booklets (The Joseph Smith Papyri and Joseph Smith's Eye of Ra), Nelson had indicated that he agreed with Joseph Smith's interpretation of the four sons of Horus when they appeared on Facsimile No. 2 as representing "this earth in its four quarters"** (which was the thesis Nibley was advocating in the *Improvement Era*

---

*Actually, there is evidence to show that even the ancient Egyptians confused the identity of the second pair of the canopic deities from time to time — though the correct identification of them is by far the predominant one encountered.

**Smith, did not identify them as "the four sons of Horus," nor did he identify them as conopic jars, nor did he even come close to giving them their proper names of *Amset, Hapi,* article just mentioned).

The basis for their charge is simply that when Nelson was describing the canopic jars and their funerary function in his lecture, he neglected to mention that, in Egyptian mythology, the four sons of Horus were also considered to be the gods of the four cardinal points of the compass, a point which he had mentioned in two of his booklets, and which had apparently struck him as being similar to a rather singular portion of the Joseph Smith explanation on Facsimile No. 2. (It should be noted that, at the time these pamphlets were written, Nelson was himself a Mormon and was likely looking for whatever points of similarity he could find, even remote or coincidental ones — just as Hugh Nibley was doing.) The Tanners are likewise criticized by the Browns for failing to mention this when quoting Nelson's description of canopic jars in their 1972 edition of *Mormonism: Shadow or Reality?* The Browns write:

> Jerald and Sandra Tanner in their book, *Mormonism: Shadow or Reality,* are very typical of all anti-Mormon propagandists. They like to quote out of context or distort the truth entirely (p. 157).

And,

> "WHAT!!! NELSON SAID JOSEPH SMITH IS CORRECT IN HIS INTERPRETATION? You certainly didn't get that idea from reading Tanner's account of Nelson's quote in MORMONISM: SHADOW OR REALITY did you! In Nelson's lecture, he forgot he agreed with Joseph Smith, too. Why didn't the Tanners use the entire reference? Why did they omit the part where Nelson verifies the fact that Joseph Smith did correctly identify the four canopic jars? In case there is any doubt in your mind that this is a clear case of intended deception, Nelson made this same statement in his other booklet . . ." (p. 158, emphasis Browns').

Also,

> Isn't it easy to see that both Nelson and the Tanners are guilty of deception? They knew what they were doing. They just didn't count on anyone checking their references so closely (p. 159).

Here again, part of the Browns' ire seems to stem from their own unwavering acceptance of the "Any Egyptian Connection" brand of rationalizations offered by Hugh Nibley. To say, as the Browns do, that "Joseph Smith did correctly identify the four canopic jars" would be stretching the actual truth far beyond its limit, and to repeat the fact that Nelson at one time recognized a similarity of treatment on one aspect of this point (as did Samuel A. B. Mercer during Spalding's 1912 study) would have very little bearing on a description of the funerary function of canopic

---

Duamutef, and *Qebehsenuef;* instead he called them "the idolatrous gods of *Elkenah, Libnah, Mahmackrah,* and *Korash.*" Nibley's article unsuccessfully attempted to build a case for the "possibility" of Smith's names standing for geographic regions.

jars, or on the identification of their correct Egyptian names. Moreover, neither Nelson nor the Tanners can fairly be accused of withholding the information, since the Browns themselves admit that *"The Joseph Smith Papyri* and *Joseph Smith's Eye of Ra* [both of which mention this subject] by Dee Jay Nelson have been published by the Tanners for years" (p.159).

It makes little sense for someone to "publish for years" something they use as a reference if they are "counting on" people not checking into it.

This theme of "deception by the Tanners" is carried on by the Browns in an even more unconvincing manner in yet another charge they make:

Brown's Charge No. 5: *The Tanners knew of Nelson's false credentials . . . the Tanners had the most to gain from pushing Nelson into the forefront with regards to the Book of Abraham, and little to lose if Nelson crashed* (p. 154, 160-163, and elsewhere).

What the Browns are implying here is that the Tanners (and other "anti-Mormon elements") found Nelson to be such a desirable part of their "false case against the Book of Abraham" that they would have hated to see anything come up that would "weaken" that case for them. (This, of course, reflects their own belief that the credibility of any challenge to the Book of Abraham somehow rests upon the credibility of Nelson.) But in making reference to Nelson, the Browns point out there was one way in which the Tanners had always been different from everyone else. Under the headline DID THE TANNERS SUPPRESS THE TRUTH ABOUT DEE JAY NELSON? they write:

> While this author was reading all the information about Dee Jay Nelson, it occurred to me that the Tanners were the only anti-Mormon propagandists that didn't refer to Nelson as 'Prof.' or 'Dr.' Nelson. We thought it quite strange that with all the publicity surrounding Nelson, they would be the only ones not to fall for his phony credentials. Every other writer referred to Nelson as 'Dr.' or 'Prof.' Nelson when quoting him (p. 160).

A letter from Sandra Tanner is then shown that is dated January 3, 1981 — well after Nelson's false credentials had been exposed — in which she wrote, "By the way, we never claimed he was a Ph.D. . . . all he claimed to us was he was self-taught."

The Browns are unable to view this situation as a case of the Tanners having merely made a successful effort to be accurate. Instead, they see their failure to make use of Nelson's false credentials as incriminating evidence that they were aware of them, and that they attempted to cover up the entire matter in order, presumably, to continue using the "strength" of Nelson for their "false case." The Tanners could hope, perhaps, that the subject would never be noticed or become an issue, but if it ever did they could blithely state that "we never claimed he was a Ph.D." — thus letting themselves off the hook. The Browns then demand:

> Sandra, why did you keep it a secret from everybody? For the past three years [as of the Browns' writing in July, 1981], all over the country and especially in Utah, Nelson has

been advertising his false degree as well as his other false credentials. Have you never heard his wild claims? (p. 161)

Following this they observe that "putting a little pressure on the scales of checks and balances helps make people honest," and point out that Tanners' book *Changing World of Mormonism,* which had gone through two printings in 1980, had been revised for its third (1981) printing. Nelson's use of false credentials was discovered, the new edition said, following the Tanners' own investigation, and therefore he was no longer being quoted by them.

This prompted the Browns to raise another headline question, WHY ALL OF A SUDDEN DID THE TANNERS DECIDE TO INVESTIGATE NELSON? which they answer as follows:

> In making the above revision, the Tanners also received encouragement from the Moody Bible Institute which published their book . . .This author, in the latter part of 1980, sent information about Dee Jay Nelson to Moody Press. A call to Moody Press indicated that the material had been passed on to Jerald and Sandra Tanner with the instructions to revise the section concerning Dee Jay Nelson . . . Between the Moody Press and us, it looks like the Tanners had no choice but to come clean (p. 161).

Again, the Browns emphasize the importance of what they believe to be their own role in this:

> . . . when Moody Press discovered the truth about Dee Jay Nelson (with help from this author), they insisted that the Tanners remove references to him (p. 163).

Thus, according to the Browns, we are asked to see three things:

1. The Tanners knew of Nelson's false credentials, and deliberately failed to expose them so that they might continue taking advantage of Nelson as an "authority."

2. The Tanners never used Nelson's false credentials themselves, so that if they were ever uncovered by anyone they could plead ignorance.

3. The Browns "put[ting] a little pressure" on the Tanners by providing information on Nelson to Moody Press in the latter part of 1980, is what then forced the Tanners to "come clean" in a "hastily revised" edition of their book.

What is wrong with the above picture? Practically everything! The first point is clearly totally subjective. The Browns, caught up in their own bitterness and suspicion towards any and all so-called "anti-Mormon propagandists," apparently cannot help but ascribe ulterior motives to the "elements" that they see as being a part of their "anti-Mormon" conspiracy. The same is true of the second point; one suspects that if the Tanners *had* picked up on and repeated Nelson's self-awarded academic titles, the Browns would have *criticized* them for doing so — just as they criticized other non-Mormons (but never Mormons!) throughout their book for falling for them. Moreover, the Browns fail to take into account the simple fact that the Tanners' writings about Nelson were all pretty much completed with their 1972 edition of *Mormonism: Shadow or Reality?* at least six years before Nelson began claiming to have earned a Ph.D. In it they generally referred to him as "the Mormon Egyptologist, Dee Jay Nelson." Since the Browns take at least as great exception to Nelson's unwarranted use of the title "Egyptologist" (which turns out to be one of the points their book does an effective job of demonstrating) as they do to "Dr." or "Professor," should they not in fairness be able to concede that the Tanners evidently did, in fact, fall for his phony credentials, just as others had?

The third point, though is an objective claim that can be examined and tested. Did the Tanners suddenly decide to investigate Nelson, and subsequently disassociate themselves from him, as a result of the Browns having contacted Moody Press in the latter part of 1980?

Again, material that can be found in the Browns' own book proves otherwise. Furthermore, as we shall see, there were also other materials, both in the Browns' possession or available to them, to establish the fact that the Tanners were responsible for initiating their own investigation into Nelson's credentials, and that, in fact, they were the first to prove that Nelson had received a bogus Ph. D. from a diploma mill.

Let us begin by looking at "the latter part of 1980."

On Saturday, November 1, 1980, the *Mesa Tribune* (Mesa, Arizona) ran a full page paid advertisement that was placed by a group called "Concerned Christians of Mesa." This advertisement (reproduced in the Brown's book on pp. 250-252) attempted to establish among other things, that Nelson's papyri translations and overall treatment of Egyptian were valid, and that therefore the question of Nelson's academic credentials "had no bearing on his ability to speak as a witness to and a translator of the papyri in question."

Robert Brown prepared a rebuttal to this article, which also was published in the *Mesa Tribune* (though no date is given), and which is shown in the Brown's book on pages 254-263. Here he chided the "Concerned Christians" group for continuing to appeal to Nelson's work (though he did note that they had stopped referring to him as "Dr." Nelson) since Jerald and Sandra Tanner, "the most outspoken of the anti-Mormon groups in the U.S., were suddenly prompted to disown Nelson because he could not prove his credentials" (p. 255). To underscore his point, Mr. Brown then went on to explain:

> *The Tanners had written a six-page, single spaced letter to Nelson asking him to explain his credentials.* If the Tanners have chosen to disassociate themselves from Nelson, it would seem logical that the people of this area should also question the validity of his statements. *A copy of their letter was voluntarily sent to me by the Tanners.* Excerpts are shown below . . . (*Ibid,* emphasis added)

Mr. Brown reproduces on pages 256-258 of his book some five pages of this six-page letter from the Tanners, along with a second one-page letter (from Jerald Tanner), as he had prepared them to appear in his *Tribune* article.

While it is interesting, in light of the Browns' persistent allegation that the

Tanners were involved in a conspiracy to suppress the whole Nelson affair, that Mr. Brown admits that "a copy of their letter was voluntarily sent to me by the Tanners," the letter itself is even more revealing.

First, the letter is dated *March 11, 1980*. This is less than three weeks after Nelson's lectures were given in Arizona, during which the Browns first decided to investigate him. This does very little to aid the Browns' contention that the Tanners were forced to act on the basis of something the Browns did "in the latter part" of that same year. Rather, it indicates that the Tanners, with no outside pressure from anyone (including Moody Press or the Browns), acted on their own initiative to investigate Nelson's claims as soon as it came to their attention — just as the Browns themselves did. It is no more appropriate to insinuate that the *Tanners* should have become suspicious of Nelson earlier than they did, than it would be to charge that the *Browns* should have noticed his false claims earlier than they did.

Second, contrary to any "conspiracy" notion of the Browns,' Jerald Tanner is quoted as bringing up repeated instances of discrepancies to Nelson regarding his experiences and credentials, particularly in regards to his "Ph.D." and the school from which he supposedly obtained it, and insisting upon receiving some satisfactory answers from him. At one point in the letter, Tanner writes:

> It is now March 12 as I finish the last part of this letter. As I indicated at the beginning, *it now appears that you do not have a legitimate doctoral degree. Even if you have a piece of paper making such a claim it apparently does not amount to anything.*
> I must confess that I feel disappointed and sad because of this whole matter . . . In any case, *I feel it is my obligation to make this information available to the public. I will, therefore, probably be printing hundreds or even thousands of copies of this letter to distribute to the general public.* I am convinced that our case against the Book of Abraham is absolutely devastating, and *I would not want to weaken it in any way by trying to cover up or remain silent concerning such an important matter.*
> . . . Even though I still believe in the general accuracy of your translation and conclusions concerning the Joseph Smith Papyri, *I will not be reprinting any of the books.* (letter by Jerald Tanner dated March 11, 1980, as shown on pp. 257-258 of Browns' book, emphasis added.)

All of this hardly supports the Browns' theory that the Tanners were trying to "hide" things for their own benefit. The copy of this letter which Mr. Brown received, and which he admits was "voluntarily sent" to him, was part of the "hundreds or even thousands" of copies that the Tanners distributed in their effort to "make this information available to the public."

A third interesting point is shown in the second, one-page letter the Browns reproduce on page 258, which shows that the Tanners' investigation was already close to being *completed* by March 20, 1980. This letter (bearing that date) was also among the material that the Tanners "voluntarily sent" to Brown, and which was being freely distributed by the thousands. In it Tanner told Nelson:

> On the 18th we received the certificate which purports to be your diploma . . . After examining the diploma and the other paper you included, we became suspicious that this

was not a genuine university. Sandra contacted a noted educator from the University of Utah, who in turn called the Executive Secretary of the Northwestern Association of Schools and Colleges in Washington. He learned from him that Pacific Northwestern University was only a 'diploma mill' which the Federal Government had investigated for mail fraud . . .

In conclusion it appears that your claim to a doctor's degree in anthropology cannot be substantiated . . . (*Ibid.*, dated March 20, 1980)

The Tanners did much more than merely write and distribute these letters, though. By the first part of April, 1980, they had written an article exposing Nelson's false credentials, published it beginning on page 7 in their newsletter *Salt Lake City Messenger* for that month, and mailed out approximately 10,000 copies of that paper — including a copy sent to Moody Press, publishers of their book *Changing World of Mormonism*. With some adaptations, this article became the basis of the revision that appeared in the 3rd printing of the book the following year.

Thus, if the Browns "forced the Tanners to come clean" by sending material to Moody "in the latter part of 1980," as they claim, how is it that the Tanners were declaring to Nelson their intention to print and distribute "hundreds or thousands" of copies of letters exposing him as early as March; or how is it that by the end of March the Tanners had already discovered the truth behind Nelson's "diploma" and "school" if they were "all of a sudden" prompted to investigate several months later by the Browns; and how is it that the Tanners' newsletter exposed Nelson in April, in the *early* part of 1980, if the Browns were responsible for "putting a little pressure on the scales of checks and balances" to "make them honest" late in the year? That the Browns could even make such a claim is altogether incredible, especially when they could so easily check the date on the letter the Tanners provided them!

It is also quite likely that the Browns had at some point prior to this obtained their own copy of the Tanners' expose of Nelson in the April issue of *Salt Lake City Messenger,* as well, since a portion of that article read:

. . . We contacted a noted educator from the University of Utah who checked with Dr. James Bemis, Executive Director of the Higher Commission of the Northwest Association of Schools and Colleges, and found that Pacific Northwestern University was only a 'diploma mill of the worst kind.' We confirmed this report by calling the U.S. Postal Department in Seattle and the King County Attorney's Office. *(Salt Lake City Messenger,* April, 1980, p. 7. More information concerning this matter will be sent to the reader by the publisher free by upon request.)

The "information sent free upon request" which the Tanners mention, included the letters the Browns partially reproduced in their book. The only way the Tanners would have been able to send them was if the Browns had requested them, and the most obvious way for the Browns to have found out how to request them would be through the Tanners' April *Messenger*. If the Browns were aware of this early exposure, to suggest that the Tanners did nothing about Nelson until forced to by Moody Press at the instigation of the Browns is nothing less than an outright misrepresentation.

Going back to these letters for a moment, or more particularly to the longer one, the one dated March 11, the reader will recall that we mentioned the Browns reproduced approximately five pages of material from what was originally a six-page letter. What about the portion they did not include? Was it merely a repetition of areas already covered, innocuously left out to conserve space? Or was there another reason the letter was trimmed?

Material the Brown's Withheld

A look at the omitted portion of Jerald Tanner's letter (see pp. 220,221), though, shows that the Browns apparently have practiced what amounts to a double standard when it comes to withholding information. Note that virtually everything mentioned in the portion of this letter which the Browns withheld, is damaging to the view of things their book presents. For instance:

First, it makes detailed reference (in paragraphs 1-5) to "Dr. Webb," the man with the bogus Ph.D. that for many years LDS authorities endorsed and supported for his "defense" of Joseph Smith's work. The Brown's entire premise loses its moral force when we learn that "a disreputable man with false credentials" *defended* the Book of Abraham, and that he was hired to do so on behalf of the LDS Church authorities, who were fully aware of the deception!

Second, it demonstrates that Hugh Nibley went on record as defending "Webb" (paragraphs 6, 7) on the basis of the position that not only his *credentials,* but even his *true name* was completely irrelevant in relation to what it was he said. Again, this argument is exactly opposite the one used by the Browns to justify their condemnation of Nelson's views of the papyri.

Third, it spells out in very precise terms (paragraphs 8, 9) the fact that Nibley considered Nelson's initial work with the papyri to be "usable and reliable," a point which the Browns did mention on page 111 of their book but which is here placed in a context that is much more difficult for them to obscure.

Fourth, the letter emphasizes the point (in paragraph 10) that the Tanners consider any work by Nelson to be quite incidental to the case against the Book of Abraham, and that others — including Baer, Wilson, and Parker — have all the "authority" necessary to use as evidence in that case.

While each of these points represents an area that the Browns either failed to address successfully in their book or else neglected to deal with at all, the first one would seem to be by far the most damaging to them. Thus, by omitting the portion of Tanner's letter that mentions "Webb," the bogus Ph.D. that defended the Book of Abraham, the Browns are not only free to attack Nelson, the phony Ph.D. that was critical of it, they are also free to create an image of "anti-Mormon" deception and cover-up as well. In order to do this convincingly, however, their readers must be kept ignorant of the entire matter. To do this, it was necessary to suppress this particular portion of Tanner's letter to Nelson, which included statements like the following:

If I were to overlook misrepresentation on the part of non-Mormon writers I would be operating on a double standard. You will no doubt remember what we wrote about 'Dr. Webb' — the great defender of the Mormon faith . . . (Tanner to Nelson, first paragraph of omitted portion of March 11, 1980 letter)

And,

If it turns out that you do not have a Dr.'s degree, honesty would demand that I make a public statement to that effect. Otherwise, I would find myself in the same position as the Mormon leaders who concealed the true identity of 'Dr. Webb' . . . (*Ibid.*, paragraph 5)

> versity, but we could not find it listed among current universities. Lorri Keck of Rocky Mountain College also told me that they were unable to locate it.
>
> You state that you "COULD NOT CONTACT REGISTRAR ON WEEKEND," but a number of days have passed since then and you have still not provided any information that would help me locate the school.
>
> You mention that this "IS MATTER OF LITTLE IMPORTANCE ANYWAY AS I HAD NO DOC-TORAL WHEN DID TRANSLATION." I must vigorously disagree with that statement. While it is true that I have never published anything about you having a Dr.'s degree, any statements you have made about this matter subsequent to the translation of the Joseph Smith Papyri could have a tendency to reflect upon my integrity in the eyes of many people.
>
> In your Mailgram you state that "ONE OF PUBLISHED BOOKLETS WAS PART OF MY THESIS." You are apparently referring to your publication, Pyramid Science Experimenter. I notice, however, that while it claims to contain "an illustrated abstract of my doctorate thesis", it does not state the name of the university. If such a thesis does exist, how can I obtain a copy of it?

GOES HERE

Above: Section of Jerald Tanner's letter to Nelson as it appears in the Browns' book, page 256. **Next Page:** Section of the letter omitted by the Browns in their book.

And,

I doubt that the Mormon Church leaders will ever have the courage to directly attack you concerning the issue of credentials because of their use and support of 'Dr. Webb.' Even Dr. Hugh Nibley defended 'Dr. Webb' . . . (*Ibid.*, paragraph 6)

Also,

At any rate, even though the Mormon Church will probably remain silent concerning your credentials,* I feel that my conscience will not allow me to keep silent if there is a problem . . . (*Ibid.*, paragraph 8)

And, as we have seen, Tanner did not keep silent. Within two weeks of writing this letter, enough proof of Nelson's fraudulent credentials had been gathered by the Tanners to expose him fully — a point which the Browns have not only overlooked,

---

*And, officially, the Mormon Church has remained silent. At the very beginning of the Browns' book, Robert Brown mentions that he is not writing as a spokesman for the LDS Church, but that his work is being done on his own initiative.

You mention that this "IS MATTER OF LITTLE IMPORTANCE ANYWAY AS I HAD NO DOC-TORAL WHEN DID TRANSLATION." I must vigorously disagree with that statement. While it is true that I have never published anything about you having a Dr.'s degree, any statements you have made about this matter subsequent to the translation of the Joseph Smith Papyri could have a tendency to reflect upon my integrity in the eyes of many people.

If I were to overlook misrepresentation on the part of non-Mormon writers I would be operating on a double standard. You will no doubt remember what we wrote about "Dr. Webb"—the great defender of the Mormon faith. It is summed up in our new book, The Changing World of Mormonism, page 333:

"The other Egyptologists whom Spalding contacted rendered a similar verdict—i.e., the 'Book of Abraham' was a work of Joseph Smith's imagination and had no basis in fact. ...Mormon historian B.H. Roberts admitted that there 'were no Egyptian scholars in the church of the Latter-day Saints who could make an effective answer to the conclusions of the eight scholars who in various ways pronounced against the correctness of Joseph Smith's translation...' (A Comprehensive History of of the Church, vol. 2, p. 139).

"The Mormons, however, did receive help from a writer who called himself 'Robert C. Webb, Ph.D.' Fawn M. Brodie claimed that Robert C. Webb's real name was 'J.E. Homans,' and that he was 'neither an Egyptologist nor a Ph.D.' (No Man Knows My History, 1957, p. 175). From this it is rather obvious that the Mormon leaders were guilty of deception. Strange as it may seem, Dr.

OMITTED PORTION

Mr. Nelson, page 3

Sidney B. Sperry, of Brigham Young University, confirmed the fact that Robert C. Webb was no Ph.D: 'He wrote a wonderful book,...under the name Robert C. Webb, Ph.D. I regret that the brethren let him put down Robert C. Webb, Ph.D., because he was no Ph.D.' (Pearl of Great Price Conference, December 10, 1960, 1964 ed., p. 9). On page 6 of the same publication, Dr. Sperry stated that Dr. Webb's 'real name was J.C. Homans.'

"At any rate, the Mormon church was able to survive Spalding's attack on the 'Book of Abraham' with very little injury because church members felt that 'Dr. Webb' had answered the critics. Writing in the Improvement Era, April 1913, N.L. Nelson stated: 'Dr. Webb has, indeed, vindicated the prophet better than he knew himself."

If it turns out that you do not have a Dr.'s degree, honesty would demand that I make a public statement to that effect. Otherwise, I would find myself in the same position as the Mormon leaders who concealed the true identity of "Dr. Webb." It is my firm belief that "there is nothing covered, that shall not be revealed; and hid, that shall not be known." (Matthew 10:26) I feel that the Lord wants Christians to be honest even though it costs us a great deal.

I doubt that the Mormon Church leaders will ever have the courage to directly attack you concerning the issue of credentials because of their use and support of "Dr. Webb." Even Dr. Hugh Nibley defended "Dr. Webb" in the Church's own publication, Improvement Era, Jan. 1968, p. 22:

"Thus reassured, Bishop Spalding proceeded to demolish R.C. Webb: 'We feel that we should be in a better position to judge the value of the opinions of Robert C. Webb...if we were told definitely who he is....If Dr. Talmage...would inform us what the author's real name is, where he received his degree, and what academic position he holds, we should be better able to estimate the value of his opinions.' Here it is again: The bishop is not interested in Webb's arguments and evidence, but in his status and rank—considerations that are supposed to bear no weight whatever with honest searchers after truth—Nullus in verba! What on earth have a man's name, degree, academic position, and, of all things, opinions, to do with whether a thing is true or not?"

At any rate, even though the Mormon Church will probably remain officially silent concerning your credentials, I feel that my conscience will not allow me to keep silent if there is a problem. I realize, of course, that the question of your credentials does not affect the validity of your translation, and that the Church is in a real bind with regard to the matter since its chief defender, Dr. Hugh Nibley, has written that your work is reliable:

"The publication of the Joseph Smith Egyptian Papyri has now begun to bear fruit. Two efforts at translation and commentary have already appeared, the one an example of pitfalls to be avoided, the other a conscientious piece of work for which the Latter-day Saints owe a debt of gratitude to Mr. Dee Jay Nelson....This is a conscientious and courageous piece of work—...Nelson has been careful to consult top-ranking scholars where he has found himself in doubt. He has taken the first step in a serious study of the Facsimiles of the Pearl of Great Price, supplying students with a usable and reliable translation of the available papyri that once belonged to Joseph Smith." (Brigham Young University Studies, Spring 1968, pp. 245 & 247)

Although we have used your translation of the Joseph Smith Papyri in a number of publications, we do not feel that our case against the Book of Abraham rests upon it. We have the testimony of some of the world's greatest Egyptologists—i.e., Professor Richard Parker of Brown University and Professors Klaus Baer and John A. Wilson (now deceased) of the University of Chicago's Oriental In-

---

Mr. Nelson, page 4

stitute. Even before you came on the scene our friend Grant Heward had identified the papyrus Joseph Smith used in the production of the Book of Abraham as the "Book of Breathings"—a pagan funerary document (see Salt Lake City Messenger, March 1968). I had studied the Egyptian language on my own before you came to Salt Lake and was able to test your work at various points. I knew therefore that it was generally a "reliable translation" as Dr. Nibley has admitted.

In your Mailgram you state that "ONE OF PUBLISHED BOOKLETS WAS PART OF MY THESIS." You are apparently referring to your publication, Pyramid Science Experimenter. I notice, however, but have obscured and misrepresented.

There are still other instances where the Browns have used their book knowingly and deliberately to suppress information that would otherwise discredit their own representations — and one in particular is even more flagrant than the one we just discussed. It too goes back to one of the statements that appeared in the "Concerned Christians" article we mentioned earlier, and can be found in the Browns' book on page 251: "Thomas Stuart Ferguson, a Mormon lawyer and founder of the New World Archaeological Foundation, has lost faith in the Joseph Smith translation [of the Book of Abraham] and Mormonism . . . '' (excerpt from Concerned Christians of Mesa article)

Brown's Claim No. 6: *Ferguson remained a convinced Mormon until his death.* Robert Brown took exception to this point due to the fact that Nelson had made a similar comment during his lecture in Mesa several months earlier, but since that time the Browns had come up with something which they believed to be proof to the contrary. In his rebuttal, Brown wrote:

> We contacted Mr. Ferguson and in a letter to us dated October 23, 1980, he states: 'I do not recall ever meeting Dee Jay Nelson or ever corresponding with him. I am an active member of the Mormon Church and always have been.' (*from* Brown's undated rebuttal in the *Mesa Tribune,* as shown on p. 261 of his book)

On the surface this letter does give one the impression that Mr. Ferguson was still a "believer" since he described himself as an "active Mormon." The fact remains, however, that Thomas Ferguson no longer believed the cardinal truths of **Mormonism, as his letters on pages 182-187 of this book reveal. It would be wrong** to fault the Browns on this point, however, because when Robert Brown responded to the "Concerned Christians" article it is unlikely that they had ever seen Ferguson's *other* letters.

At just about the same time — in the "latter part of 1980" — the Browns also sent their material about Nelson to Moody Press, and included a copy of their letter from Ferguson, since the Tanners had also been among those who had previously mentioned his lack of belief in Mormonism.

Contrary to what the Browns indicate in their book, Moody Press did *not* become alarmed about the "Nelson affair" at this point and subsequently insist the Tanners produce a "hastily revised" section for their own book. The Tanners, after all, had already provided Moody with a copy of their own exposé of Nelson several months earlier, and at that time the revision was well along, if not already completed. Moody did forward the Browns' concerns to the Tanners, though, and included what was then to them a new objection — the letter from Ferguson.

The Tanners responded by sending to both Moody Press and to the Browns, on December 8, 1980, copies of a number of Thomas Stuart Ferguson's personal letters **to close friends or acquaintances that they had collected over the years (see pp. 182-187 of this book).**

By the second week in December of 1980, then, the Browns had *in their possession* information showing that the Tanners, "Concerned Christians" — and even Nelson — had all been telling the truth about Thomas Stuart Ferguson no longer believing that the Mormon religion was true or of God.

How did the Browns respond to this information?

When the first edition of their book was published in July, 1981, the Browns printed a full-page copy of *their* letter from Ferguson on page 228, and on the page immediately preceding it they made this statement: THOMAS STUART FERGUSON IS OFTEN REFERRED TO BY JERALD & SANDRA TANNER AND OTHER ANTI-MORMON WRITERS AS A STALWART MORMON, DEFENDER OF THE BOOK OF MORMON, AUTHOR AND LECTURER OF THE LDS CHURCH, THAT HAS LOST HIS FAITH IN MORMONISM AND JOSEPH SMITH. DOES THIS LETTER SOUND THAT WAY TO YOU?

Ferguson's other letters, the ones sent to Browns by the Tanners, are ignored completely, as though the Browns had no knowledge of them, or they had never existed.

This same example of what is thus characterized as an "anti-Mormon lie" is emphasized two other times in their book, as well — once in a comment they make upon a remark by Nelson from his lecture on page 149, and again on page 261 when they reprint Robert Brown's response to the "Concerned Christians" article.

Why would the Browns — or anyone else — do this? What real difference could it possibly make to them what one man happens to believe or not believe? Were they simply so intent upon discrediting the claims of "anti-Mormons" that they did not care if there was actually validity to those claims?

Perhaps part of the answer lies in just what Thomas Stuart Ferguson represented, and continues to represent, in the eyes of many Latter-day Saints.

The reader will recall that Ferguson was, among other things, an LDS writer, and that the major focus of his writing was his effort to link ancient American legends, prehistory, and archaeology to the themes of the Book of Mormon.

One of the more successful subjects he helped to popularize involved the sixteenth-century legends of *Ixtlilxochitl,* and the "feathered serpent" of Aztec lore, the mythical god *Quetzacoatl.* This *Quetzacoatl,* he attempted to demonstrate, was actually *Jesus Christ* during his visit to the Americas following his crucifixion — a prominent Book of Mormon theme. There have been other LDS writers who have used the same treatment of *Quetzacoatl,* but Ferguson did so more convincingly than any of them, and his writings, though they are no longer in print, were eagerly accepted. The concepts he presented became enormously useful to the Church's missionary effort, as well as being helpful in establishing or strengthening the "testimonies" of members.

Though Ferguson's own letters show that he privately rejected such ideas later on, the LDS Church certainly never has. In the minds of many Latter-day Saints, Quetzacoatl is a tangible link between something recognized by the world and something appreciated only by themselves. A visitor to Salt Lake City today can go to Temple Square and view a film presentation of "Christ in America" which features the legend of *Quetzacoatl* as sober fact.

Where does this leave the Browns? Though their book is primarily an attempt to defend the Book of Abraham, they have also made an effort to provide at least a few tantalizing bits of "evidence" to support the Book of Mormon, as well. Thus, when reviewing and commenting upon their transcription of some of the points raised during Nelson's Mesa lecture, they end up discussing and promoting *Ixtlilxochitl* and *Quetzacoatl,* along with other sources that Ferguson had written about.

And since Ferguson was so closely associated with these particular "intellectual approaches" to creating credibility for the Book of Mormon, and could even be considered an expert regarding them, the Browns must have realized that it would be disconcerting to many Latter-day Saints who felt that their testimonies had been strengthened by such things, to discover that the man who had helped popularize them no longer believed them himself.

So Ferguson's letter to the Browns is prominently displayed and hailed as "proof" of his belief in what the Browns believe, and the other letters — the ones the Tanners provided that show otherwise are never mentioned by the Browns.

We could go on and on giving further examples of the types of flaws that are so prevalent throughout *They Lie in Wait to Deceive,* but we feel our point has been made. Many of these faults can be passed off as fairly innocent mistakes, the result of poor and often inadequate research; while others are reflections of the writers' unavoidable bias against any but their own view, an intolerance repeatedly expressed through bitterness, hostility, suspicion, and sarcasm. But while neither of these first two conditions are particularly commendable, they, unlike a third, are at least to some degree excusable. The other, the use of deliberate and intentional misrepresentation, is not. The frequent resort to such measures within *They Lie in Wait to Deceive* could easily suggest to the reader that the Browns' title was autobiographical.

Is there anything good that can be said about the book? As a matter of fact there is. In spite of their tendency at times to go overboard and leap to false conclusions, the Browns have nevertheless provided a convincing demonstration that fraudulent claims have been made by Dee Jay Nelson, a demonstration that is both appropriate and useful.

In what way do we mean appropriate? And just how is this information useful, and to whom?

It must be remembered that Nelson was primarily a professional lecturer. During the two lectures the Browns attended in Mesa early in 1980, they admit that though they disagreed with his message they were impressed by his ability to entertain an audience. He had apparently made the greatest part of his living for quite some time doing lectures, and could have successfully presented almost any subject he chose that was of interest to him.

His involvement with the Metropolitan Papyri, including his association with Hugh Nibley and his arrangement with N. Eldon Tanner, are a matter of record. He also managed, based largely upon his own abilities and resources, to produce and have published the first reasonably accurate translations and interpretations of those papyri. These conditions alone would have qualified him to speak with authority and from experience on the subject of the Book of Abraham if he had chosen to do so.

Unfortunately, those qualifications alone were not what he used. From the very beginning of the papyri affair (and apparently for quite some time prior to that), it appears that Nelson purposely inflated his personal and professional image. Why he did this is unclear, and does not really matter at any rate. The fact is, it had become a habit, and once begun it was apparently impossible to break. Furthermore, the evidence that the papyri presented against the Book of Abraham was impressive in and of itself, and could easily be used to add credibility to his growing list of claims about himself. The temptation to do this — whether it was originally intended or not — existed, and in the end Nelson exploited the LDS Church's vulnerability over the issue for his personal gain.

It is appropriate that Nelson's false claims should have been exposed, then, because an issue is often judged on the basis of the person who presents it. The case against the Book of Abraham deserves to be recognized and examined on its own merit, and, particularly since the issue of people's faith is involved, it should never become a thing to be exploited for anyone's personal benefit.

Moreover, this information is useful in that it helps to place Nelson's entire involvement with the papyri in a proper sense of perspective to the case against the Book of Abraham. It demonstrates that nothing is ever achieved by making false claims; any "advantage" thus gained is really only an illusion, and is usually more than offset by the damage done to one's credibility when the truth comes out.

Yes, it is true that the Tanners exposed Nelson, and that they did so early on of their own accord and at considerable expense and effort. It is also true that at least some of the research the Browns take credit for was provided or inspired by leads originally developed by the Tanners (Nelson's "diploma" from "Pacific Northwestern University," for example, which is twice shown so triumphantly in *They Lie in Wait to Deceive,* was reproduced by the Browns from a copy that had been sent to them by the Tanners!). The Browns, however, have gone beyond the Tanners in many ways. While the Tanners exposed only the false claims made by Nelson regarding his association with the Book of Abraham controversy, the Browns made it a point to expose every claim that they could, even to the point of reproducing his high school transcripts!

There are, as we have mentioned, instances where their conclusions have been faulty or oversimplified (as with Nibley's letter, the meeting with N. Eldon Tanner, the canopic jar identifications, etc.), but in many cases they have shed light upon aspects of Nelson's misrepresentations that would have otherwise remained unknown. His self-proclaimed "mathematical ability" in personally calculating the weight of King Tut's gold coffin (which it turns out he developed from a misprint in a book!), his "gifts" from King Farouk, his alter-ego "business manager" (who was actually himself), and several other claims are very convincingly demonstrated to be false. The Browns' file of response letters from various institutions, foundations, and professionals in the field of Egyptology who have never heard of Nelson and cannot verify any of his purported achievements should alone put to rest his claim to be a well-known professional in that field.

And actually, there is a certain value to their having done this, a value which the Browns probably failed to recognize themselves. By clearly exposing as many aspects of Nelson's fraud as possible, others — be they writers, lecturers, or investigators — will be prevented from ever again allowing him to "represent" the case against the Book of Abraham. Nelson can rightfully be regarded as a footnote, and never again be confused as an "originator."

If the Browns had only set out originally with such an intent, if they had been able to avoid the false conclusions that colored their work and led them to present their own misrepresentations, their work could have been an effective, and admirable contribution to those seeking to learn the truth.

NOTES

PART I

Chapter One - How It All Began

[1]Book of Mormon, 2 Ne. 28; Morm. 8:28, 31-33. Pearl of Great Price, JS H 1:18, 19 (This is a portion of the popular version of Joseph Smith's First Vision account).

[2]*Ibid.*, JS H 1:30-34, 42.

[3]Book of Mormon — The Testimony of Three Witnesses; *Introduction.*

[4]*Ibid., Introduction.*

[5]*Ibid.*, 2 Ne. 26:15, 16. This corresponds to Isaiah 29:4, and by shifting the passage to refer to America rather than Jerusalem (even ignoring the meaning of the term "familiar spirit"), LDS are able to regard this as a "Biblical proof" for the Book of Mormon.

[6]*Ibid.*, Morm. 9:32.

[7]*History of the Church,* Vol. 1, p. 64, 77.

[8]*Ibid.*

[9]*Ibid.*, p. 124, 125.

[10]*Ibid.*, p. 181-183.

[11]*Ibid.*, p. 189. Doctrine and Covenants — sec. 57.

[12]*Ibid*, sec. 103:11-36, especially vv. 13, 18-20, 26, and 34.

[13]*History of the Church,* Vol. 2, p. 106, 107.

[14]Doctrine and Covenants, sec. 105:1-9.

[15]Pearl of Great Price, JS H 1:60.

[16]The following excerpts are from a letter written by David Whitmer (one of the original Three Witnesses) to the RLDS periodical *Latter Day Saints Herald,* which was published February 5, 1887: "Some of the revelations as they now appear in the Book of Doctrine and Covenants have been changed and added to. Some of the changes being of the greatest importance as the meaning is entirely changed on some very important matters; as if the Lord had changed his mind a few years after he gave the revelations . . . But in the winter of 1834 they saw that some of the revelations in the Book of Commandments had to be changed, because the heads of the church had gone too far, and had done things in which they had already gone ahead of some of the former revelations. So the book of 'Doctrine and Covenants' was printed in 1835, and some of the revelations changed and added to."

[17]*History of the Church,* Vol. 2, p. 235.

[18]*Ibid.*

[19]Daniel H. Ludlow, ed., *Encyclopedia of Mormonism,* (New York: MacMillan, 1992), Vol. 1, s.v. 'Book of Abraham — Origins of the Book of Abraham,' p. 132; *History of the Church,* Vol. 2, p. 236.

[20]*Ibid.*

[21]Letter written by Oliver Cowdery to Wm Frye dated December 25, 1835, as published in the early LDS periodical *Messenger and Advocate,* December, 1835, p. 235.

[22]*Ibid.*, p. 236.

[23]*History of the Church,* Vol. 2, p. 238, 318, 320, etc.

[24]*Ibid.*, p. 350, 351.

Chapter Two - THE BOOK OF ABRAHAM: A TIMELY DOCUMENT

[1] *History of the Church,* Vol. 2, p. 236 (commencement of first phase); Vol. 4 p. 518 (commencement of second phase). These were first published in two installments in the *Times and Seasons* in March, 1842. See note on p. 42, this book.

[2] This view is well demonstrated in the following observation by Sidney B. Sperry in his book *Ancient Records Testify in Papyrus and Stone,* p. 83: ". . . the authors or editors of the book we call Genesis lived after the events recorded therein [in the Book of Abraham] took place. Our text of Genesis can therefore not be dated earlier than the latest event mentioned by it. It is evident that the writings of Abraham while he was in Egypt, of which our printed Book of Abraham is a copy, must of necessity be older than the original text of Genesis."

[3] Diary of Wilford Woodruff, Feb. 19, 1842 (see quote on p. 170 of this book).

[4] David Whitmer, *An Address to All Believers in Christ* (Richmond, Missouri: 1887), p. 59-65. Whitmer writes: "This manner of 'priesthood,' since the days of Sidney Rigdon, has been the great hobby and stumbling block of the Latter-day Saints . . . This matter of the two orders of priesthood in the Church of Christ, and lineal priesthood of the old law being in the church, all originated in the mind of Sidney Rigdon." (p. 64)

[5]*Ibid.*, p. 56, 57.

[6]B. H. Roberts, *A Comprehensive History of the Church,* Vol. 2, pp. 101-103; for Joseph Smith's denials see — *Times and Seasons,* Vol. 3, p. 909 (1842); *ibid.* p. 939; *ibid.*, Vol. 5, p. 423 (1844). Hyrum Smith, *Ibid.*, Vol. 3, p. 871 (1842); *ibid.* Vol. 5, p. 474 (1844).

[7] The issue of Joseph Smith's teaching a doctrine of plurality of gods was one of the three main charges leveled against him by the *Nauvoo Expositor* in June, 1844. Smith ordered the paper and its press destroyed as a "public nuisance," and was subsequently arrested and brought to jail at Carthage, Illinois, where he was killed. (The other two charges made by the *Expositor* dealt with polygamy and Joseph Smith's land schemes.) Cf. note on p. 80 this book. (An exact reproduction of the Expositor is available on request from the publisher of this book.)

[8]Steven L. Shields, *Divergent Paths of the Restoration,* 3rd ed. (Bountiful, Utah, 1982) It has been estimated that well over one hundred different groups have claimed to have sole authority over the "Restoration" since Joseph Smith's death.

[9]Bruce R. McConkie, *Mormon Doctrine,* (Salt Lake City, Utah, 1966) p. 564.

Chapter Three - CHARGES AND REBUTTALS: THE CHALLENGE BEGINS

[1] See *Egyptian Grammar, Being an Introduction to the Study of Hieroglyphics,* by Sir Alan Gardiner, 3rd ed. (by London: Oxford University Press, 1964)

[2] William E. Berrett, *The Restored Church,* 14th ed., 1969, p. 107.

[3] In Dr. Hugh Nibley's book *Abraham in Egypt* (Deseret Book Co., 1981) — The text of the original 1842 heading was erroneously assumed by Nibley to lack the words

"that have fallen into our hands." Nibley then charged that it was the 1851 Pearl of Great Price editor, Franklin D. Richards, who originated the idea that "actual possession of the (Egyptian) records is what made translation possible," — in this way attempting to build a case for a "translation" of the Book of Abraham without having to account for Smith's papyri turning out to be merely common funeral texts (cf. *The "Catalyst Theory,"* p. 136ff, this book). See also the review of Dr. Nibley's book by H. Michael Marquardt in *The Journal of Pastoral Practice,* Vol. V, No. 4, p. 113-116.

⁴ Dr. Arthur Mace, Assistant Curator, Metropolitan Museum of Art, New York, Dept. of Egyptian Art.

⁵ Dr. A. H. Sayce, Oxford, England.

⁶ James H. Breasted, Ph.D., Haskell Oriental Museum, University of Chicago.

⁷ Dr. W. M. Flinders Petrie, London University.

⁸ *Improvement Era,* Vol. 16, February 1913, p. 343.

⁹ *New York Times,* Magazine Section, December, 1912.

¹⁰ *Improvement Era,* Vol. 16, February 1913, p. 321.

¹¹ B. H. Roberts, *A Comprehensive History of the Church,* Vol. 2, p. 139.

¹² At the *Pearl of Great Price Conference* held at Brigham Young University on December 10, 1960, Dr. Sperry, speaking of "Webb," stated, "He wrote a wonderful book, *Case Against Mormonism,* under the name of Robert C. Webb, Ph.D. I regret that the Brethren let him put down Robert C. Webb, Ph.D., because he was no Ph.D." Sperry gives his name as J.C. Homans, introducing some confusion as to his middle initial.

¹³ William E. Berrett, *op. cit.,* p. 107.

Chapter Four - THE PAPYRI REDISCOVERED: A TIMELY OPPORTUNITY?

¹ Dr. Atiya's full account of his part in the rediscovery of the papyri appeared in the January 1968 issue of *Improvement Era.* There is evidence, however, that their existence was known much earlier — see interview with Dr. Henry G. Fischer of the Metropolitan Museum in the Winter, 1967 issue of *Dialogue: A Journal of Mormon Thought.*

² Dr. Hugh Nibley, *Brigham Young University Studies,* Winter, 1968 p. 171.

³ The back of Papyrus Joseph Smith II, for example, contains a map of the Kirtland area in Ohio, and is shown on p. 25 of the January, 1968 *Improvement Era.*

⁴ Walter Whipple, *et al, From the Dust of the Decades* (Salt Lake City, 1968) p. 116.

⁵ Journal of Discourses, Vol. 20, p. 65-67 — sermon by LDS Apostle Orson Pratt.

⁶ LDS Apostle John A. Widtsoe, *Evidences and Reconciliations,* Vol. 1, p. 203.

⁷ Bruce R. McConkie, *op. cit.,* pp. 700, 701.

PART II

Chapter Five - AN IDENTIFICATION AND THE CRITICAL LINK

¹ Up to the time when photographs of the papyri finally appeared in the February

1968 *Improvement Era,* they were generally not available to the public — even though the Church had had sets of photographs for nearly a year-and-half prior to that time. See the discussion of this matter in the *appendix,* of this book.

[2] There is also evidence, from Dr. Sperry's account, that the Grammar's existence was already known of, at least by some members of the Church Historian's Office.

[3] See, for example, Jay M. Todd's *The Saga of the Book of Abraham,* p. 364. Todd writes: "Outside of a few associates, Dr. Clark had kept the fragment [contained with the Grammar material] a matter of confidence, under instructions from the Historian's Office, for over 30 years."

[4] *Dialogue: A Journal of Mormon Thought,* Summer 1968, p. 91.

[5] William E. Berrett, *op. cit.,* 1956 ed., p. 133, 134.

[6] Dr. Sidney B. Sperry, December 10, 1960, *Pearl of Great Price Conference.*

[7] See speech by Reed Durham, LDS Institute of Religion, University of Utah, March 7, 1972.

[8] Letter of I. E. Edwards, Keeper of the Department of Egyptian Antiquities, dated June 9, 1966.

[9] James R. Clark in *Progress in Archaeology,* Brigham Young University, 1963, writes: "These symbols [on the Book of Abraham translation manuscripts included with the Grammar material], judging from their translation, were a highly specialized type of ideograph where a few strokes of the pen or brush conveyed an entire concept." See also similar remarks by Clark at *Pearl of Great Price Conference,* December 10, 1960.

[10] Though later apologists have attempted to reverse this conclusion, there was no disagreement with it when first discovered (before the damaging implications had fully set in). See discussion of this point in LDS Reactions, this book.

[11] Dr. Nibley eventually adopted the position that the marginal characters were done by Joseph Smith's scribes as a pastime, and had no binding credibility. See discussion of this point in the "Scribes Did It" theory, pp. 118ff., this book.

Chapter Six - THE BEGINNING OF DISAPPOINTMENT

[1] Among Nibley's numerous published works were the books *Sounding Brass* and *The Myth Makers,* both satirical and sarcastic denunciations of "anti-Mormon" writers and writings.

[2] Dr. Nibley subsequently studied under Klaus Baer, as well.

[3] For lack of preparedness within the Church, see Nibley's comments in BYU's *Daily Universe,* December 1, 1967; *Brigham Young University Studies,* Winter 1968, pp. 171-172. Nibley never seems to have been suspicious of Nelson's extravagant claims, but apparently accepted them at face value, as did many others both in and out of the LDS Church.

[4] For context of this letter, see the discussion in the *Appendix* of this book.

[5] See discussion of this matter in the *Appendix* of this book.

[6] *Improvement Era,* February, 1968, p. 40-H.

[7] This is Nelson's account as he related it to Jerald and Sandra Tanner.

[8] It is significant that these professionals were approached by "private" individuals.

The LDS Church never did officially seek an expert and impartial verdict regarding the papyri. In a letter dated December 4, 1967, Fischer (of the Metropolitan Museum) wrote: "We have not been commissioned to translate the papyri, nor do I know of anyone else who has been asked to do so."

⁹ See *Mormonism: Shadow or Reality*, 1982 ed., p. 309.

¹⁰ *Improvement Era*, May 1970, pp. 82,83 .

¹¹ The disqualifying of Nelson's "credentials" has become a chief basis for "vindicating" the Book of Abraham to some LDS minds. See discussion of the red herring technique on pp. 138ff of this book.

Chapter Seven - THE EVIDENCE OF THE PAPYRI

¹John A. Wilson in *Dialogue: A Journal of Mormon Thought*, Summer 1968, p. 70.

²Dr. Klaus Baer, *ibid.*, Autumn 1968, p. 111.

³Hugh Nibley has assigned a date of 60 A.D. to the Hor Sensen Papyrus, placing it firmly within the Roman period. While other scholars have perhaps been slightly more liberal with the time frame they have allowed for the production of the papyrus, there is no particular reason to reject to Dr. Nibley's date.

⁴ *Ibid.*, p. 116, 117.

⁵ *History of the Church*, Vol. 4, p. 518, under the date of February 23, 1842: *Wednesday, 23* —"Settled with and paid Brother Chase, and assisted in the counting room in settling with Ebenezer Robinson, visiting the printing office, and gave Reuben Hedlock instruction concerning the cut for the altar and gods in the Records of Abraham, as designed for the *Times and Seasons*."

⁶ Richard A. Parker in *Dialogue: A Journal of Mormon Thought*, Summer 1968, p. 98.

⁷ Wilson, *op. cit.*, p. 71-85

⁸ Baer, *op. cit.*, p. 111.

⁹ This was the basis for the article in the February, 1968 *Improvement Era*, p. 40-A through 40-G, in which the full set of photographs of the papyri first appeared.

Chapter Eight - THE BOOK OF JOSEPH?

¹ *History of the Church*, Vol. 2. p. 236.

² William E. Berrett, *op. cit.*, p. 106, 107.

³ Wilson in *Dialogue: A Journal of Mormon Thought*, Summer 1968, p. 68.

⁴ As appears in *Joseph Smith's Egyptian Alphabet & Grammar*, Modern Microfilm Co., 1966; and in *The Joseph Smith Egyptian Papers*, compiled by H. Michael Marquardt, 1981, p. 109.

⁵ *History of the Church*, Vol. 2, p. 350 f.; also *Times and Seasons*, Vol. 3, p. 774.

⁶Bruce R. McConkie, *Mormon Doctrine* (Salt Lake City: Bookcraft, 1958), p. 91.

Chapter Nine - TRANSLATING EGYPTIAN: A COMPARISON

¹ An excellent, illustrated explanation of the rudiments of Egyptian grammar can be found in the book *Egyptian Hieroglyphics* by Patrick F. O'Mara, Ph. D.

[2] Egyptian hieroglyphics could be written to read in any direction — left to right, right to left, up, or down, depending on the direction the pictographs were facing. Hieratic writing, on the other hand, was virtually always written and read from right to left.

[3] Except when vowels are known through sources dating from Classical times.

[4] From the "Wentworth Letter," a letter of Joseph Smith to John Wentworth published in *Times and Seasons* on March 1, 1842, as recorded in *History of the Church*, Vol. 4, p. 537.

[5] See note no. 9, Part Two, Chapter Five, above.

[6] See photocopies in Joseph Smith's Egyptian Alphabet & Grammar, p. 1; also *The Joseph Smith Egyptian Papers*, p. 6

[7] See p. 127f. of this book.

[8] Several of these are listed on pp. 124, 125 of this book.

[9] See p. 125, 126 of this book; also remarks by Josiah Quincy and others as recorded in *The Saga of the Book of Abraham*.

[10] Daniel Ludlow, ed. *The Encyclopedia of Mormonism* (New York: MacMillan, 1992), Vol. 1, s.v. 'Book of Abraham — Translation and Publication of the Book of Abraham,' p. 134.

[11] Ibid.

[12] Ibid., p. 132.

[13] The 1992 equivalent figure in U.S. dollars is based on inflation data in *The Economist* magazine, "Economic Brief: A Short History of Inflation," (February 22, 1992), p. 68.

Chapter Ten - A CLOSE LOOK AT THE FACSIMILES

[1] This explanation is more detailed (though in the same context) than the one initally given by Dr. Klaus Baer in *Dialogue: A Journal of Mormon Thought*, Autumn 1968, p. 118.

[2] James R. Clark, of Brigham Young University, in his book *The Story of the Pearl of Great Price*, evidences this traditional view when he writes: "Another thing to be noticed about the Book of Abraham is that the Facsimiles are intended to serve as illustrations of the text . . ."

"But he, Abraham, wanted to make sure that his reader would clearly understand what the altar actually looked like so he 'drew a picture' for his reader. That picture or illustration is Facsimile No. 1." — p. 119, See, Pearl of Great Price, Abraham 1:12, 14.

[3] M. Theodule Deveria in *A Journey to Great Salt Lake*, Vol. 2, as quoted in *Deseret News*, January 4, 1913, writes: "It is evident to me that several of the figures to be found in these various manuscripts have been intentionally altered."

[4] Translation of hieroglyphics as by Michael Dennis Rhodes, *Brigham Young University Studies*, Spring, 1977, p. 265; translation of hieratic by Richard A. Parker (note no. 6, Part Two, Chapter 7, above).

[5] Explanation and translation by Dr. Klaus Baer, *op. cit.*, p. 126, 127.

[6] Originally Nibley, *Improvement Era*, February, 1968, p. 20; more recently Ed

Ashment in *Sunstone,* December, 1979, pp. 33ff.

PART III

Chapter Eleven - THE INTELLECTUAL APPROACHES

[1] Statement by Hugh Nibley, as quoted by Ian Barber in his booklet *What Mormonism Isn't — A Response to the Research of Jerald and Sandra Tanner.*

[2] *Brigham Young University Studies,* Spring 1968, p. 249.

[3] Nelson pointed this out in his booklet *The Joseph Smith Papyri,* Part 2, p. 14; the same thought was also expressed by Professor Richard A. Parker in a letter to Marvin Cowan dated January 9, 1968.

[4] *Newsletter and Proceedings of the Society for Early Historic Archaeology,* October 25, 1968, pp. 1-4.

[5] *Ibid.,* June 2, 1969, pp. 11, 12.

[6] Nibley in *Brigham Young University Studies,* Autumn 1968, p. 101, 102.

[7] As quoted in Jay Todd's book *The Saga of the Book of Abraham,* 1969, p. 386.

[8] Sidney B. Sperry, *op. cit.,* p. 68.

[9] *Ibid.,* pp. 68, 69.

[10] Hyrum L. Andrus, *Doctrinal Commentary on the Pearl of Great Price,* 1967 (1970 ed.), p. 25.

[11] See the article "Judging and Prejudging the Book of Abraham," by Dr. Hugh Nibley (undated) as published in *They Lie in Wait to Deceive,* by Robert and Rosemary Brown, pp. 236-245.

[12] *Ibid.,* p. 241.

[13] *Ibid.,* p. 239.

[14] *Ibid., p. 242*

[15] *Ibid,* p. 239.

[16] *Ibid.,.* p. 238.

[17] *Ibid.*

[18] *Ibid.,* p. 241.

[19] *Ibid.*

[20] *Ibid.*

[21] *The Voice of Truth* (1844), p. 16, 17, as quoted in *No Man Knows My History,* p. 292.

[22] As to the authenticity of Brodie's source, she was writing in 1945 and would have had no way to determine whether or not Joseph Smith's "Egyptian" phrase had ever been recorded in any other place than in the 1844 pamphlet she quoted from. The publishing of *Joseph Smith's Egyptian Alphabet & Grammar* in 1966 verified her source as authentic more than 20 years after she quoted from it.

[23] *Times and Seasons,* Vol. 4, p. 373.

[24] Nibley, *op. cit.,* p. 240.

[25] *Ibid.,* p. 242.

[26] Today, the above article is circulated primarily through the book *They Lie in Wait to Deceive,* and also through the F.A.R.M.S. (Foundation for Ancient Research and

Mormon Studies) organization.

[27]This theory is also described in the article by Nibley referenced in note no. 11, above.

[28]Harris' theory was contested by Larry C. Porter, who felt that there was evidence to indicate that the blessing referred to was not actually *written down* in the *Patriarchal Blessing Book* until September, 1835, as mentioned in Joseph Fielding Smith's *Doctrines of Salvation,* Vol. 3, p. 99.

[29]All of Barber's quotes in this section are from the work referenced.

[30]Dr. Hugh Nibley, *Abraham in Egypt,* 1981, p. 4.

[31]Daniel H. Ludlow, ed., *Encyclopedia of Mormonism* (New York: MacMillan, 1992), Vol. 1, s.v. 'Book of Abraham — Origins of the Book of Abraham,' p. 134.

[32]Ibid.

[33]Remark made in a speech by Hugh Nibley at the University of Utah on May 20, 1968, as recorded on p. 317 of *Mormonism: Shadow or Reality,* 1982 ed.

[34]Letter by Richard A. Parker to Marvin Cowan dated March 22, 1966.

Chapter Twelve - ALL IS WELL: CREATING AN APPEARANCE

[1] This is the "promise" of Moroni 10:4 (Book of Mormon) and is used extensively by LDS missionaries during the proselytizing of others to their faith.

[2] See, for instance, Todd's *Saga of the Book of Abraham.*

[3] An interesting *omission* of material from *The Restored Church* in *The Latter-day Saints* is Berrett quoting Oliver Cowdery's 1835 letter about the Book of Joseph scroll as it appeared in *The Latter-day Saint's Messenger and Advocate* (See pp. 80ff., this book). Berrett quoted a great deal of Cowdery's letter in *The Restored Church* and made proud reference to the "Book of Joseph" scroll; but after the rediscovery and examination of the *Ta-shert-Min Book of the Dead* fragments, Berrett entirely omitted all remarks concerning such material in *The Latter-day Saints.*

[4] "Do Not Spread Disease Germs" — address by Apostle Boyd K. Packer given on August 22, 1981, as published in *Brigham Young University Studies,* Summer 1981, p. 259, 262-278 (esp. p. 264).

[5]*Ibid.,* pp. 267,271.

[6]This term was used following LDS historian and scholar D. Michael Quinn's strong reaction to Elder Packer's speech (see article that appeared in the now defunct independent BYU newspaper *The Seventh East Press,* November 18, 1981) in a paper by Quinn entitled "On Being A Mormon Historian."

[7] Response to Ashment's article by Hugh Nibley, *Sunstone,* December 1979, p. 49.

[8] Ibid.

[9]Browns, *They Lie in Wait to Deceive,* statement on front cover.

[10]*Ibid.,* p. 154.

[11]*New York Times,* Magazine Section, December 29, 1912.

[12]See note no. 8, Part One, Chapter 3, above.

[13]That is, Nibley's article "Judging and Prejudging the Book of Abraham."

[14]Browns. *op. cit.,* p. 172.

[15]I have frequently heard the book *They Lie in Wait to Deceive* endorsed and

recommended by well meaning people, who have also candidly admitted they have read or heard about "very little" else relating to the subject.

Chapter Thirteen - THE CRITERIA FOR RATIONALIZATION

[1] The Reorganized LDS Church (RLDS), headquartered in Independence, Missouri, could be said to have been established on April 6, 1860, when Joseph Smith III, son of the Mormon leader Joseph Smith, Jr., became its first president. This group never embraced many "Mormon" doctrines, such as polygamy, and while in its early years it accorded the Book of Abraham limited use as a sort of semi-scriptural work, it publicly rejected the notion of the Book of Abraham being scripturally binding shortly after the rediscovery of the papyri in 1967.

[2] This subject, along with many others, is well covered in Jerald and Sandra Tanner's *The Changing World of Mormonism*, Moody Press, 1980; cf. also, the Tanners' *Major Problems of Mormonism*, Utah Lighthouse Ministry, 1989.

[3] *Ibid.*

[4] *Ibid.*

[5] *Ibid.*

PART IV

Chapter Fourteen - FACING THE TRUTH

[1] Early LDS Apostle Orson Pratt, *The Seer*, pp. 15, 16.

[2] McConkie, *op. cit.*, under the heading *Seers*, p. 701, states: "The President of the Church holds the office of seership. (D.&C. 107:92; 124:94, 125.) Indeed, the apostolic office itself is one of seership, and the members of the Council of the Twelve, together with the Presidency and Patriarch to the Church, are chosen and sustained as prophets, seers, and revelators to the Church."

[3] Though polygamy was developed and practiced only secretly during Joseph Smith's lifetime, by 1852 the doctrine was being taught and practiced openly in the territory of Utah.

Chapter Fifteen - MOVING BEYOND RATIONALIZATION

[1] Commonly known as a "Fast and Testimony" meeting and held on the first Sunday of the month, members abstain from food (fast) for two of their three daily meals prior to sharing their testimonies with each other in the meeting.

[2] McConkie, *op. cit.*, under *Testimony*, p. 785, writes: "A *testimony* of the gospel is the sure knowledge, received by revelation from the Holy Ghost, of the divinity of the great latter-day work."

Chapter Sixteen - DOES ALL THIS REALLY MATTER?

[1] Jerald and Sandra Tanner have quoted portions of these letters in *Mormonism: Shadow or Reality,* both 1972 and 1982 editions, and in *The Changing World of Mormonism*, 1980; also Wesley P. Walters in *Joseph Smith Among the Egyptians*, 1973,

and others.

[2]The following observations by a Mormon writer named Klaus Hansen, which were made during the height of the papyri controversy, appeared in the Summer 1970 issue of *Dialogue: A Journal of Mormon Thought,* p. 110, and offer some insight into Ferguson's remarks: "To a professional historian, for example, the recent translation of the Joseph Smith papyri may well represent the potentially most damaging case against Mormonism since its foundation. Yet the 'Powers That Be' at the Church Historian's Office should take comfort in the fact that the almost total lack of response to this translation is uncanny proof of Frank Kermode's observation that even the most devastating acts of disconfirmation will have no effect whatever upon true believers. Perhaps an even more telling response is that of the 'liberals,' or cultural Mormons. After the Joseph Smith papyri affair, one might well have expected a mass exodus of these people from the Church. Yet none has occurred. Why? Because cultural Mormons, of course, do not believe in the historical authenticity of the Mormon scriptures in the first place. So there is nothing to disconfirm."

ACKNOWLEDGMENTS

Many people have helped to make this book possible, people whose contributions, encouragement, and prayers have been a source of continuing reassurance and inspiration to me at times when I felt as if the job would never be finished. To attempt to name them all (even the ones that I am aware of) would be next to impossible, though I am no less grateful.

Still, certain friends stand out, and must be mentioned. To H. Michael Marquardt, for his tireless attention to detail, for his patience in reading and re-reading the manuscript as it has progressed, and for his kind advice and frequent corrections; to the late Rev. Wesley P. Walters, for his contagious enthusiasm and knowledgeable background, his generous assistance in preparing with me the papyri photographs and composites that appear in this book, and for all the long distance phone calls it took to try to teach me to overcome my split infinitives; to the Tanners, for their friendship, frankness, and the free availability of so much of their research and expertise; to Dean Roberts, for the original artwork his fine talent provided to illustrate the first part of this book; to the Bethany Bible Fellowship, for their faithful support and dedication to this work; and to my wife, for reading, understanding, critiquing, and enduring; to all these and to those I could not name, my heartfelt gratitude and respect.

But most of all, my thanks goes to the community of dear and precious Mormon friends, neighbors, and family members that I have known, lived among, and loved for these many years, now. To any that I have offended, I beg your forgiveness. It was seeing you, and thinking of you, and caring about you that has made me want to give you this book, and to share with you the promise of something and Someone that I have found.

Charles M. Larson

INDEX